Communication Across Cultures

Translation Theory and
Contrastive Text Linguistics

Karen Seago

EXETER LANGUAGE AND LEXICOGRAPHY
General Editors: R.R.K. Hartmann and Tom McArthur

Understanding Semantics
by D. Connor Ferris, 1983

The ESP Classroom: Methodology, Materials, Expectations
edited by Gregory James, 1984

Workbook on Lexicography
by Barbara Ann Kipfer, 1984

Applied Text Linguistics
edited by Alan Turney, 1988

Lexicographers and their Works
edited by Gregory James, 1989

Lexicography in Africa
edited by R.R.K. Hartmann, 1990

Dictionary Workbooks. A Critical Evaluation
by Martin P. Stark, 1990

Sound Changes in Progress
by Anthea E. Sullivan, 1992

Chosen Words: Past and Present Problems for Dictionary Makers
by N.E. Osselton, 1995

Solving Language Problems: From General to Applied Linguistics
edited by R.R.K. Hartmann, 1996

Living Words: Language, Lexicography and the Knowledge Revolution
by Tom McArthur, 1998

Communication Across Cultures

Translation Theory and Contrastive Text Linguistics

Basil Hatim

UNIVERSITY
of
EXETER
PRESS

First published in 1997 by
University of Exeter Press
Reed Hall, Streatham Drive
Exeter, Devon EX4 4QR
UK
www.ex.ac.uk/uep/

Reprinted 2000

British Library Cataloguing in Publication Data
A catalogue record of this book is available
from the British Library

Hardback ISBN 0 85989 490 8
Paperback ISBN 0 85989 497 5

Typeset in 10/12pt Linotype Times by Kestrel Data, Exeter

Printed in Great Britain by
Short Run Press Ltd, Exeter

Contents

Figures

FIGURES

Preface

Both contrastive linguistics and text linguistics are now truly in their prime; witness the conferences at Innsbruck on New Departures in Contrastive Linguistics in 1991 and at Brighton on Contrastive Semantics and Pragmatics earlier this year, or the 4-volume *Handbook of Discourse Analysis* edited by T.A. van Dijk (1985). However, the combination of the two perspectives (the contrastive and the textual), for which some of us have been pleading for many years (I suggested the term 'contrastive textology' in 1980), and whose computational implementation is now feasible, is only just beginning. A further development, the application of contrastive text linguistics to translation studies, is long overdue.

Basil Hatim's book not only addresses all these issues and controversies, but exemplifies them through the prism of Arabic, a language that has enjoyed a long and distinguished rhetorical tradition, but not the benefit of much modern theoretical work. The author is well qualified to undertake this difficult but exciting task. Ever since the days of his Exeter PhD he has explored the relevance of contrastive discourse analysis to English-Arabic translation and demonstrated it in his practical teaching.

We are gratified to be able to present Dr Hatim's ideas in our Exeter Linguistic Studies in the hope that they will enrich the debate and aid instruction in a growing interdisciplinary field.

R.R.K. Hartmann
Exeter, October 1996

Transliteration System

Using material in Arabic has been kept to a minimum and English glosses are invariably provided. However, when it is felt that a particular item needs to be quoted in the original, Arabic transliteration is used. The following system has been consistently employed:

Arabic	Transliteration	Arabic	Transliteration
ا	a	ط	T
ب	b	ظ	Z
ت	t	ع	'
ث	th	غ	GH
ج	j	ف	f
ح	H	ق	q
خ	kh	ك	k
د	d	ل	l
ذ	dh	م	m
ر	r	ن	n
ز	z	ه	h
س	s	و	w
ش	sh	ي	y
ص	S	ء	'
ض	D		

Vowels

Arabic	Transliteration
َ	a
ِ	i
ُ	u
ا	aa
ي	ii
و	uu

Introduction

While the literature on translation theory, contrastive linguistics and discourse analysis has indeed grown immensely in the last twenty years or so, very few books have actually ventured into meaningfully fusing the three perspectives. This book attempts to establish such links and explore areas of common interest. Tackling the problem from this angle, I would essentially be following a trend summed up in a statement I distinctly remember Reinhard Hartmann making as early as twenty years ago to the effect that doing discourse analysis without a contrastive base is as incomplete as doing contrastive analysis without a discourse base and that translation is an optimally appropriate framework within which the entire enterprise of languages in contrast may be usefully dealt with.

Specifically, the aim of this book is to argue that a careful consideration of what actually happens to a given text when someone attempts to mediate in communicating its 'import' across both linguistic and cultural boundaries is one way of making sure that we do not settle for a partial view of what goes on inside that text. To bring entire systems of mother-tongue linguistic as well as rhetorical conventions to bear on the act of textual transfer and to match them with those of another language, which is precisely what happens in a process such as that of translating, can only be illuminating and rewarding. This is particularly the case when it is not only the mechanical, lower-level vagaries of the linguistic system that we are concerned with, but also higher-order considerations of language in use and text in context. Translation can thus add depth and breadth both to contrastive linguistics and to discourse analysis.

In the course of the unfolding argument in this book, authentic data from written, and occasionally spoken, English is used to add clarity to theoretical insights gained from a variety of sources, including translation studies, contrastive rhetoric and critical discourse analysis. A model of text processing will be outlined, and each aspect of the model proposed will be related separately to a problem of language processing, in domains as varied as translator- and interpreter-training, cultural studies, literary criticism and language teaching. The training of future linguists and the sensitization of users of language in general to the realities of discourse are some of the global objectives which this book seeks to pursue.

We begin with a scene-setting chapter in which we outline the text processing model proposed and see this in terms of context, text structure and texture. Text type is shown to be at the centre of contextual analysis and, following a survey of disciplines considered foundational to present-day notions of discourse—rhetoric, style studies, etc. (Chs 2 and 3), two chapters are devoted to text typologies seen from the vantage point of modern text linguistics (Ch. 4) and that of classical Arabic rhetoric (Ch. 5). Text structure occupies us next and two further chapters specifically deal with the compositional planning of texts (Chs 6 and 7). Texture or the various devices which lend texts their qualities of cohesion and coherence is the concern of the following five chapters (Chs 8, 9, 10, 11 and 12) which build on the analysis of compositional formats such as paragraphing. Once the various components of the model are covered, we cast the net wider in the last five chapters. Here, the aim is to test out both theoretical and practical insights in various domains of language in social life. Text type and politeness, cultures in contact, the analysis and translation of ideology in literature, the analysis and translation of irony in non-fiction, and the oral mode of interpreting as an exercise in the use of texts are some of the issues tackled from the perspective of discourse contrastive linguistics adopted in this study.

Now, a word on the choice of the language pair used throughout may be in order. Working with a relatively distant language such as Arabic, seen vis-à-vis a European language (e.g. English) is extremely valuable and will, I believe, shed useful light on some of the thornier contrastive-discoursal issues that concern us in this book. Being a viable linguistic system of communication, Arabic is just as rich in rhetorical conventions and norms of language use as any other language. However, unlike quite a number of other world languages, and certainly unlike many of the European languages with which I am familiar, Arabic is a highly explicative language, whereas a language such as English is an example of an intrinsically implicative language. While losing none of its subtlety, the Arabic language often explicitly marks the finest fluctuations in context, be they related to socio-cultural factors, to intentions or to general communicative matters such as the formality of a given text. This occurs not only at the lexical/semantic level (rich, flowery lexis to cater for every minute nuance), but also, and perhaps more interestingly, at the grammatical/syntactic level. Word order manipulation in Arabic, to take but one example, is a highly motivated and context-dependent activity which, over and above significant effects on the basic lexico-grammatical meaning, helps to communicate a wide range of added rhetorical effects. Almost all of such modes of meaning are no doubt available in any language one cares to name, but, particularly when working with a language like English, unuttered hidden meanings are likely to be retrievable only through close scrutiny of what is implied by an utterance.

On the question of cultural distance, a point recently made by N. E. Enkvist readily comes to mind. In a review of a book on discourse and translation, Enkvist (1992: 127–8) concludes with this statement:

> The laudable emphasis on the importance of cultural differences might perhaps have been concretely exemplified with a few transla-tion problems involving culturally and structurally distant, or 'exotic' languages.

It is to reminders such as these that I respond here and offer my proposals in the hope that they might yield some useful insights into the way texts are put together in particular and into the communicative process in general. To pursue these aims, a number of questions obviously confront us and must be urgently answered: what are the relevant fluctuations of context which are either explicatively or implica-tively realized in different languages? Indeed, what is text and what is context? What is it that determines 'indirectness' in texts which is so implicitly executed in a language such as English and which a language like Arabic, while as challenging in every respect, marks on the surface of the discourse? Finally, is there any point in impressing these dif-ferences on, say, some Europeans whose languages do not usually opt for this degree of explicitness? These and other related issues will form the basis of a number of my arguments in what follows.

The chapters in this volume have all been written with one unifying theme in mind: the applicability of a theoretical model of discourse processing to practical pursuits such as translation, interpreting and language teaching. But, despite professional demarcation lines, these activities pursue goals that in reality show more unity than division. It is these common areas of interest that constitute the primary concerns of this book. The various chapters were written at different times during the past ten years, a period in which, while based at Heriot-Watt University, I had the good fortune of teaching on a wide range of courses at the universities of Edinburgh, Salford, Durham, the Jordanian University for Women in Amman and at the schools of translation in Barcelona, Tampere and Tangiers. I therefore first owe a tremendous debt of gratitude to colleagues and to students from these institutions for the warmth and understanding which they so graciously gave me.

Indeed, I owe so much to so many that they cannot all be mentioned by name. However, the following must be singled out, as without their support and stimulating influence this book would simply not have seen the light of day. One is Reinhard Hartmann, my doctoral thesis advisor and a great friend and colleague, to whom special thanks are due. Then there is my long-standing colleague and collaborator on a number of projects, Ian Mason, for his unstinting encouragement over the years. There are also my two colleagues, one from the old days, Gavin Watterson (now in the Tangiers School of Translation), the other, Ron Buckley (at present with us at Heriot-Watt): to both I am truly indebted for the time and effort they spared in making what I have had to say more comprehensible. In this respect, I would also like to acknowledge the inestimable editorial help which Charlene Constable, one of my PhD students, so generously gave me.

1

Contrastive Linguistic Decisions: The Need for Textual Competence

One useful way of seeing contrastive linguistics at work is through translation, and an interesting way of looking into the translation process is perhaps through an examination of the kind of decisions which translators make in handling texts. This should enhance our understanding not only of what actually happens when text confronts text, but also, and perhaps more important for our purpose here, of what it means to be textually competent. Our ultimate objective is to shed some light on the way forward, whether our concern lies in human translation, machine translation, the wider field of artificial intelligence, applied linguistics and foreign language teaching or indeed contrastive linguistics.

In this chapter, to preview some of the issues involved in the contrastive-discourse model to be proposed, I will analyze the following text sample from a *Newsweek* article on the subject of European unity and, at the risk of sounding too prescriptive, record the various decisions to which a disciplined reading of the text would ideally lead and which should normally be made in the specific case of translating the text into Arabic. As it turned out, these decisions were not all made initially by the group of translator trainees with whom I was working on the translation of the text. This highlights the value in areas like testing or translation assessment of such a prospective approach to analyzing the process of translation, intuitive as this might initially seem.

Sample A

Welcome to 1993
Forget the struggles over Maastricht
Europe's Single Market will change the world

1

Europe is dying, Europe is dying, Europe is practically dead. Its vaunted exchange-rate mechanism lies in tatters. The pound sterling, the lira and the peseta have dropped like stones. Britain wallows in its longest postwar recession. French economic growth is slowing, and France's president has cancer. Italy faces the worst labor disturbance in decades. Even mighty Germany is hard up for cash. The Maastricht Treaty on European political and monetary union looks like a goner. Not for years has the European scene looked so bleak. And yet, the Old Continent is on the verge of accomplishing its most spectacular feat ever—the creation of a vast "frontierless" economic space with 360 million consumers and a combined GNP of 6.5 trillion.

On January 1, 1993, the Single Market—or most of it—will come into effect. Henceforward, travelers within the 12-nation European Community and the seven- nation European Free Trade Association will travel without passports or visas throughout a vast European Space. Internal customs duties will disappear. Trucks will carry no special documents. Physiotherapists, architects and students will be able to practice or study anywhere in the Single Market on the basis of degrees they earned at home. Builders and telephone suppliers will bid for public contracts on equal terms in all 9 countries. Insurance companies and banks can establish branches anywhere in the area.

Newsweek 19 October 1992

Pre-reading

Before embarking on the translation, indeed the reading, of any text, there is a crucial pre-reading process to go through, and one cannot but wonder here how mechanical procedures such as those commonly used by machine translation will cope. In tackling a text such as the one cited above, for example, the human translator exploits a variety of clues ranging from the political leanings of the magazine and the ideology of the contributor, to the actual title and subtitles of the piece in question. No less significant is the knowledge of what is happening in the world outside which can and often does have a bearing on the way the text is handled by reader and writer alike. These and similar situational factors are all subsumed under the text analytic model of register membership to be dealt with in some detail in Chapter 3.

Text Processing

But text processing proper begins when we encounter the first element (word, phrase, etc.) in the actual text and try to make sense by fitting it into some scheme of textual activity. To put this more specifically from the perspective of translation, the translator assesses initial elements in terms of their relevance to the progression of an unfolding text and the requirements of context. Let us consider the initial sentence of sample A to see what is meant by 'text relevance' in the way the term is specifically used here:

Europe is dying, Europe is dying, Europe is practically dead

Among a number of important assumptions which the reader makes, this opening statement would be deemed somehow inappropriate (lacking in credibility, persuasiveness, etc.) if it were produced to initiate an argument *for* the likelihood of Europe's demise. Within the socio-textual practices of English, the producer of such a text would be 'ticked off' by an entire community of competent text users for 'going over the top' or 'sounding off', for being 'too dramatic', 'unsubtle' and 'sensational'. These intuitions about the way a text is put together, which have serious implications for the efficiency and effectiveness of text production and reception in general and of translating in particular, will all be dealt with under the general heading of semiotics (see specially Chapters 3, 4 and 13).

Hypothesis Testing

The establishment of relevance is essentially a heuristic or a hypothesis-testing exercise. Nevertheless, this 'feeling one's way' into the text is not entirely open-ended. To return to our example of the initial element of sample A, there are all kinds of constraints both linguistic and contextual which, in English at any rate, can render the mode of 'arguing a claim through' both inappropriate and uninteresting. It is my task in this book to explain some of these constraining factors. Suffice it here to say that translators (like all text users) generally benefit from being armed with this critical sense of anticipation when approaching a text and, as translator trainers, we should therefore endeavour to raise awareness in this area of language use.

The Unit 'Text'

Text or the set of mutually relevant intentions that serve an overall rhetorical purpose (e.g. to counter-argue) is the ultimate linguistic unit in any activity to do with communicating in language. In all such activities, and particularly in translation, there is hardly a decision taken

3

regarding any element of language in use at whatever level of linguistic organization, without constant reference being made to the text in which that element is embedded. Translation equivalence, therefore, can be adequately established only in terms of criteria related to text type membership, and in the light of how these criteria inform the kind of compositional plan (structure) and the way a text is made internally cohesive (texture). At this level of global patterning, translators also refer to two other basic socio-textual units: genre (e.g. the editorial) and discourse (e.g. that of the committed Christian). The three units (text, discourse and genre) relay vital signals which, through some form of intertextuality, link a given utterance with what it basically reminds us of, be this some social occasion conventionally enshrined in language (a genre structure), some attitudinal statement (a discoursal element) or some rhetorical purpose (a textual matter). The context surrounding the initial sentence of sample A,

Europe is dying, Europe is dying, Europe is practically dead,

may thus be seen globally in terms of:

(a) the genre of the 'polemic',

(b) the discourse of exhortation, and

(c) the text entity 'counter-argument' (thesis cited to be opposed – opposition – substantiation – conclusion).

As presented here, this picture of semiotic activity is obviously much too simplified. In reality, the negotiation taking place would most probably take the form of open sets of options which, by a process of swift and disciplined elimination, gradually become single choices with which the translator ultimately works.

It may be helpful to pause here and look in more detail at the basic triad in our model—that of 'genre', 'discourse' and 'text'. In examining these categories, about which we will have a great deal more to say, it is always of paramount importance to look at the kind of constraints which regulate their use and within which the language user normally operates. With this in mind, let us consider sample B1 and sample B2 which occurred in the context of the following textual encounter. In a press release announcing a new initiative linking two UK universities, a high-ranking official's statement on the prospects for the joint venture was quoted verbatim to include the following:

4

Sample B1
> The University of X and Y University have a proven track record
> ... which this collaborative venture *can only* enhance.

The segment which I have italicized lingered in my mind only because I saw it, on the following day, replaced by something particularly noteworthy in the university bulletin's report of the centre's inauguration. Here, the quote was now used indirectly to read:

Sample B2
> The University of X and Y University have a proven track record
> ... which this collaborative venture *is intended* to enhance.

We may initially wish to reprimand the reporter for taking such liberties with other people's quotes. But, I am sure we will reconsider our position when we discover that he was the same man who, as part of his PR brief, originally composed the entire press release and, for the benefit of the press, invented what the high-ranking official purportedly said. Operating within the constraints of:

(a) an address at a reception (genre),
(b) hortatory evaluativeness (discourse),
(c) through-argument (text).

A speaker is entitled, in fact expected, to make the kind of emphatic statement carried through by a structure such as *can only*. However, a reporter for a university bulletin would be speaking out of turn if he or she were to operate within anything other than:

(a) the news report as genre,
(b) cautious detachment as discourse,
(c) exposition as text.

These reporting requirements are adequately met by the use of structures such as the impersonal passive and the kind of non-committal lexis exemplified by *intended* (see Chapter 13 on text politeness).

From Global to Local

As the focus gradually narrows and the attention becomes more concentrated on a given item, readers tend to work more closely with a set of more localized patterns while remaining within the parameters set by

5

the kind of global structures illustrated above. But 'local' patterning and 'global' organization are not two separate activities. There is a constant interaction between the two levels, and local semantic, syntactic and textual decisions are constantly informed by the intertextual potential of genres, discourses and texts. This intertextuality is a function of some actual or virtual experience with texts we as language users will have had somehow, sometime, somewhere. Let us once again consider the initial sentence in sample A:

Europe is dying, Europe is dying, Europe is practically dead.

At the local level of textual analysis, more meaningful socio-cultural insights are generated and brought to bear on the reader's appreciation of the way the text is constructed. Thus, what we have in the above sentence is a set of features which may be characterized as follows:

(a) generic: the auctioneer's 'falling gavel' (*going, going, gone*), the excitable sports commentator reporting on the last few seconds before someone crosses the finishing line;

(b) discoursal: a contentious premise (evaluative situation-managing with an axe to grind); and

(c) textual: thesis set up as a 'strawman gambit' to initiate a line of argumentation which involves opposition to the thesis cited.

Text Structure

At this stage in the process, a structure format of some kind begins slowly to emerge. In the above text sample, for instance, a thesis cited to be opposed will pragmatically determine what kind of textual elements should follow. Pragmatic factors regulating aspects of text in context, such as intentionality or the purposes for which utterances are used, are crucial here, and these will feature most prominently in the analysis of the way texts are put together (Chapters 6 and 7), and are made operational (Chapters 8 and 9).

Text structure awareness enhances anticipation and thus acts as an effective sign-posting system which guides the reader in navigating textual terrains. Building on the status of the 'thesis cited to be opposed', we expect a counter- claim (opposition) followed by a substantiation and some form of conclusion. Schematically, this counter-argumentative structure may be represented as in Figure 1.1:

6

```
├—Thesis Cited to be Opposed
├—Opposition
├—Substantiation
├—Conclusion
```

Figure 1.1 The structure of the counter-argument

Context is thus seen to underlie our awareness of text type which, in turn, almost causally determines the compositional plan of a given text (i.e. its structure). Internalized as part of language users' textual competence are a set of structural configurations corresponding to a set of text typological foci. In effect, these serve a number of rhetorical purposes which, thankfully, are by no means infinite. Work on such schemata-, script- or scenario-like structures carried out within Artificial Intelligence, discourse linguistics, etc. is highly relevant.

Texture

The analysis of structure becomes more relevant when we embark on the next phase in the process of reworking a text—that of negotiating texture or the various devices (semantic, syntactic and textual) which together lend the text its basic quality of 'hanging together', of being both cohesive and coherent. It is in this domain of textuality that translators entertain the further assumption that texture realizes given structure formats which, as we have just seen, are more or less causally determined by higher-level contextual factors (text type and so on). It is also here that, at the realization end of the context-text chain of interaction, languages differ and decisions have to be taken as to how cross-cultural as well as translinguistic differences are best reconciled.

To illustrate the process of negotiating texture, let us consider some of the English-Arabic points of contrast which are likely to emerge in working with sample A above:

(1) The first decision which the translator has to take relates to source text repetition in sentence 1 (*dying, dying, dead*). This can either be preserved or variation opted for and, in this context, Arabic chooses variation. This is primarily motivated by generic considerations (the auctioneer's falling gavel), and is not incompatible with the nature of persuasive-polemical discourse and the lip-service, almost ironical/ sarcastic, function of the textual element in question (thesis cited to be opposed).

7

Compared with English, repetition in Arabic responds to a different set of contextual requirements. Had one opted for repetition in Arabic, the genre would have been shifted to that of the 'ideological manifesto', the discourse to that of the 'passionate appeal' and the text to that of perhaps a through-argument where emphasis serves to uphold a conviction. These communicative values obviously distort source text meaning and run counter to the perceived intentions of the writer.

(2) While the 'disjunction' in evidence between the three sub-elements in

Europe is dying, Europe is dying, Europe is practically dead

is preservable in the Arabic target text, this is a deviation from normal usage in this language and is permitted only if it is rhetorically-motivated. In Arabic, such elements would typically be conjoined with 'and'. However, given the generic, discoursal and textual constraints referred to above, disjunction seems happily to accommodate the rhetorical function involved (to sound unconvinced). An adjustment will thus have to be introduced into the system of target-language norms with which the translator usually works. But no sooner is such a readjustment in place than a case of reverting back to the norm is encountered. An important decision has to be taken regarding the connectivity between sentences 1 and 2:

1 *Europe is dying, Europe is dying, Europe is practically dead*

2 *Its vaunted exchange-rate mechanism lies in tatters.*

Here, having just had the mechanism adjusted, we find ourselves reverting to the conjunction-by-default since Arabic must have an explicit connector unless there is a good rhetorical reason to do without. Of course, it is not beyond textual competence (natural or induced) to have a dual control of this phenomenon and switch from conjunction to disjunction as and when appropriate, but this could only happen if we had the kind of context-sensitive grammars needed for this highly sophisticated level of discrimination.

(3) In opting for an explicit connector to introduce Sentence 2, however, a further complication arises. This is to do with whether (a) to use an additive (a default option), or (b) to use a substantiator (a text-motivated option). If we decide to substantiate, we must further make sure that the substantiation in this case is seen as an organizational

8

device within the thesis cited tongue-in-cheek and not as a genuine substantiator which turns the preceding element into one of a statement of conviction. To complicate matters, the same set of substantiators are used for either function in Arabic, and the only way to distinguish between the two and in this case relay a dismissive attitude would be through making other syntactic and semantic changes as we go along. This is to compensate for the deficit of not having two different sets of substantiating particles and to uphold the assumption that sentences 1, 2, etc. constitute an autonomous entity whose function is to cite a thesis which will be later opposed in its entirety.

(4) Whatever the mode of argumentation, source text disjunction between sentences 2 and 3 will have to be rendered as explicit addition in Arabic. So will the disjunction between 3 and 4, between 4 and 5, between 5 and 6 (which is already there), between 6 and 7 and between 7 and 8. Sentences 1–8 are fully reproduced here for ease of reference:

1 *Europe is dying, Europe is dying, Europe is practically dead.*
2 *Its vaunted exchange-rate mechanism lies in tatters.*
3 *The pound sterling, the lira and the peseta have dropped like stones.*
4 *Britain wallows in its longest postwar recession.*
5 *French economic growth is slowing,*
6 *and France's president has cancer.*
7 *Italy faces the worst labor disturbance in decades.*
8 *Even mighty Germany is hard up for cash.*

Given generic, discoursal and most significantly textual constraints, the structure of the text being negotiated looks increasingly more likely to be counter-argumentative, with the series of elements listed functioning as a facile substantiation of a thesis cited to be opposed and not defended. There is something about the texture which is 'tongue-in-cheek', hurried, ironical, even insincere.

(5) In ploughing through the sequence of sentences 1 to 8 above, we have had to cope with an interesting problem of texture. This is related to word order. We have appropriately opted for a Nominal sentence structure—Subject-Verb-Complement (SVC). In Arabic, however, the choice is two-way (SVC or a Verbal VSC) and this largely depends on text type and attendant discoursal and generic factors. Argumentation tends to favour the Nominal SVC. Less evaluative discourse, on the other hand, favours the Verbal VSC. Of course, this is a decision not taken automatically for entire texts, but is made for each element of text as

9

and when appropriate. However, as it happens, the entire sequence of sentences 1 to 8 above is argumentative and the Nominal structure is accordingly used throughout.

The choice of the Nominal is thus justified on this occasion. Given the isomorphism between English and Arabic in this respect, this would be welcome news for those who entertain prospects of a successful machine translation one day. But this happy state of affairs cannot always be guaranteed. For example, the sequence of sentences which starts with sentence 12 moves away from the Nominal SVC (used in the citing of and opposition to the thesis) to the Verbal VSC in the substantiation component. The move is not sudden and follows the opposition move which sums up the thesis and introduces the counter-thesis:

9 *The Maastricht Treaty . . . looks like a goner.*
10 *Not for years has the European scene looked so bleak.*
11 *And yet, the Old Continent is on the verge of accomplishing its most spectacular feat ever . . .*

The substantiation begins with a semi-Verbal (CVS)

12 *On January 1, 1993, the single market—or most of it—will come into effect.*

fafii al-awwal min yinaayer 1993 sataftaHu al-suuq al-mushtaraka abwaabahaa rasmiyyan

This is followed by another semi-Verbal (CVS):

13 *Henceforward, travelers . . . will travel . . .*

wa mundhu haadha al-taarikh sayakuun bi imkaani al-musaafiriin al-tanaqqul

and then pure Verbals in the remainder

14 *Internal customs duties will disappear.*

wa satakhtafii rusuum al-jamaarik, etc.

(6) In the negotiation of the above text, the point at which the substantiation (Sentence 12) is issued has been unhelpfully marked in English by the start of a new paragraph. Many translators always see

paragraphs to be valid units of text structure, which, alas, is not always the case. Some might argue that leaving indentations, etc. where they are is surely innocuous enough. Not in the case of a language like Arabic, however. The physical break can irreparably distort text comprehension and lead to some misguided conclusions about text meaning. For example, regardless of physical paragraphing, perceiving *On January 1, 1993* to be the start of a substantiation that is part and parcel of the text being negotiated is behind the decision in Arabic to opt not for a disjunction but for a conjunction and one which is specifically a substantiator. (For a fuller discussion of paragraphing and the translator, see Chapter 6).

By the same token, and regardless of physical paragraphing, perceiving a summation and responding to the need to signal its structure properly is behind the decision in Arabic to opt for a disjunction within one and the same paragraph between the end of *Even mighty Germany*, and the beginning of *The Maastricht Treaty*. This choice of disjunction is normally reserved for paragraph/text-initial elements but here comes to represent a rhetorically motivated deviation from the norm. Decisions like these are all informed by text type, structure and texture, an orientation which will be dealt with comprehensively as this book unfolds.

Summary

The primary aim of this introductory chapter has been to set the scene for the various themes that will form the basis of the arguments in this book. One way of making this introduction more interesting, I felt, was to choose an area of language activity that is both topical and controversial. I chose the decision-making involved in the translation process and sought to demonstrate that, for the discipline of contrastive linguistics to be a viable concern, it must get to grips with linguistic structures of a syntactic and a semantic nature, seen not within units such as the sentence and elements below it, but within the sentence and beyond. It must also encompass not only isolated surface features yielded by some intra- or inter-lingual comparison and contrast, but also the underlying strategies which regulate the entire interaction. The choice of translation as the basic skill from which to draw illustrations and examples is thus justified on the grounds that here we can most comprehensively observe the various contrastive discoursal processes at work.

Within our orientation to texts, which has its origins in the register membership of texts, wider contextual frameworks such as knowledge of the world, presupposition and inference, are bound to be involved;

so are culture and ideology. Here, in addition to text type, two other important categories are constantly referred to by the language user: genre and discourse. Thus, context almost causally determines the way a text is hierarchically organized (compositional plan or structure), and the way a text is put together (texture). Whether one approaches textual issues bottom-up (with textual manifestations as a point of departure) or top-down (starting with the context that has given rise to a particular text in the first place), an inevitable conclusion is that text is the ultimate unit of effective communication.

2

Foundation Disciplines

The choices which a speaker or writer makes from among the textual resources of his or her language have been the subject of many different approaches which originated in what may generally be referred to as the field of style studies. As a result, the notion of style itself has seen a proliferation of definitions over the years. Style has become an umbrella term under which are lumped together all kinds of factors, textual and contextual. Paradoxically, the notion of register analysis, the introduction of which was intended to rid us of some of the confusion which was rife in approaches to the meaning and function of stylistic choice, has itself experienced a similar fate.

By way of clearing up the confusion, it is perhaps helpful at the outset to recognize that register analysis was initially a reaction against conceptions of language in which linguistic behaviour was seen either as a mechanical response to external stimuli or a cognitive issue to do with the psycholinguistic ability to generate well-formed sentences. The ultimate goal was to try and resolve the tension between what is basically a rhetorical-exegetical view of style, on the one hand, and on the other, those views of language which made no concession to the fact that linguistic behaviour is imbued with social meaning. In other words, for its existence, register analysis has had to rely as much on classical disciplines such as rhetoric and the study of style as on much more recent trends within linguistics, sociolinguistics and linguistic stylistics. It is this conciliatory role which register theory was to play that finally gave rise to the notion of language variation collectively referred to as register variation.

It is appropriate, therefore, that this chapter should start with an overview of some of the foundation disciplines, such as rhetoric and style studies. This will be followed by a review of linguistic approaches to variation in language, culminating with the theory of register as propounded in the 1960s and 1970s. Finally, an attempt will be made to extend register analysis to include factors such as the semiotics of signs and the pragmatics of intention. Here, the pioneering work of Michael Halliday and his colleagues will be heavily drawn upon as it is the approach which has provided the basis both for the original conception of register analysis and for later extensions. This has indeed gone a long way towards improving our understanding of what context involves and of how contextual factors link up with text in subtle and intricate ways.

The Foundations

Rhetoric

Rhetoric has exercised such a considerable influence on language use over the centuries that one can legitimately describe it as the single most important source of inspiration for present-day approaches to beyond-the-sentence linguistics, including the school of register analysis. Underlying the remarkably rich tradition is a basic assumption that is still recognizable as valid today, namely that discourse can be com-municated in a 'right' and therefore most effective way, or in a 'wrong' and therefore ineffective way, and that the right way can be taught (Grimes 1975: 12). Although the bias in orientation here is in favour of the 'public speaker', this has nonetheless evinced a genuine interest in language as real discourse. That is, the aim of rhetorical inquiry, though never explicitly stated, was the classification and refinement of the categories of and the criteria for effective communication. Taking into consideration aspects of the communicative process such as 'speaker', 'audience' and 'message', rhetoric truly pioneered what we recognize today as basic components in many models of communication.

Thus, albeit in a rudimentary manner, discourse processes as we understand them today were never far from the rhetorician's mind. For example, Quintilian identifies discourse production in terms of a number of basic stages: the moulding, ordering, transforming and delivering of thoughts appropriate to a given communicative aim in response to factors of the communicative act such as subject matter and participants (Kennedy 1969; John 1978). Quintilian also discusses discourse as a product, this time in terms of three different kinds of oratory and the external factors relevant to each: the deliberative-persuasive discourse of the politician, the forensic-defensive discourse of the attorney, and the epideictic-ceremonial discourse of the preacher. This 'audience appeal' hypothesis (Hartmann 1980) was the underlying framework for a typology of discourse that has remained influential to the present day in the classification of texts. (For views on rhetorical traditions other than those of the West, e.g. Arab-Islamic, see Chapter 5).

New Rhetoric
Recently, the influence of classical rhetoric has manifested itself in a body of work dealing primarily with creative writing and the process of composition. While the prescriptive do's and don'ts of the classical rhetorical tradition still persist, it is becoming more accepted that formal logic and the principles of usage should be subdued in favour of a more descriptive attitude to how writers themselves feel about the way a given discourse is put together. Young, Becker and Pike (1970: xii) have this to say about the new focus:

> Rhetoric is concerned primarily with a creative process that includes all the choices a writer makes from his earliest tentative explorations of a problem in what has been called the 'pre-writing' stage of the writing process through choices in arrangement and strategy for a particular audience, to the final editing of the final draft.

The status assigned to 'pre-writing' choices is defined in terms of two types of constraints. One is imposed by the lexical, phonological and grammatical hierarchies of language. The other consists of a set of rhetorical choices which derive, primarily, from the responses and reactions which language users have to the use of the linguistic code and, secondarily, from the use of the code itself. This is how the textual surface is moulded to manifest rhetorical purposes. As will be shown later, these insights into the relationship of form and function were soon to become basic procedures in the functional analysis of discourse within the theory of register.

Style Studies
A number of attempts have been made with the aim of explicating the elusive notion of 'style' in texts. The close reading method, or *explication de texte*, to name but one basic trend within style studies, had as its aim:

> a close reading which correlated historical and linguistic information and sought connection between aesthetic responses and specific stimuli in the text. (Enkvist 1973: 28)

Within literary studies, this view of style challenged well-established traditions based on aspects of the literary work such as biography, society and psychology as related to the literary substance in question. However,

15

an element of polarity persisted between those who took the literary substance and textual detail as the basis of style analysis and those who took factors external to the literary substance to be relevant in the definition of style. It was not until Russian Formalism and Literary Structuralism emerged that a drift was discerned towards an analysis of style which takes into account the text as a whole.

The focus of the Russian formalists, for example, was on artistic devices and not on content. It was the 'how' rather than the 'what' which the student of literature was encouraged to emphasize. The relationship between style and context and the definition of style as deviation from the norm thus became salient features of literary analysis. These notions have been influential for decades and have left their mark on a number of schools of stylistics including that of linguistic stylistics.

Linguistic Stylistics
Against this background of style in text, linguistic stylistics came to extend the domain of the inquiry to include the text as a 'whole', a new vision of text in context leading linguists such as Hill (1958: 406) to redefine stylistics in terms of:

> all those relations among linguistic entities which are statable, or may be statable, in terms of wider spans than those which fall within the limits of the sentence.

This view of style has facilitated an approach to language variation which relies on text-norm comparison of relationships beyond the sentence. The approach to such phenomena, however, varied procedurally. The starting point may be an undivided mass of textual material that can yield different portions of text distinguished on the basis of the distribution of linguistic features. Alternatively, the emphasis on distinct stretches of textual material and the way these correlate with contextual categories that govern stylistic choice in the same or a different body of textual material has provided us with a valid analytical framework (Enkvist 1973: 62). It is here that a shift towards style in relation to the essential impurity of text types began to be discerned laying down the basis for further work on categories such as genre, discourse and text.

Core Linguistics

The above survey of basic notions of style is primarily intended to underline the tension which existed between a rich body of rhetorical insights, on the one hand, and views of language encouraged by the linguistic climate prevalent in the first half of this century, on the other. Labels such as Bloomfieldian Structuralism and Chomskyan Transformational Grammar, spring to mind as precursors of a stance on linguistic behaviour which was always in conflict with notions handed down to us by older schools of language study. As will be explained shortly, it is the revival of traditional analyses of form and content, using recent linguistic methods and procedures, that ushered in a new era in text linguistics. Here, we saw a valuable synthesis of views which may best be exemplified by the work of Firth in the 1940s.

Bloomfieldian Structuralism
In assessing the views of American structuralist linguists, it is of paramount importance not to overlook the purpose of their inquiry and the nature of the intellectual climate and the interdisciplinary activity going on at the time. For example, Bloomfield (1933: 170) held that the sentence is considered to be:

> an independent linguistic form, not included by virtue of any grammatical construction in any larger linguistic form.

This should not be construed as willful neglect of the upper limits in the grammatical hierarchy. Such views must rather be seen as motivated by a set of meta-theoretical considerations deemed appropriate at the time.

But, given our concern with text, it is perhaps legitimate to claim that certain structuralist practices (such as the Distributional Method and Immediate Constituent analysis) seem to have hindered rather than helped the development of studies of meaning and textual unity. To refer to structuralism again, Bloomfield advocated that three parts may be distinguished in any linguistic act of speech: practical events preceding the act, the speech itself, and practical events following the act (1933: 23). The first and last parts are termed 'speaker's stimulus' and 'hearer's response' respectively. Linguistic studies, Bloomfield insists, should be restricted to the intermediary aspect of 'speech', with no regard whatsoever to the context of the utterance. This neglect of the complex interaction between speech and context of situation is precisely where the inapplicability to discourse studies of such models of linguistic description becomes clearest.

17

Transformational Grammar

As I have already indicated, the aim in this chapter is to assess selectively what the various schools of linguistics have achieved within the terms of reference of what they set out to do. It is only then that we can begin to see what is missing in the light of our primary concern with the unit 'text'. Thus, transformational-generative grammar, to take an example of a brand of linguistics that has been extremely influential since the late 50s and early 60s, set out to formulate:

> the rules that are necessary for the explicit construction of sentences of a language, omitting the problem of formulating the rules for constructing larger linguistic entities such as paragraphs and discourses. (Langendoen 1970: 4)

Similarly, issues of language in use were left out, hence distinctions such as that between 'competence' and 'performance' were adopted. From the perspective of discourse studies, however, dichotomies like these can only highlight some basic flaws in the entire approach. In attempting to account for the communicative process involved in using language, and before rebutting the basic transformationalists' argument, Widdowson (1971: 35–6) summarizes their stance in the following terms:

> Performance is, in effect, a residual category containing everything which is not accounted for under competence. The suggestion is that it subsumes everything about language which is imperfect or irregular, all systematic features being accounted for within competence, which is the repository, as it were, of the speaker's knowledge of his language.

But, as Widdowson goes on to argue, every performance must somehow presuppose some basic competence. In the most unwieldy kinds of discourse, there is a systematicity which reflects degrees of speaker's competence that must be accounted for in any attempt to explain the social dimension of linguistic behaviour. Textual competence may thus be a more apt term to adopt if we assume as we should that, although interaction makes its own rules, it is by no means seamless. This and similar themes will be tackled in greater detail in some of the coming chapters.

Firthian Functional Linguistics

The resolution of the tension between the system-oriented views of language exemplified by the above schools of linguistics, on the one hand, and the vision of text as embedded in a context of situation, on the other, was to be the main aim of a new trend in linguistics heralded by J. R. Firth in Britain. Influenced by the work of the anthropologist Malinowski, Firth maintained that the study of meaning is the *raison d'être* of linguistics and that meaning should be viewed in terms of what an utterance is intended to achieve rather than merely the sense of the individual words making up the utterance.

Context of situation thus becomes part and parcel of what we mean. This relationship between the function of an utterance and its context now includes participants in speech events, the action taking place, other relevant features of the situation and the effects of the verbal action. Given this orientation, meaning could best be viewed in terms of 'function' in 'context'. According to Firth (1968: 92):

> What I may call the total meaning of a text in situation is broken down and dispensed at a series of levels such as the phonological, the grammatical and the situational levels.

Thus it is the recognition of the cross-fertilization constantly taking place between these levels of linguistic expression that was the hallmark of Firthian linguistics for years to come.

Halliday's Systemic-functional Grammar

Working within the parameters set by Firthian linguistics, Halliday defines language in terms of the basic distinction between context of culture and context of situation. Within the context of culture, language is envisaged as:

> a form of behaviour potential, an open-ended set of options in behaviour that are available to the individual. (Halliday 1973: 48)

Context of situation, on the other hand, is seen as:
> the environment of any particular selection that is made from the total set of options accounted for in the context of culture. (Halliday 1973: 71)

That is, while context of culture defines the 'potential', context of situation accounts for the 'actual'. As Halliday (1973) puts it, 'can do' is not a

19

linguistic notion, and for it to be related to 'can say', an intermediary concept has to be brought in: 'can mean'. Meaning potential is seen as a set of options available to the speaker-hearer, and forming, in its totality, the possibility of encoding in language what is not language. This potential thus ranges over the significant variation which all textually competent users of language command. In line with Hymes' view of 'the native theory and systems of speaking' (e.g. 1964), this variable linguistic behaviour is regulated by what came to be known as communicative competence, an in-built mechanism that determines when to speak and when to remain silent, which code to use, where, when and to whom.

Register Theory

In a well-known treatment of register, Halliday, McIntosh and Strevens (1964: 87–89) introduce the concept in the following way:

> Language varies as its function varies: it differs in different situa-
> tions. The name given to a variety of a language distinguished
> according to use is 'register' . . . It is by their formal properties that
> registers are defined.

Numerous studies with a theoretical bias and numerous textbooks and manuals have been inspired by the rapidly developing framework of register analysis (Robinson 1980). But, as will be made clear in the course of the following discussion, this notion of variety and the analytic apparatus proposed suffer from serious shortcomings, the rectification of which has occupied workers in the field (including Halliday and his colleagues) for a good part of the last three decades following the introduction of the original theory.

But before embarking on a critical assessment of the notion of register, it may be helpful to describe briefly the basic analytic framework proposed. Catford (1965:83) neatly captures the background to the emergence of register theory in the following terms:

> The concept of a 'whole language' is so vast and heterogeneous
> that it is not operationally useful for many linguistic purposes,
> descriptive, comparative, and pedagogical. It is therefore desirable
> to have a framework of categories for the classification of 'sub-
> languages' or varieties within a total language.

So what is it that determines variation in language? Within the framework of register analysis, two dimensions of language variation are recognized. The first has to do with the user in a particular language event: who (or what) the speaker/writer is. Such 'user-related' varieties (Corder 1973) are called 'dialects'. The second dimension relates to the use to which we put language. Use-related varieties are known as 'registers'. These and related issues will be discussed in the next chapter.

Summary

In this chapter, various forms of functional linguistics have been presented as important developments which are best understood against a background of classical disciplines such as rhetoric and style studies on the one hand, and, on the other, of modern trends within linguistics proper (e.g. structural and transformational grammar). Neither of these two major strands has been treated exhaustively here, and a number of important trends (Pike's tagmemics, Coserin's 'norms', etc.) have had to be left out. From the perspective of applied linguistics, register theory has been one of the more important proposals made within functional linguistics. The influence of register analysis in the sphere of language studies, however, lies in the very fact that the original notion has never been static. It has undergone numerous revisions which have incorporated new and valuable insights into the various aspects of what is meant by the saying that 'man speaks in many registers'.

3

The Myth of the Single Register

In this chapter, I intend to review basic trends within register theory, and the various attempts to expand the notion of register variation. One way of approaching this is to present the use-user dimensions as making up what is here referred to as the institutional-communicative dimension of context. Together with two other domains of contextual activity, one catering for intentionality (pragmatics), the other for intertextuality (semiotics), register envelops text and almost causally determines text type, structure and texture.

Text type is seen in terms of two basic contextual specifications, that is, 'monitoring' or 'managing' a given situation. In turn, text structure and texture respectively subsume the principles of organizing a text

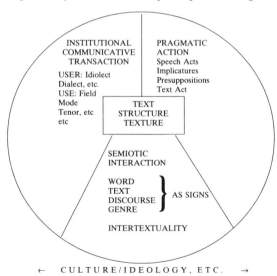

Figure 3.1 The three dimensions of context

hierarchically and the factors which regulate the continuity of the text as a communicative occurrence. As I will show in due course, this comprehensive view of register counteracts the prevalent myth of 'one situation = one language'. The various strands of text in context may be represented diagrammatically as in Figure 3.1 adapted from Hatim and Mason (1990):

One or More Registers?

The following text samples all relate to the Maastricht Treaty signed by the representatives of the twelve nations of the European Community. It may be worth noting that, in the heyday of register analysis as traditionally practised, the first three text samples (A, B, C) would all have been glossed as 'legalese', leaving us with 'journalese' as the register of the last two (D1 and D2). But, as will become abundantly clear from the arguments advanced throughout this book, these texts differ from each other in a number of basic and significant ways. What is involved may certainly cater for a particular subject matter, or level of formality, but other systems of language variation are also clearly at work.

Sample A

Part Two
Citizenship of the Union
Article 8

Citizenship of the Union is hereby established. Every person holding the nationality of a Member State shall be a citizen of the Union.

From *The Treaty of Maastricht*

Sample B

The treaty creates citizenship of the European Union. Everybody holding the nationality of a member state will be a citizen of the Union, with rights and duties conferred by the treaty. (See note 10)

Abridged by *The Independent* (11 October 1992)

Sample C

Note 10

This was designed to give the idea of the union some meaning. But it has proved to be one of the most controversial elements in some countries, since it means that 'foreigners' get the vote.

Annotated by *The Independent* (11 October 1992)

Sample D1
European Community
Decommissioned
From our Brussels Correspondent

The mood inside the European Commission has not been so glum for almost a decade. Since 1985, when Jacques Delors became its president, the Commission has enjoyed seven years of growing power and influence. Its proposals, including those that created the single-market programme, made it the motor driving the European Community. But the recent wave of hostility to interference from 'Brussels' has badly dented the Commission's self-confidence. It is reluctant to make any proposal that could upset entrenched national interests, lest EC governments seek to trim its powers. The motor has all but stalled.

Sample D2

Sir Leon Britton and Martin Bengemann, whose responsibilities are respectively competition and the single market, argue that the Commission should risk courting unpopularity and push on with its legislative programmes. Other commissioners think that would be folly. Christine Scrivener, the taxation commissioner, has called for a legislative pause. Mr Delors, the president, now stresses the need for caution.

The Economist 10 October 1992

As I have already pointed out, in the early days of register analysis, this kind of textual material would have all too readily earned single, indiscriminate labels. But anything beyond a superficial view of the way language varies would immediately reveal that such a categorization barely scratches the surface of what is actually going on inside these texts.

For the moment, however, a brief description of what is actually happening in each of these texts is in order. Sample A reflects the powers assumed by the text producer to form without option the future behaviour of the text receiver (the language of law). Sample B, on the other hand, displays the total absence of such powers since the summarizer's sole responsibility is, ideally, to the facts as he or she sees them (i.e. no particular case to argue 'for' or 'against'). Finally, in samples C and D, one is, curiously enough, in a domain not dissimilar to that of sample A (i.e. the formation of future behaviour) but with one basic difference. This relates to the option which the receivers of samples C and D enjoy of not heeding the argument if they so wish, no matter how persuasive it is intended to be. But here we may observe that, while the producer of sample C would not take exception to being ignored, as the argument is not his own but somebody else's, the writer of sample D1 has put forward an argument of his own and it is his credibility as an arguer that is at stake. Nevertheless, as will become clear in the course of the following discussion, arguing is not our Brussels correspondent's only card: he could, if he so wished, play a different hand and achieve his overall persuasive objective through a different channel (e.g. in his capacity as a reporter in sample D2).

Cast in more practical terms, these issues give rise to a number of relevant questions: What are the criteria for judging one kind of language as appropriate or inappropriate for this or that kind of writing? In what ways does our reaction to appropriateness in instances like these form part of our textual competence? Are these critical skills teachable and learnable? What are the ground rules for the assignment of register membership, if such a contextual option exists at all?

Register Membership

Use and User
Within the model of text processing developed here, context is taken both as a point of departure and a destination for text users in their attempt to communicate or appreciate the meaning of a message. In this domain of sense- making, three contextual dimensions are distinguished: who is speaking to whom (institutional-communicative), for what purpose (pragmatics) and through what kind of socio-cultural 'signs' (semiotics). The institutional-communicative dimension subsumes the various aspects of the transaction conducted between text producer and text receiver in their capacity as 'users' of a particular dialect, idiolect, etc. (e.g. the colloquialism of *foreigners get the vote* [sample C]).

But, by themselves, user-related variables are not sufficient, hence the need for a different set of defining features. Producers and receivers of texts operate within constraints imposed by the particular 'use' to which they put their language. This provides us with the second basic aspect of variation which includes 'field' (e.g. the legal jargon of sample A), the 'mode' of interaction (sample A as written to be read reflectively) and 'tenor' or level of formality (sample A being by far the most formal).

It is tenor, however, that is perhaps the more crucial factor in regulating the complex relationships between addresser and addressee. In its simplest form, this is the formal-informal stance which co-communicants adopt towards one another and which can range from casual to deferential, from the most intimate to the most impersonal.

Different terms have been used by different writers for this 'level of formality': 'style', 'status', 'attitude', 'relative social status' and so on. The various terms, however, all converge on the central point that, as Young (1985: 284) points out, tenor 'concerns the level of formality of the relation between the participants in the linguistic event'.

Functional Tenor
The level of formality is in fact an 'inter-level' in that it overlaps in a number of significant ways with field of discourse, on the one hand, and with mode, on the other. Diagrammatically, this interrelationship may be represented as in Figure 3.2:

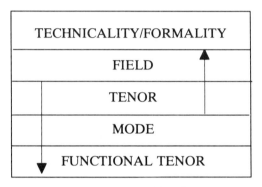

Figure 3.2 Tenor v. field and mode

The cross-fertilization taking place between tenor and field results in 'formality' and 'technicality' emerging as two aspects of tenor. This is collectively viewed in terms of stabilized patterns of 'role' relationships which Halliday (1978: 222) explains in the following terms:

> The language we use varies according to the level of formality, of technicality, and so on. What is the variable underlying this type of distinction? Essentially, it is the role relationships in the situation in question: who the participants in the communication group are, and in what relationship they stand to each other.

The overlap between tenor and mode, on the other hand, gives rise to what Gregory and Carroll (1978: 53) call 'functional tenor':

> the category used to describe what language is being used for in the situation. Is the speaker trying to persuade? to exhort?

Or, indeed, is he trying 'to regulate' (as in sample A) or merely 'to inform' (as in sample B)?

Functional tenor (e.g. persuader, discipliner, informer) thus builds into the analysis a set of role relationships obtaining in a given situation (e.g. politician v. the electorate, lawmaker v. the public, reporter v. a particular readership). The participants are now defined not only in terms of single-scale categories such as formal or informal, but also in terms of other aspects of message construction such as level of technicality and degree of formality obtaining directly in face-to-face encounters or indirectly as between writer and audience. That is, in addition to the semi-formality of the 'persuader' in sample D1, the slightly more formal tenor of the 'informer' in sample B, and the ultra-formality of the lawmaker in sample A, these text producers also engage in different role relationships with their receivers which entail particular shifts in functional tenor (e.g. the reporter-arguer role-switching in samples D1 and D2). Institutional-communicative transactions thus acquire an interactive character which is the domain of the other level of context—that of semiotics.

Interaction through Signs

Ideational, Textual and Interpersonal Meta-functions
So far, my investigation of both personal tenor and functional tenor, with technicality and role relationships forming the two basic aspects of the latter, has brought out the way in which communication materializes institutionally in terms of use and user of language. However, for rhetorical goals such as 'persuading', 'informing' and so on to be properly pursued, and for role relationships to stabilize, language users must negotiate meanings in texts and thus deal with context more interactively. As Hatim and Mason (1990: 64–5) point out from the perspective of discourse and the translator:

> Seeing the meaning of texts as something which is negotiated between producer and receiver and not as a static entity, independent of human processing activity once it has been encoded, is, we believe, the key to an understanding of translating, teaching translating and judging translations.

This negotiation between speaker and hearer or writer and reader forms the basis of one level of 'semiotic' interaction. This involves the exchange of meanings as signs between a speaker and a hearer. But, co-communicants do not merely exchange meanings which display a certain

27

level of technicality, bear the features of a certain mode of interaction (spoken v. written) or exhibit a certain degree of formality. Rather, they perceive ideational meanings within a given field, textual meanings within a given mode and interpersonal meanings within a given tenor. Field will here subsume social processes and social institutions (e.g. racism), tenor will subsume aspects of power and solidarity (e.g. the ambivalent status of the middle-manager) and mode will subsume physical distance (e.g. the proximity of the footballer to the game when describing it in the field as opposed to the commentator on the match or indeed the journalist reporting the match the following day). To illustrate the three meta-functions briefly, let us consider the following exchange between an interviewer and a middle-manager:

Sample E

Interviewer: If I asked you to draw a line in this factory between managers and below managers, where would you draw the line?

Middle-manager: Oh, I think that would be difficult . . . because, really, if you look at the management of our division, it consists, really, of several people with a figurehead.

Interviewer: What do you mean by a figurehead?

Middle Manager: Well, literally, he,—he's the face that is nailed at the front of the ship. But [this ship] is officered, if you like, by people who form the management team.

(From Jones and Kress 1981)

Here, the middle-manager is being deliberately ambiguous about his occupational status and role. True, features of language use or user are crucial contextualization cues without which no proper processing of any text is conceivable. But as we listen to such an exchange, we are not solely tuning in to, say, business administration as the field of discourse, but to a range of ideational/institutional processes such as the motivated suppression of agency in:

(a) nominalizing 'someone manages' and opting for 'management', and

(b) passivizing 'X officers the ship' and ending up with 'it is officered'.

The aim in both these linguistic processes is without doubt to maintain the ambiguity and, in the words of Jones and Kress (p. 70) they tell us 'nothing about actual management, who does what'. By the same token, features of the spoken mode or the generally informal tenor (*because, really, if you look*) must surely be seen not merely as normal features of a given register, but as a reflection of the 'masking' going on 'textually' (an aspect of mode), and the need to maintain a semblance of solidarity 'interpersonally' (tenor).

The semiotic domain of context, then, transforms institutional-communicative transactions into more meaningful engagements. The way in which levels of basic communicativeness (field, mode and tenor) acquire a semiotic specification may be represented diagrammatically as in Figure 3.3:

Field	Ideational	I N T E R T E X T U A L I T Y	Social processes Social institutions
Mode	Textual		Addresser—Addresee Physical Distance
Tenor	Interpersonel		Power Solidarity

Figure 3.3 The semiotics of field, mode and tenor

A given text or textual element is the product of all three semiotic categories. The ideational component captures cultural experience and expresses what goes on in the environment, manipulating 'transitivity' relationships to best effect (e.g. 'the ship is officered' v. 'X officers the ship'). The textual component provides texture devices which make ideational expression both cohesive and coherent in a given textual environment (the use of *really*, repetition, etc. in the middle-manager's answer above). Finally, the interpersonal component helps co-communicants to express attitudes and assess what is happening around them and through them (e.g. the middle-manger's use of 'you' to secure the endorsement of his interlocutor). (On these and related notions, see Halliday 1978).

It is in the latter domain of interpersonal activity, however, that interaction moves to a slightly higher level than simply that of a speaker negotiating with a hearer. Interaction now becomes one in which the speaker interacts not only with the hearer, but also with the utterance he or she produces. The hearer would similarly interact, not only with the speaker, but also with the utterance he or she receives. In this way, utterances become 'signs' or semiotic constructs which embody the assumptions, presuppositions and conventions that reflect the ways a given culture constructs and partitions reality.

Let us now cast our minds back to samples B1 and B2 in Chapter 1 and recall how the university Dean (or his impersonator) complemented the basic interaction between him and his audience, whom he took to be 'sceptical', 'eager', 'bored' or whatever, by a desire to tease out from his utterance an emphatic assertion. We also remember how the reporter, on the other hand, suppressed such a desire, which is once again evidence of some form of interaction going on not merely between him and his readers who are there to be informed and not entertained, but also between him and his utterance. This is all undertaken within a 'universe of discourse' that neatly seems to divide into those of the 'exhorters' and those of the 'reporters'. It is as if by some divine linguistic convention that an element of territoriality emerges from this kind of division of labour which is both well-charted and respected. Encroachings, transgressions or excesses are immediately spotted and shunned as 'going over the top' (a label which our reporter would have earned had he dared to write *this venture can only enhance*) or as 'being coy' (with which the Dean would have been described had he opted for the passive *this venture is intended to enhance*).

Intertextuality

For an optimally effective expression of meanings which bear a variety of semiotic values, utterances themselves interact with each other within and between texts. That is, in tandem with the interaction between a speaker (and utterances produced) and a hearer (and utterances received), another, far more important, level of semiotic activity emerges to facilitate the interaction of sign with sign. The principle which regulates this activity is 'intertextuality' through which textual occurrences are seen in terms of their dependence on other prior, relevant occurrences. The language of the exhorter, for example, is almost a universal code recognized as such. Within this kind of linguistic manipulation, devices such as emotive repetition and other forms of emphasis would be tokens of a type of occurrence that carries within it traces of its origins wherever and whenever these happen to be. Our ability to perceive and interact with this type of meaning depen-

30

dence on context is a prerequisite for appropriate and efficient communication.

Genre, Discourse and Text

In order to impose order on this seemingly open-ended interaction of signs, a number of semiotic structures may be recognized. These are genre, discourse and text, introduced briefly in Chapter 1, p. 4. Signs occurring within parameters and under constraints set by these categories constantly move about by means of the semiotic mechanism of intertextuality. Genres are conventionalized forms of language in use, each with its own functions and goals adopted by a given community of text users or socio-cultural grouping to cater for a particular social occasion. The ineffective orator opting for 'coy' impersonal constructions (the passive, etc.) or the over-the-top reporter waxing lyrical with emphatic constructions (repetition, etc.) are all instances of mishandling genres.

Such generic structures are ideational in origin. If we recall the example of the 'auctioneer's falling gavel' genre in sample A discussed in Chapter 1, the ideational categories actor-process-goal, blown up to macro-level, are very much in evidence. Ideational expression seems to be a prerequisite for genres to be effective vehicles of signification. But no less basic to generic structures are two other aspects of semiotic activity: one textual, the other interpersonal. Before proceeding to define

FIELD		S		GENRE
		O		
		S		
		I		
		O		
MODE		T		TEXT
		E		
		X		
		T		
TENOR		U		DISCOURSE
		A		
		L		
		PRACTICE		

Figure 3.4 Deeper levels of semiotics

31

these intertextual sign types, however, Figure 3.3 above may be usefully upgraded to reflect this added level of semiotic analysis—that of socio-textual practice:

The textual component reflects fluctuations in rhetorical intention from, say, 'arguing' (e.g. samples D1 and, to a lesser extent, sample C) to 'narrating' (e.g. sample B and, to a lesser extent, sample D2). These rhetorical purposes impose their own constraints on how a sequence of sentences becomes a text. Texts are units of interaction, both intended and accepted as coherent and cohesive wholes only when realizing a set of mutually relevant communicative intentions appropriate to a given rhetorical purpose.

But, in the same way as the pursuit of a given rhetorical goal in a text requires that this be conducted within a particular generic framework, it must also strike an ideological note of some kind. That is, in their attempts to serve a given rhetorical purpose, within the do's and don'ts of a particular genre, text producers and receivers necessarily engage in the composition or analysis of 'attitudinal meanings' (e.g. the Euro-sceptic in sample C). This attitudinal, interpersonal component is what I shall call discourse.

Genres and texts, then, ultimately involve attitudinally-determined expression or discourse. The polemic as the genre of sample D1 above, utilizing argumentation as a text-type focus, has entailed a particular attitudinal stance (the evaluative discourse of situation-managing). On the other hand, the report as the genre of sample B, utilizing narration as a text format, has engaged its producers and receivers in a different set of attitudinal meanings (the non-evaluative discourse of monitoring). Discoursal values relay power relations and help define ideology. This aspect of meaning is properly the domain of what Halliday (1978: 112) refers to as the 'participatory function of language, language as doing something'.

Intentionality and Action

As I have pointed out, the two basic levels of semiotic interaction—that of the text producer with a text receiver and that of utterance with utterance—necessarily involve another level of interaction, namely that of speaker or hearer with utterances produced or received. For its success, this latter kind of interaction primarily relies on intentionality —the ability to 'do things with words', the capacity to deploy one's utterance for a 'purpose'. Here, semiotics or signification through signs acquires a pragmatic dimension which Stalnaker (1972: 380) defines as:

the study of the purposes for which sentences are used, of the real world conditions under which a sentence may be appropriately used as an utterance.

Utterance signs within sample A are thus pragmatically different from those of the other texts in our sample. Apart from the locutionary acts involved, or lexical and grammatical well-formedness, distinct communicative forces (illocutionary acts) are always in evidence (e.g. 'directing' and 'representing'). Directive speech acts are intended to form future behaviour. Representatives, on the other hand, seek simply to depict a state of affairs for the benefit of the text receiver. Such illocutionary forces inevitably lead to what has been termed a perlocutionary effect or the ultimate communicative objective sought (e.g. persuading, informing). Text samples such as B and D1 may now be seen to involve two distinct kinds of audience: those to be informed and those to be persuaded.

Managing and Monitoring

From the perspective of creative writing and literary discourse, Britton (1963: 37) puts forward an interesting audience dichotomy akin to the two kinds of audience we have envisaged for texts such as the summary B and the counter-argument D1. Britton explains these in the following terms:

> If I describe what has happened to me in order to get my hearer to do something for me, or even to change his opinion about me, then I remain a participant in my own affairs and invite him to become one. If, on the other hand, I merely want to interest him, so that he . . . appreciates with me the intricate patterns of events, then not only do I invite him to be a spectator, but I am myself a spectator of my own experience . . . As a participant I should be planning . . . As a spectator I should be day-dreaming.

The distinction between participant and spectator is almost identical to another distinction from artificial intelligence made popular and more accessible by recent· work in text pragmatics (e.g. Beaugrande and Dressler 1981). This is the difference between 'managing' or 'monitoring' a given situation, a distinction that we have been using in a rudimentary fashion so far and to which we shall return in more detail in the coming chapters. The goal of the producer of sample D1 is clear enough: to manage by arguing for the need for firmness in government. The goal of the producer of sample D2, on the other hand, is far less personalized though not totally void of ulterior motives: it is primarily to monitor a situation by reporting a sequence of events. It should not be overlooked, however, that what is involved in D2 is not merely introducing a speaker, but introducing someone whose ideas are going to be examined rather critically.

Summary

In this chapter, the notion of register was presented in terms of both the original framework proposed in the early 1960s and the modifications on the original model that were made some twenty years later. The latter developments are seen here within a model of discourse processing that owes a great deal to the view of language as social semiotic put forward by Halliday and his colleagues as well as to contributions made to the science of texts by text linguists such as Beaugrande and Dressler.

4

Argumentation Across Cultures

This chapter presents a model of text types which supplements the model of contextual analysis presented so far. In the following discussion, argumentation is dealt with in greater detail to reflect both the importance of this particular type of text as a vehicle of persuasive strategy and our interest in cross-cultural differences in utilizing such a strategy. Such differences exist not only between different languages but also within the same language and seem to point to deep divisions among the various subcultures within a society.

Texts can be seen as carriers of ideological meaning, a factor which makes them particularly vulnerable to changing socio-cultural norms. A case in point may be the dormancy of a particular text form in a particular language. As will be made clear in the course of the following discussion, the mode of arguing by citing an opponent's thesis, then countering it—a format which is common in languages such as English—is fairly uncommon in Arabic, for example. Communicative deficits such as this have serious implications for a pragmatics of language in social life, particularly in domains of language use such as intercultural communication.

A Text Typology

Many attempts have been made to develop a text typology. But, primarily due to the absence of coherent descriptions of context, almost all attempts have suffered from serious shortcomings. As Hatim and Mason (1990) point out, classifying texts according to situational criteria such as 'field of discourse' amounts to little more than a statement of subject matter, with unhelpful examples such as 'journalistic' or 'scientific' text types. Similarly, categorizing texts in terms of an over-general notion of 'domain' leads to text types such as 'literary' and 'didactic', categories which are too broad to yield a useful classification (for a criticism of early register analysis and the text typologies advocated within this trend, see Crystal and Davy 1969).

In the text-type model adopted in this book, a view of context is taken which is sufficiently broad to accommodate communicative use-user distinctions, pragmatic notions such as intentionality, and semiotic categories such as genre and discourse. Intertextuality ensures that the various domains of context are in constant interaction, ultimately leading to the emergence of text types. In this way, an utterance within a sequence of utterances would be described as a series of semiotic 'signs' pragmatically 'intended' by someone to 'communicate' something to someone, sometime, somewhere. In the process, a text-type focus slowly emerges which may, at a very general level of abstraction, be identified in terms of a tendency either to 'monitor' or to 'manage' a given situation. Beaugrande and Dressler (1981: 162) define these terms in the following way:

> if the dominant function of a text is to provide a reasonably unmediated account of the situation model, SITUATION MONITORING is being performed. If the dominant function is to guide the situation in a manner favourable to the text producer's goals, SITUATION MANAGEMENT is being carried out.

More specifically, text type focus, or the predominant rhetorical purpose served by a given text, is identified in terms of what Werlich (1976: 19) refers to as 'specific factors and circumstances from the whole set of factors' in a communicative situation. Recognizing a broad distinction between texts which set out to 'monitor' a situation and texts which set out to 'manage' a situation, a typology of texts is proposed in which the following are distinguished:

Exposition
These may focus on the analysis of given concepts. Conceptual exposition of this kind can be illustrated by sample A below, which combines synthesis (paragraph 1) with analysis (paragraph 2):

Sample A
> The chief causes of this pollution are alleged to be the non-enforcement of the law for the prevention of smoke from factories, the imposition of inadequate penalties, the neglect to limit works which produce noxious vapours to special areas where they can be closely supervised and so do the least possible amount of harm; and

lastly, the absence of any provision in the law compelling the occupants of dwellings to produce the least possible quantity of smoke.

On the point of prosecutions, it was stated that there are people in Manchester who systematically pollute the air and pay the fine, finding it much cheaper to do so than to put up new plant. The trial of such cases before benches of magistrates composed of manu-facturers or their friends creates an atmosphere of sympathy for the accused, and it was alleged that magistrates who had sought to give effect to the law encountered the indifference and sometimes the positive opposition of their colleagues. It was explained that . . .

> (*Pollution of Atmosphere*, from the Report of the
> Inter-Departmental Committee) (Eyken 1973)

Alongside this kind of 'conceptual' focus, two other expository variants may be identified: *description*, dealing with 'objects' or 'situations', and *narration*, dealing with 'actions' and 'events'. These two forms may be illustrated respectively by sample B and sample C below:

Sample B

The hours will be long, fifty-five per week, and the atmosphere he breathes very confined, perchance also dusty. Employment of this character rarely fosters growth or development; the stunted child elongates slightly in time, but remains very thin, loses colour, the muscles remain small, especially those of the upper limbs, the legs are inclined to become bowed, the arch of the foot flattens and the teeth decay rapidly.

The girls exhibit the same shortness of stature, the same miserable development, and they possess the same shallow cheeks and carious teeth.

> (*Conditions of Employment*, from the Report of the
> Inter-Departmental Committee, 1904) (Eyken 1973)

Sample C

There were fifteen of us boarders. We paid 150 a year, and we never had enough to eat. We rose at 7 a.m. and had breakfast at 8.30, consisting of weak tea, a thick bit of bread with a thin smear of butter. Butterine was substituted for butter until complaints were made, and then we had salt butter. Once a month a boiled egg was given at breakfast. Dinner, which came at one o'clock, consisted of two courses, soup and meat, or meat and pudding . . .

> (From *Parsimony in Nutrition*) (Eyken 1973)

In examining these samples, you will have noted that, while a primary text-type focus on conceptual exposition, description or narration is always discernible, these forms intermesh and shade into one another in a variety of ways. Furthermore, the global processing patterns utilized by all three types of exposition are *frames* (knowledge stating which things in principle belong together) and *schemata* (knowledge establishing a sequential order for the occurrence of events).

Argumentation

This focuses on the evaluation of relations between concepts. Thus, argumentative texts are 'those utilized to promote the acceptance or evaluation of certain beliefs or ideas as true v. false, or positive v. negative. Conceptual relations such as reason, significance, volition, value and opposition should be frequent.' (Beaugrande and Dressler 1980:184). The global processing pattern exploited in this type of text is the *plan* (how events and states lead up to the attainment of a goal).

To appreciate how evaluativeness is effected within the argumentative plan, let us consider the following example:

Sample D

The first step in finding a cure for those defects is to recognize the fact that the real root of the evil does not lie in the condition of what is called military education, but in a general deficiency in the mental training of the English youth at large.

It is, however, not with our universities, or with popular conceptions of education, that we are now more immediately concerned, but with those great institutions known by the name of public schools, to whom the education of our ruling classes is committed. It is these which must be held responsible for the initial stages of our military as well as of our general education.

(From C. C. Perry's 'Our Undisciplined Brains') (Eyken 1973)

Instruction

It is perhaps worth noting if only briefly the striking similarity between argumentative texts such as sample D and texts belonging to another 'operative' type, namely the *instructional* (e.g. the article from the Maastricht Treaty [sample A, Ch. 2]). The similarity, however, may be seen in terms of the 'goal' aimed at and not the 'means' adopted. That is, while argumentative and instructional text types, each in its own way, both set out to 'manage' and thus focus on the formation of future behaviour, the means of achieving such an aim are different: instructional texts attempt to 'regulate' through instruction without option (as in contracts, treaties); argumentative texts 'evaluate' through persuasion with option (as in advertising, propaganda).

The three basic text types and sub-types discussed so far may be represented schematically as in figure 4.1:

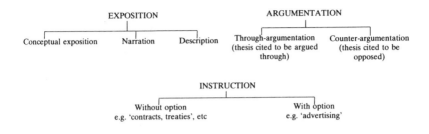

Figure 4.1 Basic text types

Argumentation: A Typology

Within the text typology proposed here, two variants of argumentation may be distinguished:

(1) Through-argumentation. This is initiated by stating a viewpoint to be argued through. There is no explicit reference to an adversary, a format which may be diagrammatically represented as in Figure 4.2:

THROUGH-ARGUMENT
⊢—Thesis to be supported
⊢—Substantiation
⊢—Conclusion

Figure 4.2 Through-argumentation

Sample E is an example of through-argumentation:

Sample E
The decentralizing approach has not one fundamental defect, but two. Either of them by itself would have crippled the reforms. Together, they interact powerfully and guarantee failure. First, as Karl Marx might have put it, is the question of property relations;

second, the related issue of the enterprise's financial environment. In short, who owns the firm, and can it go bust?

The Economist 28 April 1990

(2) Counter-argumentation. This is initiated by a selective summary of someone else's viewpoint, followed by a counter-claim, a substantiation outlining the grounds for the opposition, and finally a conclusion. This configuration may be diagrammatically represented as in Figure 4.3:

COUNTER-ARGUMENT
⊢—Thesis cited to be opposed
⊢—Opposition
⊢—Substantiation of counter-claim
⊢—Conclusion

Figure 4.3 Counter-argumentation

Sample F is an example of counter-argumentation:

Sample F
In the decentralized, self-managed model, workers and managers control the enterprise and have a direct personal interest in the income it produces. But they do not own the enterprise. That may seem an academic distinction, but it turns out to be crucial. Because of it, the self-managed enterprise suffers from catastrophic short-termism.

Owners are free to sell their assets. They are therefore interested not just in the income their assets generate, but also in their market value . . .

The Economist 28 April 1990

Within counter-argumentation, two sub-types are further distinguished:

(i) The Balance. Here, the text producer has the option of signalling the contrastive shift between what may be viewed as a claim and a counter-claim either explicitly (as in sample F above) or implicitly as in sample G below (cf. Nash 1980):

Sample G
Mismanaged Algeria
The country's troubles are so glaring that it is easy to forget

40

Algeria's strengths. At three o'clock in the afternoon in the poor, over-crowded Casbah of Algiers, children leave school not to beg but to do their homework. Investment of some two-fifths of GDP a year during much of the 1960s and 1970s gave Algeria the strongest industrial base in Africa north of the Limpopo. The Northern coastal bit of the country, where 96% of its 23m people live, is rich and fertile. It used to feed the Romans. It could feed Algerians if it were better farmed.

These strengths are being wasted.

The Economist 10 December 1988

(ii) The Explicit Concessive. In this sub-type, the counter-claim is anticipated by an explicit concessive (e.g. *while, although, despite* etc.). Sample H illustrates this counter-argumentative pattern:

Sample H

FEARLESS FIXX

Sir: While it was, as the Weasel implies (Up & Down the City Road, 17 February), ironic that Jim Fixx (author of The Complete Book of Running) had his heart attack while out running, it could have occurred at any time or place. His family had a history of heart disease, and his father died of a heart attack . . .

The Independent Magazine 24 February 1990

In dealing with the various text forms identified as variants of the argumentative type, we are often confronted with one intriguing phenomenon: The various argumentative formats appear not to be equally available for all language users to choose from, and the preference for one or the other varies within, as well as across, languages and cultures (Martin 1985). But the choice does not seem to be haphazard and the preference for one or the other form is motivated by all kinds of factors. These range from politeness to ideology and power, and sometimes include aspects of social life such as the political system or the nature and role of the family. Our text typologies must therefore be sufficiently rigorous to be able to handle this multi-faceted socio-linguistic phenomenon that imbues text types with a crucial discoursal meaning.

Text-type Hybridization

So far, I have deliberately glossed over the phenomenon of 'text hybridization' and the essentially 'fuzzy' nature of text types. Hybridization is a crucial issue in any attempt to work out a typology of texts and this will now be properly addressed and illustrated. In the typology espoused here, an important admission is made at the outset: texts are essentially multifunctional, normally displaying features of more than one type, and constantly shifting from one typological focus to another. To account for this hybrid nature of all texts, and on the basis of the analysis of argumentation and exposition presented so far as idealized text types, the following discussion concentrates on how a given predominant text-type focus could be shifted to admit other subsidiary typological effects.

The distinction between 'predominant' and 'subsidiary' text-type focus is an important one. My own analysis of a variety of text types involving a sizeable sample of actual texts has clearly shown that no text can serve two equally predominant functions at one and the same time. By the same token, no text can be sustained by two subsidiary functions without one of these somehow becoming predominant. For texts to function efficiently, the duality of function together with the 'subsidiarity' issue must always be born in mind. In the words of Beaugrande and Dressler (1981: 186), text type is only:

> a set of heuristics for producing, predicting and processing textual occurrences, and hence acts as a prominent determiner of efficiency, effectiveness and appropriateness.

But, for this heuristic to be used as an adequate determiner of the viability of texts, a number of organizing principles must be recognized, and one of these is inevitably the notion of the 'predominance' or the 'subsidiarity' of a given text function.

Text-type hybridization takes many forms. One particularly complex arrangement is that which will be referred to here as 'embedded' hybridization. This is when, in subtle ways, the function of a text is shifted to accommodate another function. The two functions vie for recognition, but this will ultimately be granted to one of them only. A common occurrence of this kind of hybridization is when text-type focus (e.g. to monitor or review within the type 'conceptual exposition') admits contextual instructions atypical of the 'normal' context for the type in question. For example, consider sample I:

Sample I

> Jean Jacques Rousseau was the revolutionary, the impertinent, who, for the first time, directly and effectively challenged the accepted rationalist view held by the enlightened century in which he lived. He made a real breach in that long tradition of reasonableness

42

which, building up in North Italy before 1600, dominated the French and English academies in the seventeenth century and was carried on actively by Voltaire and the Encyclopaedists in the eighteenth century. Partly under Rousseau's pounding, the formal structure of French salon life gave way to a more equalitarian society, and its belief in science and satire yielded to a view which seemed to glorify instinctive, irrational and emotional behaviour.

In processing this text sample, a text-type focus as neutral as expository monitoring is generally opted for in response to generic, discoursal and textual norms endorsed almost by default in this kind of writing (factual narration of events). This requirement, however, is gradually relaxed to admit values which relate to a slightly different text-type focus, responding to different textual, discoursal and generic factors (evaluation of events). Fluctuation between 'informing' and 'manipulation' is now in evidence replacing what could otherwise have been a straightforward exposition of facts. But, I must stress that the 'other' function is allowed to manifest itself up to and not beyond a certain point. That is, the two functions cannot be seen to enjoy equal predominance, and the original function will thus remain supreme. The success of this particular text sample may therefore be ascribed to introducing an 'axe to grind' appeal of a passionate biographer while still operating within the boundaries of detached monitoring.

True, interaction makes its own rules. But, relegating phenomena such as hybridization to the rubbish bin of 'performance fuzziness' is a defeatist attitude to adopt. Stubbs (1982: 15) lends this argument support by calling for the need to recognize higher-level patterns in discourse:

> It has sometimes been maintained that there is no linguistic organi- zation above the sentence level. However, I suspect that some people believe this because they have never looked for such organization.

Text-type hybridization may be little understood at this stage in the development of text typologies, and certainly further research into its causes and manifestations is urgently needed. However, the mere fact that impurity exists lends credence to the psychological reality of text types. In the midst of fuzziness, we seem to operate with a system of expectations constantly upheld or defied in a motivated manner. To be able to do this, we must be referring to some 'norm' against the background of which deviations are assessed as motivated departures.

Argumentation across Cultures

Pending further quantitative and qualitative research, my own investigations into the argumentative text type in English and Arabic from the perspective of translation points to a noticeable tendency in English towards counter-argumentation. Furthermore, of the two counter-argumentative formats, English seems to prefer the Balance (thesis–opposition–substantiation–conclusion) to the Explicit Concessive (e.g. although . . .). Modern Standard Arabic, in contrast, tends more towards through-argumentation (thesis–substantiation–conclusion). No doubt, counter-argumentation is also in evidence in Arabic, but when this occurs, it is usually the Explicit Concessive which seems to be the more preferred option stylistically. The distribution of preferences may be displayed diagrammatically as in Figure 4.4 which, although based on the analysis of a sizeable number of text samples, does not purport to be conclusive in reflecting the trends involved:

ENGLISH	ARABIC
A The Balance Counter-argument	Through-argumentation
B Through-argumentation	The Explicit Concessive argument
C The Explicit Concessive argument	The Balance argument

Figure 4.4 Order of text-type preference

To demonstrate how the textual resources of Arabic are particularly stretched when handling counter-argumentation in general, let us consider Sample J below. It was presented as sample G above. Here, it is reproduced with the deleted segment of the argument restored and set in bold type. Thus, sample J may be taken as an example of complex counter-argumentation in English where a micro-Balance is embedded within another macro-Balance:

Sample J

Mismanaged Algeria

The country's troubles are so glaring that it is easy to forget Algeria's strengths. At three o'clock in the afternoon in the poor, over-crowded Casbah of Algiers, children leave school not to beg but to do their homework. Investment of some two-fifths of GDP a year during much of the 1960s and 1970s gave Algeria the strongest

44

industrial base in Africa north of the Limpopo. The northern coastal bit of the country, where 96% of its 23m people live, is rich and fertile. It used to feed the Romans. It could feed Algerians if it were better farmed.

These strengths are being wasted. **Some 180,000 well-schooled Algerians enter the job market every year. Yet a hobbled economy adds only 100,000 new jobs a year, and some 45% of these involve working for the government.** Algeria lacks the foreign currency it needs to import raw materials and spare parts to keep its factories running. The collective farms have routinely fallen short of their targets, leaving Algeria ever more reliant on imported food.

The Economist 10 December 1988

The macro-Balance (the entire sample) is a form difficult enough to translate. Far more difficult to deal with, however, is the embedded micro-Balance above (the sequence underlined). The difficulties encountered in dealing with this textual strategy relate both to source-text comprehension and to target-text production. To handle this case of multi-level argumentation, the micro-Balance would have to be transformed into an Explicit Concessive in Arabic. Sample K is a back-translation of the Arabic rendering of sample J above:

Sample K

Mismanaged Algeria

These strengths are being wasted. For although some 180,000 well-schooled Algerians enter the job market every year, a hobbled economy adds only 100,000 new jobs a year, and some 45% of these involve working for the government.

On this particular point, and to avoid giving a false impression regarding what actually happens in Arabic, I feel I must state that, regrettably, a yawning gap exists between the rich rhetorical tradition of the Arabs and the way the language is currently used. Counter-argumentative texts of the Balance type are almost exclusively found in the discourse of Western-educated literate Arabs and those versed in classical Arabic rhetoric. But negligence in this area of language use is not a permanent position. What we have now is a situation in which a particular set of textual resources are lying somewhat idle. The classical Arab rhetoricians have advanced what could unreservedly be described as one of the most elegant theories of text in context, a set of valuable insights which will have to be somehow, sometime, resurrected for positive change to occur.

45

Summary

In this chapter, a model of text types has been presented which recognizes two basic kinds of texts: exposition and argumentation. Within the latter, two further forms are identified: through-argumentation and counter-argumentation. Further, counter-argumentation is divided into the Balance counter-argument and the Explicit Concessive. The basic aim has been to demonstrate that, while Arabic shows a particular preference for through-argumentation, with the Explicit Concessive preferred if counter-argumentation is at all involved, counter-argumentative texts of the Balance type are not unknown in classical Arabic rhetoric. What is in evidence in the rhetorical practices of present-day Arabic as a 'text-type deficit' is therefore only a by-product of social and political (i.e. pragmatic and discoursal) conditions that have contributed to a temporary stifling of a certain text type. But a semiotics of culture capable of smothering certain forms of expression is also capable of breathing life and vigour into them.

5

Argumentation in Arabic Rhetoric

Within the text-type model adopted here, two basic forms of argumentation have been distinguished: through-argumentation and counter-argumentation. A through-argumentative text is characterized by extensive substantiation of an initial thesis. A counter-argumentative text, on the other hand, involves the rebuttal of a cited thesis, followed by a substantiation and a conclusion. These two forms were discussed in Chapter 4 and it was suggested that the use of one or the other is likely to be closely bound up with societal norms such as politeness or 'saving face'. It was also suggested that other factors of a socio-political nature such as attitude to truth, freedom of speech and so on may similarly be involved.

I have discussed some of these issues in greater detail elsewhere (e.g. Hatim 1991), and will return to the topic of intercultural communication in the following chapters. For the moment, however, it is perhaps sufficient to indicate that interrelationships such as that between language and truth can be used to explain the tendency in certain languages and cultures to adopt, say, a more direct through-argumentative style. Modern Standard Arabic is a case in point. In contrast with English, this particular language variety displays a distinct preference for through-argumentation, a text form which either advocates or condemns a given stance, glossing over beliefs entertained by an adversary. But, as I pointed out in Chapter 4, it would be wrong to assume that counter-argumentation is altogether alien to the rhetorical system of Arabic. The main aim in this chapter is to substantiate this claim by describing a model of argumentation outlined in the work of an Arab rhetorician of the classical period. In the course of the discussion, I also hope to provide a comparative account of argumentation in terms of what was recommended at a certain stage in the development of Arabic rhetoric and what is actually found in the way Arabic is used today.

The Text Receiver

As contributors to a rich tradition of studying text in context, Arab rhetoricians (e.g. al-Jurjaani, al-'Askarii, al-Sakkakii) were always aware of the intimate relationship between the degree of evaluativeness with which the text producer imbues his utterance and the state of the receiver in terms of his preparedness to accept or reject the propositions put forward. Three particular types of context, each with its own typical linguistic realization, were identified:

(1) Utterances addressed to 'one who denies' (*munkir*) must be made maximally evaluative (through emphasis, etc.). The degree of evaluativeness will depend on the degree of denial displayed.

(2) Utterances addressed to 'one who is uncertain' (*mutaraddid*) must somehow be evaluative. Once again, the degree of evaluativeness will depend on the degree of uncertainty displayed.

(3) Utterances addressed to 'one who is open-minded' (*khaali al-dhihn*) must be minimally evaluative.

What we have here may best be seen as a continuum with highly evaluative discourse at one end, least evaluative discourse at the other, and with the category 'uncertain' occupying a place somewhere in-between. Put in terms of our own linguistic model of text types, deniers and those who are somewhat uncertain, are likely to be confronted with texts displaying varying degrees of evaluativeness or 'managing'. This manifests itself through the use of various forms of emphasis, parallelism, and other linguistic devices of intensification. In the case of the open-minded, however, minimal use of such evaluative devices will be made since the aim of the text would invariably be to 'monitor' a situation —describe, narrate or deal with a set of concepts objectively through various forms of exposition.

A view of Argumentation

Later rhetoricians built on these insightful analyses of the text receiver and developed what may even by today's standards strike us as serious attempts to develop text typologies. But among the sources which inspired such work on the art of argumentation is a much older one:

Naqd al-Nathr, a book on 'the criticism of prose' by Qudaama b. Ja'far, an Arab rhetorician of the eighth-century AH (14th century AD). Although the rhetoric of Aristotle was perhaps the most important source of influence on the thinking of the author, Qudaama fully understood the Greek rhetorical tradition and remoulded it in terms of Arab rhetorical thinking, giving rise to one of the earliest attempts to relate text to context and the essential idea that a speaker's utterance must always be compatible with its context of situation. To Qudaama, Arabic rhetoric became:

> The art of producing utterances which relay intended meanings through selecting those forms of expression that are among the most effective, systematically ordered and linguistically eloquent.

In his work on argumentation, the author of *Naqd al-Nathr* used proposals put forward by Islamic orators and theologians, drawing heavily on the Quran, the traditions of the Prophet (*Hadiith*) and the works of numerous philosophers and men of letters. A new rhetoric was in the making aimed at defining what constitutes a true orator, writer or poet: clarity of thinking, eloquence of speech and an ability to express what goes on in the mind and in the heart with elegance and economy. Also discussed were the most effective means of expression and delivery. However, it is worth noting that most of these proposals went unheeded at the time by Arab writers who persisted in writing the way they had always done.

According to *Naqd al-Nathr*, from which we shall quote extensively in this section,

> Argumentation is a type of discourse intended to present proof for settling differences of belief between arguers. It is used in ideological doctrines, religious debates, legal proceedings, disputes and defences. It is also found in both prose and poetry.

> Argumentation is divided into commendable (*maHmuud*) and condemnable (*madhmuum*). The first kind is truthful in upholding what is right. The second type, on the other hand, settles for the kind of prevarication in which the end justifies the means and through which renown is sought.

> This is not the case with exposition (*baHth*). Correct exposition builds its premises on what is more immediately accessible to the mind of the expounder because what he seeks is the truth and what

he aims for is clarity and clarification, in disregard of his opponent's approval.

It would perhaps be helpful at this stage to view these proposals in terms of our own model of text types. Expository texts start off with a so-called topic sentence whose function is to 'set the scene'. Various aspects of the scene are then non-evaluatively presented. Ideally, the aim of such texts is to analyse concepts, to narrate, to describe, or perhaps even to combine the three communicative goals in as detached a manner as possible. Argumentation, on the other hand, starts off with an evaluative thesis whose function is to 'set the tone' for an unfolding argument. That is, while exposition is intended simply to monitor a situation, argumentation engages text users in situation managing, guiding the receiver in a manner favourable to the text producer's goals.

The Rhetoric of Rebuttal

At the heart of this rhetorical model of argumentation lies the analysis of rebuttal, or what we have termed 'counter-argumentation'. Sample A below provides an illustration of this text format from English:

Sample A
The Cohesion of OPEC
Tomorrow's meeting of OPEC is a different affair. *Certainly, it is formally about prices and about Saudi Arabia's determination to keep them down. Certainly, it will also have immediate implications for the price of petrol, especially for Britain which recently lowered its price of North Sea oil and may now have to raise it again.* **But this meeting, called at short notice, and confirmed only after the most intensive round of preliminary discussions between the parties concerned, is not primarily about selling arrangements between producer and consumer.** It is primarily about the future cohesion of the organization itself.

The Times

The citation of one's opponent (in italics) and the opposition which follows (bold type) constitute a counter-argumentative structure favoured by arguers within the Western rhetorical tradition (where it even has a name—the 'strawman gambit'). But, for many Arab users of English, this seems to be a blind-spot. To give a practical example of the kind of problems encountered, the majority of a group of Arab postgraduate students of English tested in the comprehension of this text misjudged the main thrust of the counter-argument. In subsequent

50

discussions, it transpired that what they did not perceive was that the text-initial *certainly* is anything but an emphatic signal expressing conviction. To most of the students taking the test, this lack of understanding rendered the key concept *but* confusing if not meaningless. The end result was a seriously flawed reading in which the crucial point, namely that 'OPEC is in disarray' was completely lost (for a fuller discussion of this and related issues, see Hatim and Mason 1990).

The irony in all of this is that this kind of counter-argumentation was not unknown to the classical Arabic rhetorician. As indicated above, *Naqd al- Nathr* presents a pioneering attempt at recognizing, discussing and prescribing the use of this argumentative strategy. The author portrays counter-argumentation in the following terms:

> Proper argumentation is that which anchors initial premises in what the opponent agrees with. Argumentation is most effective in confronting the opponent with evidence by initially citing his very own words.

That is, since the intention of the arguer is to steer his opponent into accepting the argument put forward, presentation of the evidence which cites the opponent's own words must surely be the most effective way of achieving the arguer's objectives. To illustrate the use of this device, Qudaama quotes a Quranic verse which counter-argues with the Israelites by citing a thesis from the Torah, a book which they endorse. Here, Quranic inimitability lies in the very fact that the Israelite thesis cited includes the strictures which are being argued for.

Thus, the citation of one's opponent, Qudaama is careful to note, is never altogether without motive. Generally, the text producer cites his opponent in a way which does not betray too much conviction so as to render the subsequent rebuttal of the opponent's thesis ineffective. The content of the citation is therefore normally presented with an air of subtle dismissiveness, even irony, showing up serious conceptual gaps. This most valuable insight into the necessarily opaque nature of 'citing one's opponent without giving too much away', which classical Arab rhetoricians obviously knew and analyzed, is the hallmark of counter-argumentation in languages such as English, and, as sample A above shows, a potential pitfall for many a user of other languages.

Argumentation and Language Use

In response to a hypothetical claim that 'in X (a particular country), there is no freedom', a committed supporter of the regime in that country might very well argue along the following lines:

Sample B

    X is not in the hands of Y (the leader). It is in the hands of the people, because it was the people who handed the country over to the person who is their servant, and who seeks only what is good for them.

Following Koch (1987) who analyzes a similar text, the argument in sample B reaches the conclusion ('X is not in the hands of Y') through the juxtaposition of a minor premise ('the people handed the country over to Y') and a major premise ('if people put themselves under someone else's control, they have shown that they are free'). Koch remarks that the claim (conclusion) and the datum (the minor premise)

    are related through a concept of freedom with which we [in the West] are not so familiar . . . Our difficulty with this notion is what makes it so odd to hear East Bloc officials claiming that their countries are free, and it is at the heart of the debate about religious cults and 'de-programming'. (p. 177)

So far so good. But Koch and a few others writing on contrastive rhetoric (a subject to which I shall return in Chapter 14) seem always to imply that this kind of 'lopsided' reasoning is a cognitive characteristic of the users of certain languages and is ultimately explainable in terms of those languages being characterized by 'ideational vagueness and formalistic rigidity' and in which persuasion 'works aesthetically' (i.e. by presentation and not by proof). Rarely if ever do we come across blame being attached where it properly belongs, to an incompetent language user. The kinds of communication breakdown illustrated by sample A and sample B above are precisely what a careful reading of books such as *Naqd al-Nathr* would help us avoid. In this book, the anatomy of counter-argumentation is lucidly displayed, and the theory of logical sustainability (*'illa*) is perhaps one of the more sophisticated analyses in Arabic of the process of reasoning since Aristotle.

Summary

Building on the model of text types presented earlier, the aim in this chapter has been to demonstrate that Arabic shows a particular preference for the kind of argumentation in which the arguer either advocates or condemns a given stance without making any direct concession to a belief entertained by an adversary. It may be true that this form of argumentation generally lacks credibility when translated into a context which calls for a variant form of argumentation in languages such as English. However, for Arabic, through-argumentation remains a valid option that is generally bound up with a host of socio-political factors and circumstances, not with Arabic *per se*. It is therefore speakers and not languages which must be held accountable. From text-type focus, which has occupied us in the last two chapters, I shall now move on to deal with the hierarchic organization of texts or their compositional plan.

6

The Paragraph as a Unit of Text Structure

Having dealt with the various aspects of context and the way in which these determine text-type focus, we can now move on to another aspect of the relationship between text and context—that of text structure. The structural organization of a text or its compositional plan is related, on the one hand, to contextual categories such as text-type focus and the degree of text evaluativeness, and, on the other, to surface manifestations of cohesion as cotextual clues for underlying coherence.

To appreciate the structural organization of texts is one way of imposing order on how the various elements of a text concatenate to serve a given rhetorical purpose. In this chapter, the particular problem addressed is the paragraph as a unit of text structure. The analysis firstly reconsiders the traditional distinction between the 'orthographic' or 'typographical' paragraph and the 'structural' paragraph, and seeks to demonstrate that it is the latter which contributes most to our perception of a text's hierarchic organization. Next, the topic-shift approach to the segmentation of discourse into structural paragraphs is presented and its shortcomings pointed out. This will lead into a discussion of text type and how this can be used as a more useful basis for our perception of 'rhetorical purpose' in texts through their structural plan.

Reading for Function

As I have so far suggested, discourse context is defined in terms of language users' intentionality (pragmatics), the status of the utterance as a sign (semiotics) and a number of communicative factors such as subject matter and level of formality. For such contextual values to be realized in actual texts, however, a further category is usually invoked —that of text-type focus. Text types are global frameworks utilized in the processing of rhetorical purposes in discourse. In what follows, I shall develop this argument and propose that, as the ultimate contextual specification, text-type focus almost causally determines text structure and lays down the principles which regulate the way texts are organized as cohesive and coherent wholes.

When we first approach a text, we identify a series of *elements* (words, phrases, clauses) in the order in which they appear. But this progression does not tell the whole story, and the sequence of the various elements is not, as is widely believed, solely linear. Rather, it is essentially hierarchic, with some elements enjoying a higher communicative status than others. In ploughing through this hierarchy, we as text users are always conscious that each element is active in performing a particular rhetorical function. We are also conscious that each element enters into a discourse relation with other elements to perform rhetorical functions at a higher level of text organization (that of the *chunk*). In turn, sequences combine to serve an overall rhetorical purpose, ultimately realized by the unit *text*.

This view of the way a text is put together is probably shared by both the analytical interpreter as text receiver and the more active composer or text producer. That is, whether we see it from the perspective of receiving a text as a finished product, or that of actively engaging in the

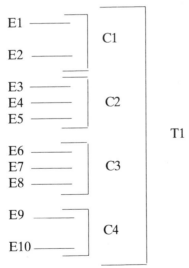

E = element. C = chunk. T = text

Figure 6.1 The negotiation of text structure

composition process, the hierarchic organization of texts will be seen as negotiated along lines which essentially group together a number of elements to realize a chunk, and a number of chunks to realize a text. Diagrammatically, this process of negotiation may be represented as in Figure 6.1

Text Structure—An Illustration

To illustrate the grouping of elements into chunks and, ultimately, into texts, let us first consider the following characterization of a possible context before it is transposed into text.

Pragmatic Action: Defending the premise that 'measures adopted by Israel are doing little to quash the Palestinian uprising in the West Bank'.

Semiotic Interaction: Juxtaposing the sign 'claim' and the two signs 'counter-claim' and 'substantiation' (Palestinians face a new deprivation —ban on fax. However, like other Israeli measures, this one will not work. This is because . . .').

Communicative Transaction: Locating the text within the appropriate 'field of discourse' (the dynamics of Middle East politics), 'tenor' or level of formality (semi-formal, confidence-inspiring news commentary) and 'mode' or channel (the quality magazine article, projecting a sense of balance and detachment).

Text Type: Counter-argumentation

Figure 6.2 A possible context

Let us now consider how the contextual values listed above are transformed into functional elements of texture within a given con-figuration of structural elements:

Element 1: Thesis Cited: 'Palestinians face new deprivation'

Element 2: Enhancer: 'Israel has clamped down on the use of fax'

Element 3: Enhancer: 'Aim of ban: to stop transmission of leaflets'

Element 4: Statement of Opposition: 'Like other measures, this one is bound to fail'

Element 5: Substantiation as Evidence: 'Israelis tried same tactics with telephones'

Element 6: Further Substantiation: 'They gave up when Palestinians used East Jerusalem'

Figure 6.3 Negotiating a structural format—the basic level of elements

Once pragmatic and semiotic values are properly negotiated to yield something like the meanings contained in the glosses suggested above, this sequential ordering of elements is seen in terms of relations which obtain on a higher level of text organization, that of chunks:

Chunk I: Elements 1,2,3 : Thesis Cited to be Opposed

Chunk II: Element 4 : Opposition

Chunk III: Elements 5, 6 : Substantiation of Opposition

[In this model of structure, a chunk may be realized by one element only]

Figure 6.4 Negotiating a structural format—the higher level of chunks

In turn, these Sequences enter into other discoursal relations at an even higher level, ultimately giving rise to the unit text: Sample A below will be seen as a counter-argument.

Sample A

Israel and the Palestinians
EXHAUSTION

Palestinians in the Israeli-occupied Gaza Strip are facing a new deprivation. Israel has decided to restrict their use of facsimile machines, in the hope of stopping the transmission of leaflets and instructions between activists in the occupied territories and the leadership of the Palestine Liberation Organization abroad.

Like many of the measures adopted by Israel since Palestinians started their uprising in December 1987, the ban on faxes looks pretty easy to circumvent. Israel tried to stop international telephone calls from the occupied territories early on in the *Intifaada*, but gave up when Palestinians started making all their calls from East Jerusalem, formally part of Israel and therefore unaffected.

The Economist 2 September 1989

It is worth noting that the procedures for negotiating text structure outlined above are all components of a theoretical model. In practice, this can only provide us with a heuristic, the empirical backing for which awaits further research. Nevertheless, as it stands, this model of the way texts are hierarchically organized derives its basic theoretical validity from a number of studies of text structure (Sinclaire and Coulthard 1975; Winter 1982; Hoey 1983; Crombie 1985; Hatim and Mason 1990). The model also represents a synthesis of insights gathered from practical experience of actually working with texts which we as producers, receivers or translators hopefully all share.

The Paragraph As a Structural Unit

> Were we to probe deeper into the linguistic nature of paragraphs, we would surely find that in certain crucial respects paragraphs are analogous to exchanges in dialogue. The paragraph is something like a vitiated dialogue worked into the body of a monologic utterance. Behind the device of partitioning speech into units, which are termed paragraphs in their written form, lie orientations toward listener or reader and calculation of the latter's possible reactions. The weaker this orientation and calculation are, the less organized, as regards paragraphs, our speech will be.
>
> V. N. Volosinov (1929/trans. 1973: 111)

It has long been recognized in discourse analysis that an ability to identify the formal boundaries of chunks of discourse is one way of lessening reliance on subjective, *a priori* specification of content in the segmentation of texts. Formal markers of topic-shift, for example, have been used as a structural basis for dividing up stretches of discourse. Brown and Yule (1982: 94–5) define this segmentation procedure in the following terms:

> between two contiguous pieces of discourse which are intuitively considered to have two different 'topics', there should be a point at which the shift from one topic to the next is marked.

This approach to the analysis of writing is extremely valuable in applied disciplines such as language teaching. One obvious strength of such a view of text organization lies in its ability to distinguish between structural and orthographic paragraphs. In order to arrive at the true intentions of writers from a consideration of how they develop their texts, we are no longer concerned merely with the identification of boundaries marked by indentations. After all, as Longacre (1979: 116)

58

observes, orthographic paragraphs may be motivated purely by mechanical aspects of the writing process, such as 'eye appeal' or printing conventions, with little or no regard for the meanings being exchanged through texts.

From the perspective of contrastive textology in general and that of translation in particular, an awareness of the distinction between structural and orthographic paragraphs is essential. This is because, regrettably, it is the 'appearance' aspects of texts which too often guide our search for their meaning. To illustrate this point, sample A above was given to a group of postgraduate translator trainees as a translation assignment into Arabic (their mother tongue). The majority of those tested could not perceive the true development of the source text and thus did not preserve it in the target language. This was partly due to an inability to appreciate that the entire text was a single structural paragraph made up of two orthographic paragraphs. More specifically, the students taking the test were unable to make the appropriate connection between chunk I (elements 1, 2, 3 as Thesis Cited) and chunk II (elements 4, etc. as Opposition). The problem is compounded by the fact that the signal of Opposition (e.g. *but, however*, etc.) which would normally introduce chunk II happened to be suppressed in the English source text.

The students assigned the task of translating sample A also committed another, more serious error in reading comprehension. Basically, this too was related to their taking indentation as a marker of the boundary between one stretch of discourse and another and thus misreading the connection between them. The connection this time was not between two complete orthographic paragraphs, but merely between the final section of one such paragraph and the whole of the next one. That is, a new text emerged at the end of sample A, since, in fact, it was immediately followed—without an orthographic break—by sample B, set in bold type below and cited together with sample A:

Sample A

Israel and the Palestinians
EXHAUSTION
Palestinians in the Israeli-occupied Gaza Strip are facing a new deprivation. Israel has decided to restrict their use of facsimile machines, in the hope of stopping the transmission of leaflets and instructions between activists in the occupied territories and the leadership of the Palestine Liberation Organization abroad.

Like many of the measures adopted by Israel since Palestinians started their uprising in December 1987, the ban on faxes looks

COMMUNICATION ACROSS CULTURES

pretty easy to circumvent. Israel tried to stop international telephone calls from the occupied territories early on in the *Intifaada*, but gave up when Palestinians started making all their calls from East Jerusalem, formally part of Israel and therefore unaffected.

Sample B (a continuation of sample A)

Twenty months after it started, the Intifada is still unquashed. Even so, Israeli pressure is having an effect.

The Palestinians have lately begun to show signs of stress, fatigue, even desperation. Until recently, Israeli officials who said it was only a matter of time before that happened, were doing little more than thinking wishfully. Now some Palestinians are starting to question whether it is all worth it . . .

The Economist 2 September 1989

Acting on the basis of orthographic features, the students added the meaning of the first two elements of sample B to their already flawed comprehension of sample A. In doing so, they overlooked an interesting feature of the evaluative journalistic paragraph in English, namely that the two elements concerned in fact perform a dual function: not only do they conclude the argument of sample A, but they also initiate the argument contained in sample B.

In general terms, this functional duality could plausibly be explained in terms of the text producer initially intending to conclude a particular argument, but suddenly realizing either that the conclusion itself exhibits 'gaps' that have to be handled by further discussion, or, as here, that the conclusion is too powerful and needs to be somewhat constrained. In either case, since to continue within the same orthographic paragraph would still be perfectly acceptable in English, it is mere orthographic considerations of 'appearance' (length, lay-out, etc.) that primarily motivate the decision to start a new paragraph.

Thus, from the point of view of comprehension, sample B should preferably have been negotiated as an independent unit with its own counter-argumentative structure:

Chunk I: Thesis Cited to be Opposed

Element 1: Statement of a Claim: Twenty months . . .

Chunk II: Opposition

Element 2: Counter-claim: Even so, Israeli pressure

Chunk III: Substantiation

60

Element 3: Substantiator: The Palestinians have lately . . .

Element 4: Further Substantiation, etc.

Figure 6.5 The structural organization of sample B

That is, instead of chunk III being considered as the start of a new text (the reading which the students opted for), it should have been treated as a 'substantiator' of the 'opposition' (element 2) to a 'cited thesis' (element 1). In Arabic, this requires the use of a special substantiation signal (the particle *fa*), but not necessarily the start of a new orthographic paragraph.

Topic-shift

On the definition of topic-shift cited above (the existence of a perceptible change of topic between adjacent portions of discourse), it could be argued that the only way to approach sample A would be to see it as a single topic unit, and that the mistake committed by the students was therefore not unavoidable. But would topic-shift help to explain the mistake made in translating sample B? We know for a fact that, here again, there is no overt topic-shift between the end of sample A and the beginning of sample B—which in itself is sufficient ground for the two orthographic paragraphs to be seen as a single structural unit. Nonetheless, given the way the article develops, we feel, intuitively at least, that a new text has emerged at the end of sample A. If this is the case, the question now becomes: how is the emergence of that text signalled?

Of course, one could argue that a formal signal (the adverbial expression *twenty months after it started* . . .) is there to indicate that there is some kind of topic-shift. Such adverbial expressions, however, are not sufficiently reliable to be consistently used as a partitioning principle. Moreover, in terms of content, topic does not really shift in moving from sample A to sample B. What, then, are the criteria for determining that one stretch of discourse (sample A) has ended and another has begun?

Topic-shift and Text-type

While useful as a heuristic device, the concept of topic-shift seems to suffer from a number of basic shortcomings. The first is the stipulation that shifts from one topic to the next are somehow formally marked.

This condition may easily be met in narration or description, but it is not always achievable in other kinds of discourse such as argumentation. How, for example, could one classify *twenty months after* . . . in text B: is it a signal of a change of direction within a single argumentative text or between two argumentative texts? Even in our present, fairly well-developed, state of knowledge of how adverbials work, the question posed by Brown and Yule (1982: 98) has not yet received a satisfactory answer. They asked,

> do all these adverbial expressions function in the same way? After all, we would like to distinguish between adverbials which indicate a connection between one sentence and the next and those adverbials used to link a set of sentences to another set.

A second weakness of the topic-shift approach is the continued implicit reliance on 'content', i.e. the *a priori* nature of topic. Two portions of discourse are somehow intuitively felt to have two different topics. It seems that only then are formal signals sought to confirm a preconceived specification of the way a text is put together.

Going by the kind of errors discussed above, it is clear that a reliance on orthographic paragraphing did not help the students in approaching either sample A or sample B. Nor apparently did reliance on topic-shift as defined above. With the translator in mind, I suggest that, for the category 'topic' to be useful in determining the way a text is organized structurally, it has to incorporate more precise pragmatic and semiotic specifications of the way arguments are structured. In addition to uniformity of topic, and the existence of certain lexical or syntactic partitioning signals, what essentially binds chunks I and II together (sample A or B), is a series of important links including those of the writer's intention to 'rebut' a cited thesis and the requirement of the sign 'rebuttal' that a claim and a counter-claim be juxtaposed.

Such a combined semiotic-pragmatic specification of context gives rise to what we have been referring to as text-type focus. In the case of sample A and sample B, it is the counter-argumentative thrust which determines both structure and, as we shall see in future discussions, texture. As competent users of language, our experience with texts has taught us that, for example, once the text-type counter-argument is seen to be involved, we must, to maintain what Hörmann (1975) calls 'text constancy', search for a claim, a counter-claim, a substantiation of the counter-claim and some sort of conclusion. This method of negotiating text structure is illustrated by sample C. Here, two texts emerge despite the fact that the example consists of a single orthographic paragraph, is devoted to a single topic (as hitherto defined by proponents of the topic-shift approach) and exhibits hardly any formal partitioning signals:

Sample C
> The Prime Minister who betrayed her own Government
> MARGARET THATCHER will never fully recover from the resignation of the Chancellor of the Exchequer. Last night, her method of running the Government had its logical outcome: an explosion. She could not indefinitely go on treating Cabinet ministers in the way she has done for a decade without at some point suffering politically disastrous consequences. Her manner of governing has been a means of infusing the administration with energy, and of carrying through vast and in many respects admirable reforms. It did not, however, involve winning the trust of colleagues, carrying them with her, proving to them that since she had appointed them, they could count on her support. Her method, whether conscious or not, has always been to manipulate subordinates and to stab them in the back when they had outlived their usefulness.
> *The Independent* 27 October 1989

At the risk of oversimplifying what in reality is a complex process of reception, the Opposition may be taken here as an analytically convenient starting point:

> *It did not, however, involve winning the trust of . . .*

Within the conventions of the counter-argumentative text type, this condemnatory statement must be seen in opposition to a statement of 'facile praise', or a 'strawman gambit':

> *Her manner of governing has been a means of infusing the administration with energy . . .*

By our own definition of 'topic', the apparent praise stands in contrast to the preceding discourse—eminently condemnatory in vein (. . . *She could not indefinitely go on treating . . . without suffering politically disastrous consequences*). To be more precise, the fundamental contrast is not really one of topic, but of a shift in text-type focus from a through-argument about 'natural justice' to a counter-argument about 'winning votes v. winning trust'. Thus a single orthographic paragraph yields two distinct texts differentiated not by their themes but by topic defined as the statement of an overall rhetorical purpose in a text. Such differentiation is normally carried out in terms of our knowledge of how text types evolve, which provides us with the means to determine the intention of the text producer at any given juncture in the discourse as well as the text sign employed for that purpose.

Summary

In this chapter, we have argued that the inability to appreciate the distinction between orthographic paragraphs and structural paragraphs is often the root cause of serious errors of comprehension committed at the level of discourse by the advanced language user. The topic-shift approach to the analysis of discourse structure is shown to be valuable in making us less reliant on intuition and more reliant on the evidence of formal markers. However, as our analysis of a number of texts has shown, for the notion 'topic' to be usable as a tool in the partitioning of discourse, it must be supplemented by a pragmatic, intentionality-based, as well as a semiotic, sign-related, specification of text type.

7

Background Information in Expository Texts

Still pursuing the topic of text structure, this chapter addresses the specific problem of the embedded sequence of elements (chunk) when, within a larger stretch of discourse, this begins to acquire a certain prominence. By 'prominence' we mean that the chunk stands out, displaying its own somehow independent context, structure and texture. To reflect the change in status from the main text to those embedded sequences, language users must first perceive the shift in text-type focus, and the concomitant variation in structural organization and cohesive harmony.

In translation, the shifts taking place within one and the same main text can be a source of particular difficulty and must therefore be heeded if source text integrity is to be optimally preserved. As we have seen in the discussion of paragraphs, the problems are compounded when working into languages such as Arabic which, to reflect contextual fluctuations of this kind, tend to mark surface formats more explicitly than, say, English.

In dealing with the text-type theme, I have so far extensively discussed the issue of culture-specific modes of argumentation and the hierarchic organization of argumentative texts. This justifies that we now turn our attention to the other basic text type—exposition—and use this to illustrate well-formedness of texture and multi-level text structure. Within exposition, the sub-type 'narration' will feature prominently. The discussion, however, will focus on genres other than literary ones (e.g. 'event reviews' such as those found in news reports). The discourse involved will therefore be of the more detached, non-evaluative type, and not, say, of the emotive, fictional variety.

The Structure of Exposition

In purely socio-cognitive terms, text types are global frameworks for the analysis and appreciation of rhetorical purposes. As such, text types become useful grids within which both the structure of texts and the way texts are moulded to exhibit a variety of texture patterns are seen and examined. The principles of composition are thus followed in response to a given text-type focus, and with the aim of capturing the way texts are organized as cohesive and coherent wholes. To illustrate the process of negotiating structure, let us remind ourselves of the kind of compositional plan displayed by the typical expository text:

THE EXPOSITORY TEXT
⊢—Scene-setter
⊢—Aspect I of the Scene set
⊢—Aspect II
⊢—Aspect III, etc.
⊢—Conclusion/Summation

Figure 7.1 Exposition

Thus, beyond the surface sequence of words, phrases, clauses, etc. (to be conveniently referred to here as sentence elements), text users negotiate higher-order relations on the basis of the rhetorical functions which a given element or a group of elements performs within a text. These functions are defined in terms of the contribution they make to the realization of the overall communicative goal or rhetorical purpose (cf. Crombie 1985). They could be 'steps' in an argumentative plan, 'events' in a narrative, sets of 'attributes' in a description, 'aspects' of a conceptual entity in an expository text and so on. Consider, for example, how a text sample such as the following sounds incoherent simply because the 'opposition' step, which is an essential ingredient of a counter-argumentative text, is not properly marked:

Sample A
(Government minister's statement back-translated from Arabic)

> Travelling between the Gulf States is the easiest thing to do, and the Gulf citizen does not need a visa. *And then*, the passport is considered a proof of identity, and as such is indispensable.

66

The use of *and then*, instead of something like *but then, however*, has marred cohesion and rendered the 'opposition' ineffective in English. (For more on the ideological implications of motivated departures from norms, see Chapters 15 and 16).

Add-on Background Information

To return to exposition, and to illustrate the term 'rhetorical function' in relation to text structure, let us specifically consider 'background information'. This is a kind of information commonly found in genres such as event reviews (e.g. news reports). The segment in italics in sample B illustrates one way of presenting background information in expository texts:

Sample B

Moroccan Planning Minister received

Morocco's Minister of Planning & Regional Development, Mr. Taieb Bencheikh, visited the Chamber on 22 September 1981 for a reception in his honour. *Mr. Bencheikh, who was on his first visit to the UK, has been concerned with Moroccan economic planning for many years.*

From the Bulletin of the Arab-British Chamber
of Commerce, November 1981

This is an example of the most basic format of presenting background information in English: one or two rhetorical functions are added on and are normally paragraph-final. Although often just one or two sentences, this particular kind of 'background' information is nevertheless problematic when translating into more explicative languages such as Arabic. In English, this background function is not usually marked in any conspicuous way. But in Arabic, for example, even this linearly presented piece of background information is frequently introduced by one of a number of conventional phrases such as *wa jadiirun bil dhikr* (literally 'it is worth mentioning'). When translating into English, the Arabic background signal should normally be dropped and the circumstantial detail is either set off as a separate entity if it is of a substantial length or incorporated parenthetically. In fact, sample A is a translation from the Arabic where the background information is typically presented in the manner just explained.

But, leaving aside for the moment text reproduction in the translation process, the background information in sample B, for example, would be least problematic to process for comprehension purposes. As pointed out above, this kind of information is usually an extraneous, add-on sequence of elements serving a single rhetorical function which the main text happily accommodates as such. Diagrammatically, this may be represented as in Figure 7.2:

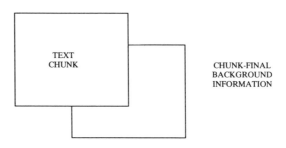

Figure 7.2 Add-on background information

Multi-layered Background Information

Presenting background information is not always as straightforward. It can be slightly more intricate and therefore more difficult to process in both productive and receptive terms. Background information may be relayed through a number of sentence elements, each of which tackles a particular aspect of the background macro-function (e.g. Background I, Background II, etc. chronologically sequenced). To illustrate the problems involved in the translation of this particular kind of background format, let us consider sample C divided into three parts for easier reference. Part I (C1) consists of the first five sentence elements which together perform the overall rhetorical function 'scene setter'. This is the initial chunk of an expository text reporting the macro-event of 'Greek freighter hit'.

Sample C1

GREEK SHIP HIT

A Greek freighter was hit by Iraqi bombs on Saturday and ran aground off the Iranian port of Bandar Khomeini, a Greek shipping Ministry spokesman said. The 21 crew of the 10,000-ton Evangelia were all safe and awaiting repatriation, he added.

Part II consists of the two sentence elements which follow C1 and together perform a dual function: they provide us with a second aspect of the event being reported, and, at the same time, relay a useful stretch of background information (Background I):

Sample C2
    Iraq said on Saturday that its aircraft sank an unidentified vessel in the Gulf.

The news report is finally concluded with Part III consisting of a further set of two sentence elements which again perform the dual function of providing us with the third and final aspect of the event being reported and of relaying another useful stretch of background information (Background II):

Sample C3
    It has declared the north-eastern sector of the Gulf a military zone and has threatened to sink any ship entering the area.
                                                  The Guardian

In presenting the text piecemeal like this, I am in effect trying to reconstruct the reading process which we go through before embarking on any reworking of the text for purposes such as translation. A number of interesting points emerge from this text structure analysis. These may be seen against the background of a general point which is worth making first. While every single sentence-element individually has a role to play in shaping the overall rhetorical configuration of the text and thereby helping us perceive the ultimate rhetorical purpose, to view the series of sentence elements as a monolithic, one-dimensional sequence is utterly misleading (cf. Beaugrande 1978).

That is, the kind of relationship which ties element 1 to 2 in sample C1 (I below), for example, is different from that which ties element 3 in sample C1 to element 1 in sample C2 (II below).

    I. (1) A Greek freighter was hit by Iraqi bombs on Saturday
        (2) and ran aground off the Iranian port of Bandar Khomeini,
    II. (3) The 21 crew of the 10,000-ton Evangelia were all safe and awaiting repatriation
        (1) Iraq said on Saturday that its aircraft sank an unidentified vessel in the Gulf.

The two sets C1 and C2 serve two different rhetorical functions, one straightforward reporting, the other background information. Two different levels within the unfolding narrative are thus involved. The same goes for the kind of relationships which tie the various elements of sample C3 together and differentiate these from those of sample C2.

The situation portrayed in sample C is thus different from that of sample B. In B the rhetorical function 'background' is realized by a single element, albeit a complex one, which is attached to and can therefore be easily detached from the other adjacent elements. In Arabic, as I pointed out earlier, the relationship is handled by the use of the explicit background signal *wa jadiirun bil dhikr* (it is worth mentioning). In sample C, on the other hand, the background information is presented in a number of chunks, each of which is realized by a number of elements, a situation which gives rise to a status problem and makes a signal like *wa jadiirun bil dhikr* somehow awkward if not impossible to use.

It might be argued that there is no reason why the background phrase should not be similarly appropriate for sample C, given that the only difference between this text and that of sample B relates to the length of the background note. But, even if we suppose that this were possible, the solution would still be partial as the scope of the signal would only include C2, and would not extend to C3. This makes sample C particularly difficult for the translator who must here look for alternative signalling devices. Such devices would not only cater for the background information scattered throughout, but would also mark the various levels of narration which distinguish the event related in C3 from that of C2 and both these events from that of C1.

What is more significant for the translator in all of this is the need both to perceive and relay the various narrative levels outlined above. In languages such as English, mere sequencing without explicit linkage is often adequate for making distinct the various contours of texts. When a language such as Arabic is involved, however, special linking devices must be used to mark background information and simultaneously indicate that we are operating on a particular level of narration or that we have moved on to another, more distant, narrative plane. There is no problem with regard to the first chunk (C1). The simple past which dominates the time-tense aspect of sample C1 would be sufficient by itself to indicate that the narrative is progressing within what I shall call narrative Level I.

However, a problem is faced in dealing with the second chunk—C2. We need a connector which introduces this sequence as 'aspect of the scene set' and at the same time pushes the narration back slightly from the basic level of sample C1, signalling in the process the emergence of narrative Level II: in Arabic, the particles *wa qad* are used here for this purpose. Furthermore, to introduce the third chunk (C3), we need a connector which introduces another 'aspect of the scene set' and, at the same time, pushes the narration even further back, signalling that we have moved on to narrative Level III: *wa kaana . . . qad* are used here to relay this. Diagrammatically, the three levels of narration may be represented as in Figure 7.3:

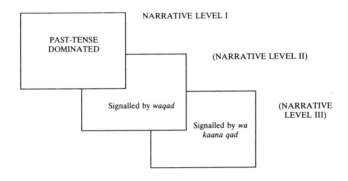

Figure 7.3 Three levels of narration

To remind ourselves of the process of dealing with sample C, the background signals used in preference to the conventional *wa jadiirun bil dhikr* perform the following basic functions:

(a) setting off background information from the rest of the text, and

(b) differentiating the various levels of the narrative.

But in dealing with a text like that of sample C, translators should also note that an element of evaluativeness inevitably creeps in which shifts the genre and the discourse slightly. Strictly speaking, we are not dealing with a straightforward news report as a genre, or with detached reporting as discourse, but with an ideologically motivated use of language in which the text producer is trying to apportion blame while ostensibly relaying a sequence of events.

To put this differently, introducing C2 as a stage 'once removed' from C1, and C3 as a stage 'twice removed' from C1, pragmatically implicates someone for what happened to the Greek ship. Semiotically, C1, C2, and C3 thus become signs which begin to relay new meanings over and above those of their propositional content merely by being juxtaposed and set off from adjacent signs. This added meaning is expressed implicitly in English but must be made more explicit in languages such as Arabic, hence the need on the part of the translator to be vigilant and specially sensitive to how texture disguises all kinds of motives and how these are reflected in the compositional plans chosen in order to relay higher-level rhetorical purposes.

Embedded Background Information

The problems discussed above are by no means insignificant and translators working with languages such as Arabic ignore them to the detriment of preserving the full meaning of the text. In the texts analysed above, however, background information happened to be chunk-final (sample B) and text-final (sample C). More specifically, this information is relayed as the final rhetorical function of the 'biographical' chunk of text B where it is realized by a manageable sequence of elements. In sample C, although performing more than one rhetorical function and spread over more than one chunk, the background information also occupies final position in the text. In addition to structural considerations, both texts similarly display sufficient co-textual clues (related to the texture of this kind of news reporting) to guide the translator and chart the routes through which the various rhetorical functions are to be negotiated with the aim of discovering the ultimate rhetorical purpose of the text.

But the hierarchical organization of texts can be a little more opaque than that of the sample texts discussed so far. Embedding of varying degrees of complexity can often make the process of discovering the structural hierarchy of a text extremely difficult. Embedding is particularly problematical when a main text (say, an expository event-review) includes within it a subordinate text which, while not different in overall function (i.e. still expository), nevertheless displays independent features of texture (tense and other devices of cohesion) which cater for a different, independent compositional plan (structural hierarchy) and serve a different, independent set of contextual instructions (text-type focus). For example, the subordinate text could display a deeper, more distant level of narration (in italics) within a basic event-review as in sample D:

Sample D

Bridging the gap between local villagers
and the spraying teams

Extensive effort went into establishing channels of communication with the local chiefs. The consultants remained a month in the village of one chief who undertook to teach them the local dialect. *Proud of his guests, he spent many hours a day with them and invited visitors, including other chiefs and their captains, from his own and nearby villages.* The establishment of friendly relations in this way was accompanied by a free exchange of ideas about the government and the malaria eradication programme . . .

WHO's Health Education: A Programme Review (1974: 59)

The difference between this form of embedding and that of samples B or C above is that, while in B and C, the rhetorical function 'background information' is realized by sentence elements which are accommodated as an add-on within one and the same text, background information in D is relayed through elements performing more than one rhetorical function, none of which is part of the overall main text plan. In fact, the main text is resumed as though nothing has happened once the background intrusion (in italics) is out of the way. By the same token, removing the background chunk would not substantially harm the overall structural organization, nor indeed the cohesion of the text. This is primarily due to the capacity of the background information in question to be self-sufficient in both structure and texture, which enables it to acquire the status of an almost autonomous text. To appreciate the difference between the three texts, compare Figures 7.2 and 7.3 with Figure 7.4 below which diagrammatically represents the relationship between main and subordinate (background) texts:

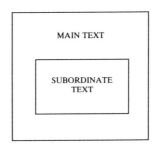

Figure 7.4 Main and Subordinate Texts

73

But it is this very autonomy which is perhaps at the root of the problems faced in working with a text like D. The texture of the English source text shows no marked differences when moving from main to subordinate text. However, in Arabic, for example, the target text would have to distinguish between the two entities while not disturbing the overall patterns of cohesion. The separation is done through the use of explicit linking devices, which push the subordinate text into the background, leaving the main text very much in the foreground:

English source text	Arabic target text	Gloss
proud of his guests	kaana ya'tazzu	'had been proud'
he spent	kaana yaqDii	'would spend'
invited	kaana yad'uu	'would invite'

Figure 7.5 Background signals in embedded texts

As the gloss above indicates, the mechanisms of marking these relationships are as available in English as they are in Arabic. In Arabic, however, this kind of explicit marking is essential and is required by the linguistic and the rhetorical conventions of the language.

Here, I might add that, while the conventional background signal *wa jadiirun bil dhikr* was appropriate for sample B, and could conceivably be used in sample C, generic and discoursal constraints to do with the 'event review' as a main text and the 'personal narrative' as a subordinate text rule out the use of such a signal. Genres such as the 'personal narrative' and the evaluative discourse associated with them are conventionally distinguished from other semi- narrational types of text such as the 'news report'. Like all structural distinctions, however, this one is not without pragmatic or semiotic significance. As in the case of sample C, the shift from the 'main' event review to the 'subordinate' and to deeper levels of narration is motivated. The writer is inviting 'intimacy', which is sparked off by the signal 'the chief undertook to teach them the local dialect'. This kind of intentionality entails that the 'aside' is seen as a sign, self-sufficient and viable in its own right.

The appropriateness of texts is thus viewed not only in terms of extra-textual factors such as intentionality (context) which determine the way they are put together (structure and texture) but also in the light of a number of constraints, both generic and discoursal. It is only when the various pieces of the jigsaw are put in place that we can begin to talk about translations being faithful to the original.

Summary

In this chapter, I have examined text hierarchic organization and suggested that this is essentially determined by contextual categories such as text type. I have also suggested that text structure, in turn, determines the kind of texture devices used to make texts operational as communicative occurrences. Perceiving text hierarchies in this way is shown to be an important aspect of the kind of text analysis which translators need prior to working with texts, particularly in languages with more explicit patterns of texture such as Arabic. The particular problem discussed here is a text that is embedded within another text to serve a slightly different function from that of the main text. Translators must identify the boundaries which separate one text from another and must use appropriate signals which ensure that such delimitation is made apparent to the target reader.

8

At the Interface Between Structure and Texture: The Textual Progression of Themes and Rhemes

It is hoped that the discussion in the previous chapters has gone some way towards showing us how text-type focus and text structure are intimately related. Contextual factors such as monitoring and managing tend to find expression in the way texts ultimately shape up in terms of some compositional plan. But for text structure to play its part in turning a sequence of sentences into a viable communicative occurrence that is effective, efficient and appropriate, the resources of texture must be systematically tapped. Texture ensures that a given sequence 'hangs together' as a cohesive and a coherent whole, as a series of mutually relevant 'steps' in an argument, 'events' in a narrative or 'instructions' in regulative discourse. In all these cases, we would be working towards achieving the ultimate goal of all texts, namely, the realization of an overall rhetorical intention.

To illustrate the role of texture in complementing the process of negotiating text structures, this chapter looks into one aspect of the interface between the two categories of cohesion and text organization, that is, theme-rheme progression in texts. This 'staging' or 'orchestration' of texts is primarily related to the choice and ordering of utterance points of departure or 'themes' within a given textual sequence. But the concatenation of thematic elements in a text is not haphazard. On the contrary, 'thematic' elements form patterns that, in highly complex ways, reflect higher-order contextual specifications such as text type and the hierarchical organization of text (i.e. structure).

Sentence Typology in Arabic

By way of setting the scene and to illustrate the kind of problems which will be addressed in the following discussion, let us briefly consider one aspect of Arabic grammatical analysis that is of particular relevance to our topic in this chapter. This is sentence typology.

Grammarians of Arabic, classical and modern, generally distinguish two basic sentence types. The first is the Nominal, where the subject precedes the predicate, e.g. *Zaydun mariid* (Zayd is ill) or *Zaydun inbaraa faSiiHan yudaafi'u 'anhu* (Zayd waxed eloquent in his defence). The second type of sentence is the Verbal, where the predicate precedes the subject, e.g. *zaara Zaydun 'Amr* (literally 'visited Zayd 'Amr').

Accounts of the conditions under which either of these sentence types is chosen are scarce and when available are plagued with vagueness. Operating within the sentence as the ultimate unit of analysis, those grammarians of Arabic with whose work I am familiar have nothing of particular significance to say about the distinction between the two types. A modern linguist, Beeston, captures this air of ambivalence when he suspects that 'in literary prose the choice of a verbal sentence structure is the more favoured', but immediately follows this with the remark that 'the operative factor in the choice is still very obscure' (1970: 108).

Professionals working with texts in the general field of Arabic studies are utterly frustrated by the lack of coherent explanations regarding which sentence type to use, where and when. This is particularly the case when the translator or the advanced language user is faced with the problem of having to make choices and would therefore need clearer distinctions informed by more explicit criteria. The problem becomes even more acute when experienced writers or translators perceive the difference only intuitively, respond to the various contextual requirements unsystematically and in the process set standards that are at best spurious. For example, in translating sample A and sample B below, the majority in a group of postgraduate translator trainees used the Arabic Nominal and Verbal interchangeably and thus indiscriminately for the initial sentence of the two texts. When subsequently quizzed, those taking the test could not come up with a consistent explanation of why they opted for this or that structure, which can only reflect the state of uncertainty surrounding this area of language use.

Sample A
> Much credit flows to the State of Israel for the vigour of the Kahan commission's enquiry and the rigour of its conclusions. There is not another country in the Middle East (and not too many beyond)

where the rulers could be subjected to questioning of such a kind, and in Lebanon, at whose citizens' hands the massacres were committed, the parallel enquiry has turned into a charade.

The credit attaches to the state, though, and not the government which at first refused to have its complicity attainted; . . .

Guardian (editorial)

Sample B

Several consequences flow from this new proposal. One is that, if we are to have a site for the trace, a movement rule cannot obliterate the site from which something is moved . . . Another consequence is that . . .

Brown 1984

Theme/Rheme: Current Conceptions

In an attempt to identify the 'operative' factors which regulate the choice of the Nominal and Verbal sentence types in Arabic, I will draw heavily on the Prague theory of theme and rheme and in the process suggest that, for this theory to have any practical value, it must be drastically modified and recast in terms more sensitive to text in context. First, though, it may be useful to summarize current views on theme and rheme.

The organization of the sentence in terms of theme and rheme has come to be collectively known as functional sentence perspective (FSP). The term is used to indicate that sentence elements function within a certain perspective of communicative importance. Procedurally, this means that, in the unmarked case,

(1) the basic sentence structure exhibits a predominant order in which the theme precedes and is commented on by the rheme;

(2) the thematic elements are identified as those which present 'known' information, while rhematic elements carry 'new' information ('known' and 'new' being a function respectively of recoverability and irrecoverability of information from the textual or extra-textual environment); and

(3) 'context-dependent' theme elements are of lesser communicative importance than 'context-independent' rheme elements.

Thus, in the English sentence *He backed away slowly*, with *backed away* functioning as a transitional element, *he* would be identified as 'theme', as 'recoverable' or 'context-dependent' and as of lesser communicative importance than *slowly* (Firbas 1975: 318).

Sentence segmentation into theme-transition-rheme and the relative importance of these elements have been discussed under what is referred to as communicative dynamism (CD) (Firbas 1975). This is the quality which pushes communication forward as the text unfolds, with certain known, context-dependent elements contributing less to the advancement of communication than other context-independent elements occurring subsequently. Three principles are invoked in the determination of CD:

(a) Gradation of position and an ensuing rise/fall in CD (e.g. *He backed away slowly* v. *He slowly backed away*);

(b) Semantic content and a concomitant rise/fall in CD (e.g. *A boy stood at the corner* v. *A boy came*);

(c) Context-dependence which, irrespective of position, exercises a de-dynamising effect (e.g. *the boy* v. *a boy*).

From this brief outline of mainstream FSP theory, it is clear that, particularly in Firbas' formulation, context is posited as a crucial determinant of CD and the way it is distributed among the elements of the sentence. Yet, complex phenomena such as 'context-dependence' are left virtually undefined, and the rich possibilities offered by the marked/ unmarked distinction remain largely unexplored. In terms of CD, there is little to distinguish the initial sentence of sample A from that of sample B, for example. But, even a cursory look at the two texts would immediately reveal that something of great rhetorical importance is at work here and needs to be explained more adequately. There is therefore an urgent need to re-examine the basic premises of grammatical theory in this area and to establish a new set of constraints for the way clauses are put together in actual texts. Communicative phenomena such as these seem to transcend surface word order, ultimately linking up with deeper, underlying factors of text coherence.

These basic shortcomings in theme-rheme analysis may in part be ascribed to an inherently sentence-oriented approach to the analysis of texts. FSP theorists emphasize categories such as 'communicative purpose' as fundamental determinants of context. But nowhere are such notions adequately defined and, as Firbas (1975: 318) tauntingly puts it:

> In deciding context dependence or independence, the last court of
> appeal is the communicative purpose imposed on the utterance by
> the immediate communicative concern of the speaker.

Thus, the missing link in formulations such as these seems to be the
relationship between contextual categories such as the communicative
purpose of the speaker and other aspects of context pragmatics and
semiotics (e.g. intentions upheld or flouted, the intertextual potential of
a given utterance). Once identified, these would then have to be related
to the hierarchic organization of texts (structure) and, ultimately, to the
various mechanisms that lend texts the quality of texture (e.g. theme-
rheme progression, cohesion). The absence of such an overall framework
led Palkova and Palek (1977: 212–3) to conclude that:

> Very generally, it can be said that the theories of FSP are directed
> to the description of the sentence from the point of view of its
> (potential) use in a message (framed in a text or a situation) while
> TG (Text Grammar) aims to describe the structure of texts in all its
> aspects. Whereas it may be supposed from this that some of the
> findings of FSP are of importance for TG, it must also be noted that
> there is a fundamental distinction between the two approaches: from
> the point of view of FSP theory, the sentence is the unit of the
> highest order, while in TG it is principally a fundamental component
> in a unit differently conceived.

While I endorse the general drift of such arguments, I still feel that the
establishment of binary distinctions between FSP and Text Grammar
may not be a fruitful line to pursue. FSP is a potentially useful analytical
procedure and an FSP in which text and context are properly defined
can be accommodated most happily within a comprehensive model of
discourse processing.

Thematic Progression

Many attempts have been made at formulating FSP and developing the
original theory, ensuring as wide a coverage as possible of various
essentially beyond-the-sentence phenomena. Most notable in this respect
is the set of procedures proposed by Daneš (e.g. 1974) under the label
Thematic Progression (TP), which he defines as follows,

> . . . the choice and ordering of utterance themes, their mutual
> concatenation and hierarchy, as well as their relationship to
> hyperthemes of the superior text units (such as the paragraph,

80

chapter . . .) to the whole text, and to the situation.

(Daneš 1974: 113)

For Daneš, thematic progression yields a number of patterns. Firstly, a simple linear TP with linear thematization of rhemes:

T1 --------- R1
     /
     T2 (=R1) --------- R2
              /
              T3 (=R2) -------------- R3

Figure 8.1 Simple linear TP

This pattern may be illustrated by the initial two sentences of sample A above:

S1 T1 (*Much credit*) >>> R1 (*State of Israel*)
S2 T2 [R1] (*There is not another country*) >>> R2 (*questioning*)

Secondly, TP with a continuous theme:

T1 ----------------------- R1
     /
     T2 (T1) ------------------ R2
     /
     T3 (T1/2) ---------------- R3

Figure 8.2 Continuous-theme TP

The two initial sentences of sample B above illustrate this pattern.

S1 T1 (*Several consequences*) >>> R1 (*proposal*)
S2 T2 [T1] (*One*) >>> R2 (*movement*)

As will become clear in the course of the following discussion, the notion of Thematic Progression is a potentially useful analytic tool for unlocking texts and revealing their texture. The analytical procedures suggested by Daneš, however, still suffer from the absence of a comprehensive attempt to relate the various thematic patterns to an overall framework of text in context. That is, the system of Thematic Progression, as it stands, is not variety-sensitive and cannot answer the question why, for example, sample A and sample B above display patterns 1 and 2, respectively.

Variety-sensitive Approaches to Thematic Progression

One study which answers some of the questions raised in our critique of Firbas and Daneš is that of Deyes (1978). Here, the analysis of theme and rheme is made more responsive to the way in which fluctuations in communicative dynamism relate to 'features which reflect varying contexts and situational parameters' (1978: 325). This is illustrated by focusing on the development of text structure in samples of English writing such as narration and argumentation.

Without doubt, Deyes' proposals have taken us a long way towards ridding basic FSP theories of their sentence-orientedness and introducing an element of sensitivity to context and variation singularly missing in Daneš' formulation. However, the basic analytic tools used by Deyes were still informed by the standard theme/rheme conceptions current at the time. This is most evident in the treatment of 'transitional' elements where the procedures used neither reflect the degree of importance possessed by the verb as the 'fulcrum' of the clause, nor explain the basic text typological differences engendered by factors such as rhetorical purpose. The difference in the verbal element between the initial sentences of sample A and sample B above is a case in point. As will be made clear in the next section, 'flowing' in sample A is a 'virtual' event and is there to support the evaluativeness of the rheme. In sample B, on the other hand, 'flowing' is very much an 'event' and is there to join forces with the theme, buttressing the unfolding narrative.

Text Type and Thematic Progression

In the model of text processing outlined in this book, texture is seen as providing the means for realizing in discourse a set of mutually relevant intentions, signs and features of a given register. Together with an attendant text-type focus, these elements of context almost causally determine the hierarchical organization of texts. Finally, texture charts the routes through which context is made more accessible and structure more transparent. For the text receiver, the negotiation of texture marks the transition from the stage of forming hypotheses about texts (macroprocessing) to the crucial stage of the step-by-step testing of hypotheses and the discovery of texts as meaningful units (micro-processing).

In micro-processing proper, we begin with how the words and the elements within words cohere in realizing higher-order elements within the clause and beyond, and how these ultimately realize the unit 'text'. This process is constantly guided by top-down instructions (context to text) as well as bottom-up instructions (text to context). From the top-down, text users generally concentrate on text-type focus, while from the bottom-up, users focus on the various elements of texture which contribute to the overall impression that a text 'hangs together'.

In the light of the foregoing, let us re-consider the following sentences, represented schematically in Figure 8.3. Sentence 1 is the initial 'tone-setter' of sample A and sentence 2 is the initial 'scene-setter' of sample B above:

1 Much credit flows to the State of Israel

i1	i2	i3	i4	i5	i6	i7	i8
		i3	i4	i5	i6	i7	i8

i1	i2

2 Several consequences flow from this new proposal

i1	i2	i3	i4	i5	i6	i7
			i4	i5	i6	i7

i1	i2	i3

[In this representation, the letter i stands for item. The figures indicate linear sequence. The middle line represents a hypothetical level below which items are perceived as communicatively less prominent (e.g. thematic) and above which items will be perceived as communicatively more prominent (i.e. rhematic).]

Figure 8.3 The tone-setter and the scene-setter

In negotiating the texture of sample A, the process is set in motion by assigning values yielded by text-type focus to the first clause (sentence 1 above). Item 1 is assigned the status 'thematic' and is thus taken to be 'least prominent' communicatively. However, and here I part company with mainstream FSP theory, a number of additional features manifest themselves:

(a) Given the contextual specification of the text (a *Guardian* editorial, a rebuttal, contentious discourse, etc.), and within the constraints of 'tone-setting' as part of an unfolding argument, *much* sparks off evaluativeness and joins forces with item 2 (*credit*), which is also assigned a thematic status, conveying the effect we associate with what may be described as a 'catalyst' to get the argument going, as it were.

(b) Being a 'non-doer', the thematic *much credit* searches not for an 'action' to be performed, but for what may be labelled a 'virtual event'. This is located in a universe of hypotheses, analogy, metaphor, etc. to be constructed and negotiated by both text producer and receiver as the text unfolds.

These interpretative procedures seem to point to a serious disruption of the theme-transition nexus in this context. The item *flows* may be said to repel or be repelled by *much credit* and appears to join forces with *to the state of Israel* in what can be termed a *progressive directionality* (transition > rheme). This new alliance seems to dynamise the rheme maximally, presenting it as something that needs to be further developed lest the argument should weaken, if not misfire. With this rhetorical aim in mind, and with the rhematic element having acquired sufficient communicative thrust, *flows to the State of Israel* becomes deployable as the theme of the subsequent element. In this way, communication is pushed forward and rheme-becoming-theme produces a *zigzag pattern* that reflects an element of 'turbulence' necessary for evaluative discourse. In clause 2 of sample A, *there is not another country* picks up the rheme and re-uses it as theme.

The initial clause of sample B (Sentence 2 above) seems to receive an entirely different treatment. Here, given the contextual specification of the text (summary review, etc.), and within the constraints of 'scene-setting' as the function of the initial utterance, the theme *several consequences* appears to defuse any potential tension between the actual text and the narrative context. Such tension would have been likely had the actual occurrence been situated within a more evaluative context (e.g. 'several consequences are no doubt in sight. However, focusing on consequences seems to fudge the issue'). But, in sample B, the process of monitoring is genuinely set in motion and is upheld by the logic of the event, namely, that of the review. We have no trouble associating the action *flow* with an actor element such as *consequences*, and a theme > transition nexus is thus properly perceived.

The theme-transition nexus plays an important role in the processing of sample B. It establishes a *regressive directionality* which may best be understood in terms of the magnetic nature of the narrative event. It is the ability of the actor-action nexus to take us back to a world of facts, happenings and assumptions valid for a world already constructed—that of the narrative act. This is a world that is uniform and least turbulent, a semiology which finds expression in a 'theme-becoming-theme' progression. Unlike argumentation which relies on our discursive competence, exposition involves our narrative competence.

Diagrammatically, the discursive, zigzag pattern, and the narrative, uniform pattern may be represented as follows:

Sample A
Theme 1 (*Much credit*) >>> Rheme 1 (*flows to the State of Israel*)
Theme 2 [Rheme 1] (*there is not another country*) >>> ....

Sample B
Theme 1 (*several consequences*) >>> Rheme 1 (*flow from this* ...)
Theme 2 (*One* . . .) >>> ....

Figure 8.4 The zigzag and the uniform patterns

Negotiating Texture

As interaction makes its own rules (Candlin 1976) and as these rules are almost always discoverable and systematic (Stubbs 1983), the procedures for the negotiation of texture, and indeed of the various other aspects of text in context, are necessarily a heuristic, a disciplined form of intuition. Text users embark on the negotiation process armed with a set of hypotheses about the way a given text is likely to be developed within a given context. These hypotheses are either confirmed and taken on as a basis for further hypotheses, or disconfirmed by the realities of the interaction and are therefore discarded.

Of course, it is the task of further research to test these interpretative procedures empirically. However, scattered bits of evidence already exist which can assure us that we are certainly on the right track. For example, Deyes (1978: 323) points out that

> most notably in C [an argumentative text], the rheme of one field becomes the theme of subsequent fields.
> (insertion in square brackets are my own)

Let us compare this with what Deyes has to say about exposition:

> The sequencing in passage B [an expository descriptive text] is much less pervasive, since rhemes tend to be thematized only in the immediately following sentence which generalizes rather than particularizes the information [a hybrid 'tone/scene-setter' in my own terminology]. (p. 323)

Deyes' observation which seems to support our distinction between a world 'yet to be constructed' in argumentation and an 'already constructed' narrative universe in exposition (progressive v. regressive directionality, respectively), goes as follows:

> The communicative fields of A [an expository narrative text] produce the recurrent thematic question 'when?' On referring back to the opening, *since early morning . . .*, the identification of *which* morning is left unresolved, but only because this is an extract from a longer novel [i.e. is otherwise resolvable, which supports backward directionality and narrative competence]. (p. 322)

Finally, in dealing with the argumentative text in his sample, Deyes observes that:

> the initial sentence still fulfills the thematic role outlined above, in that it answers 'under what circumstances the propositions are being made' [i.e. under what conditions the assertions made are to hold valid]. (p. 322)

The findings of Deyes' study thus lend credence to a number of the hypotheses with which we have been working. In particular, they offer empirical backing to two basic claims: that argumentative texts exhibit 'forward directionality' towards a universe of discourse yet to be constructed (hence the unpredictable and therefore challenging nature of this particular text type), and that expository texts exhibit 'backward directionality' towards a universe of discourse already constructed (which is how we initially feel about, say, narration and its essentially familiar plots).

A Contrastive Slant

The relevance of the above re-formulation of theme-rheme theory and its application to the textual function of the Verbal and Nominal sentence types in Arabic may be seen most convincingly in the process of translating Sentence 1 of sample A and B above into a language whose texture is more explicative than that of English. Let us first clarify what the choice involves when a language user or a translator is faced with the option of using either the Nominal or the Verbal in a language such as Arabic. These are not interchangeable, as the general picture which emerged from our students' rendering in the above experiment seems to suggest. Idiomatically, competent text users would opt for the Nominal in rendering the initial sentence of sample A above and for the Verbal in rendering the initial sentence of sample B. The reasoning behind this decision has to rely first on attested reactions of textually competent native speakers of the language. But there is also a text-linguistic explanation which relies on theme-rheme analysis of the kind proposed in the present study.

If I am correct in regarding sentence 1 of sample B as displaying a theme-transition nexus and a backward directionality towards the narrative act, then to ensure that this is maximally preserved, the Arabic translator must opt for a Verbal sentence type (*wa yataratabu 'adadun min al-nataa'ij 'alaa muqtaraHaatinaa haadhih*—literally 'flow several consequences from our proposal'). In Arabic, the Verbal unequivocally assigns a thematic status to the verb and, with the subject as junctional, prevents any likelihood of a recourse to any context other than that of the narrative act. A text-typological commitment to an unevaluative, expository text is thus made and upheld.

In translating sentence 1 of sample A into Arabic, on the other hand, the translator would be responding to a different set of contextual factors. Here, the thematic status is not assigned to an 'actor' as such, as the event (if we could call it that) is not retrievable from a context already known (the narrative act) but from one yet to be constructed within some hypothetical universe of discourse. The resulting forward directionality reflected in the transition-rheme nexus needs to be preserved and the Nominal structure in Arabic fulfills this task admirably (*saylun min 'ibaarati al-thanaa' yanhaalu 'alaa dawlati israa'iil*—literally 'much credit flows to the State of Israel'). The marked status of this structure severs the theme-transition nexus and in so doing enhances the communicative thrust of the rheme by the addition of the transitional force.

To conclude, verbs in the Nominal format, unlike their counterparts in the Verbal format, no longer 'mean' what they 'say' they 'do'; they acquire an added text-semantic specification (connotations, for short) which in the case of Sentence 1 of sample A runs something like 'credit will continue to flow to the State of Israel *undeservedly* unless the statement is curtailed by the proviso that it is to the State and not to the government that credit must go'.

Summary

The aim of this chapter has been to demonstrate that theme-transition-rheme is a variety-sensitive variable of texture which responds to specific sets of demands made by specific text structures and by specific contextual directives. Like other aspects of texture, such as cohesion and kinds of information, for theme and rheme to provide us with a useful analytic tool in dealing with texts, they must be seen as a realization of a higher level semiology. This stratum of textual activity is no doubt 'seamless', 'fuzzy' and 'nomadic', but certainly not shapeless. Thus, it is only templates such as text type that can provide us with the means of imposing order, controlling diversity and discovering patterns.

9

Cataphora as a Textural Manifestation

The model of text processing presented so far endorses the notion that, while contextual categories are indeed universal, the linguistic realization which these categories engender is bound to be language-specific. Thus, taking the 'rebuttal' as an example, one can 'rebut' in any language. As a textual procedure, however, rebuttals are realized differently in different languages. There will be variations in both the way rebuttal texts are 'put together' (structure), and in the way they are made to 'hang together' (texture), to achieve the rhetorical purpose intended.

This chapter, like the previous one, is primarily concerned with texture. The specific aim of the discussion which follows is to examine how variation in rhetorical purpose (text type), on the one hand, and the concomitant variation in the compositional plan (structure), on the other hand, play a role in the way linguistic expression is moulded to make texts cohesive and coherent. The particular aspect of texture to be focused on is cataphora—the use of the pro-form before the co-referring expression (e.g. 'In his speech, Clinton hinted that . . .'). This is an interesting area of contrastive linguistics at work and one that can be particularly revealing in comparing those languages which tend to be more implicative in texture, such as English, with those that are intrinsically more explicative. Stated briefly, the specific issue addressed in this chapter relates to translation and to the absence in certain languages of linguistic means sanctioned by rhetorical conventions to express cataphora. This problem becomes particularly acute when cataphoric expression in a given source language is functional and must somehow be preserved.

Context, Structure and Texture

As I hope to have made amply clear so far, context may be defined in terms of pragmatic notions such as intentionality and acceptability, in terms of semiotic notions such as intertextuality, and, finally, in terms of the communicative transaction which materializes as a by-product of pragmatic action and semiotic interaction. Further, I have suggested and tried to demonstrate that the intention of a given language user to achieve some rhetorical purpose and thus to use a particular text-element as a sign within a particular communicative setting almost causally determines text structure and texture. The text-type counter-argumentation may be a good example with which to illustrate the above constituents of textuality:

Sample A
> The Arab East is a region with an unsurpassed ability to export wars and recessions. Yet, it is one whose inner workings the outside world understands only dimly. Because their history is interwoven with the history of Islam, and therefore sharpened five times a day by prayer, Arabs have a keen sense of the past. They exult in the memory of the seventh and eighth centuries, when they carried the word and the sword of Islam out of the Arabian fastness and built an empire from Persia to the Pyrenees.
>
> *The Economist* 6 February 1988

After citing a given thesis first ('The Arab East is an exporter of troubles'), the text producer of sample A introduces a counter-thesis ('but it is a region little understood'). The grounds for the opposition follows as a substantiation. The semiotic interaction of these 'signs' (thesis, counter-thesis, etc.) may be approached from the vantage-point of intentionality (taking issue with the West's myopic view of the 'other'). Semiotics can also be defined in terms of the register membership of the text (*The Economist*'s expert in dialogue with the Western policy-maker). The text-type focus on evaluativeness, which cumulatively builds up, determines that, for the text form 'rebuttal' to emerge as a successful token of the type 'argumentation', a particular structure format is used: Thesis–Counter-thesis–Substantiation, together with texture devices that maintain cohesion and coherence (e.g. *yet, because, therefore,* which establish grammatical as well as conceptual continuity). (See Crombie 1985, and Hoey 1983, for alternative models of text structure).

Subject matter and other factors of register membership, however, are only part of overall contextual specification. Even within the same subject area, for example, the text producer's intentions may vary. This entails having to operate with different sign systems, and ultimately leads

90

to the emergence of different text types. Let us consider sample B which illustrates this particular point:

Sample B
> The Scottish Development Agency was set up in 1975 as the government's principal instrument of industrial and economic development in Scotland. As well as its own wide-ranging powers to invest directly in new enterprise, the Agency provides factory space, industrial management advice and acts as a central Scottish information centre for international business . . .
> *Bulletin of The Arab-British Chamber of Commerce* (1981)

Here, the intention of the text producer is 'to define' an entity in a fairly detached manner, the signs used involve various aspects of a scene set in the first sentence, and, given the use and user normally involved in this particular kind of text, the text-type focus is on non-evaluativeness. For the text to be recognized as a successful token of the type 'exposition', it must first conform to the structure format Scene-setter–Aspects of the Scene Set. Secondly, the text must exhibit the kind of texture that is appropriate for what we take to be a cohesive and coherent 'definition' as a text form. In sample B, texture patterns may be illustrated by the switch from past tense to present tense and the consistent use of the latter in relaying the various aspects of the Agency's work.

Thus, two basic text types are recognized within the model of text processing proposed in this study: involved argumentation and detached exposition. As we have already shown, two basic structure formats are also recognizable as typical of the two types:

COUNTER-ARGUMENTATION	CONCEPTUAL EXPOSITION
(e.g. Rebuttal)	(e.g. Definition)
Thesis Cited	Scene-setter
Counter-thesis	Aspect I of Scene Set
Substantiation	Aspect II etc.

Figure 9.1 Argumentation and Exposition

Texture and Cataphora

To illustrate the category of texture with which the present chapter is primarily concerned, I shall first provide a theoretical overview of what is involved in the use of cataphora as a cohesive device. This will be followed by a comparative statement of the way cataphoric constructions are used in the two text types, argumentation and exposition, and in the two languages, English and Arabic. With reference to sample A and sample B cited above, we will focus on the following examples of cataphoric use:

Sample A

Because their history is interwoven with the history of Islam, and therefore sharpened five times a day by prayer, Arabs have a keen sense of the past.

Sample B

As well as its own wide-ranging powers to invest directly in new enterprise, the Agency provides factory space.

Beaugrande and Dressler (1981: 61) define cataphora, after Halliday and Hasan (1976), as the use of the pro-form before the co-referring expression, and explain the mechanism involved in the following terms:

[In dealing with cataphora], processing would require the creation of a temporarily empty slot—a position on a hold stack . . . until the required content is supplied.

Such an anticipatory mechanism may be used within the boundaries of a single sentence, or may look ahead to an entire event beyond the single sentence. In either case, the motivation in using cataphora seems to be one of generating uncertainty and thus arousing the interest of the text receiver. This function of upholding informativity is doubtlessly related to the notion of markedness and saliency (Prince 1981). But, like markedness itself, informativity seems to be closely bound up with 'text type' as a contextual category which determines the way texts actually emerge. That is, when dealing with cataphora, or indeed any other aspect of texture, receivers of different text types (argumentation, exposition, etc.) will perceive different degrees of markedness in some or other block of content. Markedness can thus range from minimal in texts which are least evaluative (detached exposition) to maximal in texts which are most evaluative (involved argumentation). Inevitably, there will always be cases in between: the use of cataphora in semi-evaluative exposition as in story-telling, for example, is bound to be somehow marked, impelling the reader to read on (Hatim and Mason 1997).

Text Type and Cataphora

The relationship between cataphora, informativity, markedness and text type may now be illustrated from sample A and sample B above. In general, receivers of all texts expect that what they hear or read is somehow structured. These structure formats, though actually discovered only as one proceeds, are nevertheless internalized templates stored as part of our textual competence. To conform to the requirements of such global patterns and ultimately realize the overall rhetorical function of a text, sentences would singly or collectively perform various rhetorical functions (e.g. set a scene, oppose, etc.).

But sentence sequence is only a partial representation of what actually goes on inside texts. In approaching a text, what receivers first seek to discover is some form of hierarchical organization, with some elements contributing more and in a major way, some contributing less and in a minor way, to the achievement of a text's overall rhetorical purpose. But, as often happens, a 'more' or 'less' relationship could easily be confused with 'content' and thus become misleading too. A more adequate way of explaining these terms would be to view them in relation to wider structures such as those of text types.

Within an argumentative text, for example, what in 'formal' terms seems to be a minor element, making a lesser contribution to the sequential arrangement of the sentences' purpose, can within the unit 'text' take on important functions such as 'making a proviso', 'making an exception', 'trying to cover oneself by the provision of an important detail', and so on. That is, what on the surface looks like an inconsequential minor detail (say, a parenthesis) could in fact be an important 'step' in an argument. Given the primary objective of the text, namely to argue a point through, this becomes an important sign-post which steers us in a direction most favourable to the text producer's goal.

The cataphora in sample A may be taken as an example of this 'marked' use of subordinate elements. The following is a representation of the various stages of the 'counter-argument', with the function of the cataphora highlighted in italics:

Thesis Cited: 'It is obvious that the Arab East is an exporter of troubles'
Counter-thesis: 'However, it is a region little understood'
Substantiation: *'Given the dominance of Islam over the hearts and minds of all Arabs, these people live in a past which they revere'*

Figure 9.2 Cataphora in argumentation

In detached exposition, on the other hand, formally minor elements actually contribute less to the overall rhetorical purpose of the text. They are genuinely subordinate elements in that they merely provide supporting details to prop up the main narrative. They may well be making provisos, making exceptions or even providing extra details, but, unlike their argumentative counterparts, they are extraneous to the primary objective of the expository text. Exposition is to relate in as detached a manner as possible a series of, say, events or aspects of a scene. In including such minor elements, the text producer would thus merely want to fill us in on the background.

The instance of cataphora in sample B is an example of this 'unmarked' use of subordinate elements. The following is a representation of the various stages of the 'definition', with the function of the cataphora highlighted in italics:

Scene-setter: 'The Scottish Development Agency was set up in 1975 by the government to be the principal instrument of industrial and economic development in Scotland'

Detail: '*in effect, this means having wide-ranging powers to invest directly in new enterprise*'

Aspect I: 'One of the SDA's main functions is the provision of factory space'

Aspect II: 'Another function is the provision of industrial advice'

Aspect III: 'A third function is acting as an information centre'

Figure 9.3 Cataphora in exposition

Cataphora in Arabic: The Translation Angle

Thus, to an arguer, cataphora would be a means of highlighting a particular detail. To achieve a variety of rhetorical purposes, a specific block of content is focused upon which makes what is formally minor substantively on a par with, if not slightly more prominent than, adjacent major elements. To the text producer engaging in detached exposition, however, minor elements de-emphasize both content and rhetorical value and prevent these from blocking the main flow of information. Here, the text producer attempts to make concepts less prominent; information and function are both shelved, as it were.

In Arabic, while the linguistic means of using pro-forms which point forward to a co-referring expression are formally available, rhetorical conventions discourage their use in establishing cohesion and coherence in the way used in English. Both in classical and in modern times, grammarians of Arabic strongly advise against the use of cataphora, while stylisticians and rhetoricians discourage its use. Only those uses of cataphora deemed to possess a high degree of stylistic informativity are allowed, and these are only a handful! For example, one notable exception where cataphora is allowed is the case of what is referred to in both the grammar and rhetoric of Arabic as the Pronoun of Prominence (*Damiir al-sha'n*). But this use of cataphora is constrained by all kinds of genre and discourse factors which restrict it either to the highly emotive or to the more formal style of writing. Consider the following Quranic verse as an illustration:

innahu laa yaflaHu al-Zalimuun
'indeed it is that the wrong-doers never shall prosper'

At this point, it is worth raising the question of how, when almost all languages have the capacity to use cataphora to block some content for reasons of emphasis, etc., Arabic still manages to relay these functions while the particular use in question is not rhetorically sanctioned and the means are, to all intents and purposes, virtually unusable. To answer this question, translation seems to be an ideal procedure for tracking down the kind of content which we cataphorically block in English, enabling us to examine how it is actually expressed in Arabic. One way of handling English cataphoric elements in Arabic is to strip these of their cataphoric status by embedding them parenthetically and thus turning them into anaphoric elements. The cataphora in both sample A and sample B may be rendered as follows:

Sample A (Arabic)
> *aSbaHa li al-'arabi, wa li 'anna taarikhahum kaana qad iltaHama bi tariikhi al-islaam . . ., Hassun murhafun bi maaDHiihim.*

Back-translation
> The Arabs, because their history is interwoven with the history of Islam, came to develop a keen sense of their past.

Sample B (Arabic)
> *wa taquumu al-wakaala, bi al-'idaafati ila al-SalaaHiyati al-waasi'a allati tatamata'u bihaa min Haythu al-mubaashrati bi al-mashaari'i al-jadiida, bi tawfiiri al-araaDHi li 'iqaamati al-maSani' wa taqdiimi al-mashuura.*

Back-translation
> The Agency, in addition to its own wide-ranging powers to invest directly in new enterprise, provides factory space and gives industrial advice . . .

The solution of embedding cataphoric expression seems to be ideal in the case of translating sample B into Arabic. The parenthetical anaphoric device appropriately subordinates the background information and thus leaves ample scope for a smoother progression of elements outlining the major aspects of the scene set by the 'definition' text. In Arabic, the flow of the actions *provide factory space, give industrial advice,* etc. should normally be allowed in an uninterrupted fashion, and this is precisely what happens. Interestingly, such continuity is equally achieved in the English text, despite what on the surface strike us as being otherwise. But to deal with this more comprehensively is beyond the scope of the present discussion as it will involve us in invoking the notions of 'orality' v. 'literacy' and the 'aural' v. 'visual' text (see Chapter 14 for a fuller statement).

In dealing with sample A, on the other hand, the translator faces serious problems in adopting this particular procedure of handling cataphora. Apart from the highly unidiomatic nature of the rendering itself, the solution to embed the cataphoric element is surely a gross misrepresentation of source-text intentionality. Given its function in the English text, the cataphora subdued in this way mars the general thrust of the argument and diminishes the rhetorical force of the text. For its success, the argument relies, among other things, on the sudden and emphatic 'intrusion' of the reasoning behind *Because their history . . .*

Thus, to preserve the role of cataphora in evaluative texts such as A above and, at the same time, keep within the dictates of the grammar and rhetoric of the target language—Arabic—translators must therefore seek an alternative solution. This may be illustrated by the following rendering:

Sample A (Arabic)
> *lamma kaana taariikhu al-'arabi multaHiman bi taariikhil islaami . . . fa qad aSbaHa lahum Hassan murhafan bi maaDHihim.*

Back-translation
> Because the history of the Arabs is interwoven with the history of Islam, they have developed a keen sense of their past.

In this way, we manage to preserve the dynamism of the 'intrusion' function which the cataphora performs in the source text and at the same time avoid using the pro-form to refer forward. In adopting this procedure, however, the translation would still suffer, but only because the textual status of the source-text cataphoric element is not preserved: we no longer have the informativity of the element in question intact. The source text impels its readers to figure out the co-referent for *their*, but this is somehow lost in the translation.

But, is it always important or indeed possible to achieve this close degree of equivalence? The answer obviously depends on what kind of text, in what kind of context, and so on, which are issues that may ultimately be settled by appealing to text type and degree of evaluativeness. These variables would provide us with reasonably rigorous criteria for deciding when to insist on formal, substantive and textual equivalence. Sample A, for example, is an argumentative text, which belongs to the genre 'article in a prestigious weekly magazine' and which utilizes evaluative but balanced discourse. This makes it slightly less emotive than, say, a text which belongs to a genre such as the 'editorial in a national daily newspaper' which uses highly emotive discourse. In dealing with contexts such as the latter, a different solution to the problem of cataphoric expression will have to be found in order to preserve the added generic and discoursal significance.

Preserving cataphoric use in maximally emotive contexts may be achieved by resorting to what could initially strike us as a violation of the rules of Arabic 'usage'. But, given the specific generic and discoursal considerations which distinguish one text from another even within the same type, the use of forward-pointing pro-forms could indeed be justified. This sensitive response to the subtleties of context, however, is not the same as the willfully negligent kind of writing we sometimes find in journalistic Arabic that is heavily and uncritically influenced by Western text conventions.

The option proposed and the one which, it must be stressed, should be sparingly used, and only when generically, discoursally and textually appropriate, brings us to an area of language use that we can only allude to here. It relates to the distinction introduced by Arab rhetoricians between what is referred to as 'cohesion' (in the sense of 'usage'—*faSaaHa*) and 'coherence' (in the sense of 'use'—*balaagha*). This distinction, liberally reinterpreted here, is made in the following way in the manuals of rhetoric: what is 'cohesive' may not necessarily be always 'coherent', but what is 'coherent' is necessarily always in some fashion 'cohesive' (i.e. has an essence of its own). That is, rendering English cataphoric expression in highly emotive discourse, for example, by actually making pronouns function cataphorically in Arabic, could constitute a violation of the rules of cohesion (usage) though not of the rules of coherence (use) which are ultimately over-riding. In such contexts, coherence itself begins to have a text grammar of its own in which new standards of cohesion are set and within which apparent violations, if sufficiently motivated, would be tolerated and permitted. (For a fuller discussion of these issues, see Hatim, forthcoming).

Summary

In this chapter, the function of cataphora as a device which maintains both the cohesion and coherence of texts has been examined. In addition, the basic difference between the use of cataphora in evaluative argumentation and its use in detached exposition has been discussed. Given this text-type perspective, informativity, one of the standards of textuality that is upheld by the use of cataphora, can consequently be defined as text-type-sensitive: it is maximal in texts which are more evaluative, and minimal in texts which are less evaluative. Finally, the problems faced in this respect by translators working into Arabic, a language in which almost all forms of cataphora are discouraged, were presented. The translation procedures suggested for dealing with cataphoric expression vary from neutral ones in which the form of the cataphora is modified but its function retained to those which necessitate that rules of cohesion (usage) be slightly relaxed to accommodate cataphorizing in the interest of text coherence or language in use.

10

Degree of Texture Explicitness

Texture has been the theme of the last two chapters. Here, we continue with the discussion of texture manifestations and specifically examine how the degree of explicitness in the linguistic realization of contextual values can vary from one text type to another between and within languages. Of relevance to this domain of textual activity is the issue of how this aspect of variation can be problematic in translating from relatively more implicative languages such as English into markedly more explicative languages like Arabic.

A number of specific lexico-grammatical structures (e.g. the correlative subordinate clause '*whether X or Y*') are analysed in terms of their English-Arabic translation equivalence across a number of text types. It is found that, while one and the same surface form (*whether X or Y*) is invariably used in both evaluative and non-evaluative contexts in English, for example, Arabic has a separate form appropriate for each of these two contexts. The task of the translator working into Arabic must therefore be to appreciate text function, particularly in source languages which opt for a higher degree of implicitness. It is only in the light of such an appreciation that we can make decisions regarding what to retain, modify or jettison. From this perspective, notions such as 'literal' v. 'free' translation come to be seen not as static 'either-or' options but rather as dynamic and variable strategies. In this respect, text type seems to provide an ideal framework which informs the translator's choice of expression and to which appeal is constantly made.

Texture or the constitution of texts, we recall, relates to the cohesion and coherence of utterances. Furthermore, for these standards of textuality to be upheld, utterances must also have a role to play in the hierarchic organization of texts (structure). But it is text type which is the single most important factor in determining how contextual instructions are enacted, yielding actual structures that are both cohesive and coherent. That is, efficient language use in activities such as translation, interpreting or academic writing invariably seems to involve us as users in reacting to context in terms of the text type selected. In the processing of texts, this organizing principle, if used effectively, appears to inform the majority of decisions we take in using language appropriately.

Particularly for translators working into Arabic from a European language such as English, the fact that Arabic has a much more explicative texture constitutes one of the main problems of establishing cohesion and coherence. The often opaque relationship between form and meaning which characterizes expression in languages such as English thus becomes an area fraught with difficulties. My aim here is to suggest a framework within which translators may be able to develop their own text strategy and make more appropriate choices.

A Grammar of Texts

In Chapter 8, a case was made for the need in English, despite time-honoured beliefs about the structure of the clause being an invariant SVC, to distinguish between sentences such as those in italics in the following text samples:

Sample A

> Created by the IMF, *Special Drawing Rights are an international currency.* They can formally be used by the Fund's members for making international payments . . .

Sample B

> Certainly *tomorrow's meeting of OPEC is formally about Saudi Arabia's determination to keep prices down.* But this meeting is primarily about the future cohesion of the organization itself.

The grounds for such a distinction between two types of SVC structure, I suggest, are text-typological, with serious implications for aspects of texture such as 'staging', 'thematic progression' and so on. The initial sentence of sample A 'sets the scene' for a detached expository news report, while that of sample B 'sets the tone' for an involved argumentative rebuttal and is followed by the 'opposition' to the 'thesis cited'. The point worth recalling from the earlier discussion of these textual manifestations is that such distinctions can be systematically made only when text-type considerations are invoked. Furthermore, it is of paramount importance that translators working into a language such as Arabic make these distinctions and appreciate their significance in the text. A text grammar of Arabic, if one were to exist, would stipulate that one or the other of the two major clause types (the Verbal or the Nominal) be used, depending on what the SVC clause format is pragmatically 'doing' and in which text type.

Thus, sample A would be initiated in Arabic by a Verbal clause type (one beginning with a verb, *tu'tabaru huquuq al-saHb al-khaaSa wiHadatan naqdiyyatan dawliyya* . . .—literally 'considered the SDRs an international currency') which ushers in non-evaluative exposition and has the following text structure format:

Scene-setter > Aspect I of the scene set > Aspect II, etc.

Sample B, on the other hand, would be initiated by a Nominal clause type (one beginning with a noun, exactly like its English counterpart (*ijtimaa' OPEC ghadan—'tomorrow's OPEC meeting'*) which is followed by the opposition (also in the Nominal: *illaa anna haadha al-ijtimaa'*—'but this meeting'), ushering in evaluative counter-argumentation and displaying the following text structure format:

Thesis cited > Opposition > Substantiation

In terms of texture, the Verbal clause type which will predominate in the Arabic rendering of sample A exhibits a degree of detachment compatible with the contextual specification of the source text. The Nominal clause type, on the other hand, relays an element of involvement essential for the way arguments are normally put together.

In concluding my earlier argument regarding sentence types in Arabic (Chapter 8), I indicated that it is not grammar alone which is involved in the production of discourse meanings. In addition to language systems such as intonation or prosody, textual considerations also involve lexis. That is, concomitant with discourse intonation and text-syntactic distinctions such as the expository Verbal and the argumentative Nominal, other text-semantic distinctions are made and upheld by the language user. Examples of these inter-systemic phenomena at work are the two readings which the lexical item *formally* yields depending on the text type in which it occurs, and on the position of the sentence in the text in which it occurs: *shakliyyan* (literally 'to do with mere formalities') would be more appropriate for an argumentative context, while *rasmiyyan* (literally 'formally', 'officially') would be more appropriate in expository contexts.

Thus, it is often difficult to separate between the various language systems, an issue which is better tackled in terms of the interaction between semantics, syntax and text grammar. Within this network of relationships, the lexico-grammar would primarily be informed by higher-level contextual factors.

Explicit and Implicit Texture

The various choices which translators make regarding the grammar and lexis of source and target texts, then, are closely bound up with the notion of text type. This added level of meaning is so subtle that it is often overlooked by translators to the detriment of optimally preserving source text meaning. To illustrate the need on the part of the translator to be extra vigilant when switching from a literal mode to a freer one or vice versa, let us consider the following text segments drawn from two different text types (my italics):

Sample C
> Health education is concerned not merely with the prevention of disease but with achieving balance and harmony between all the factors that affect the health of human beings, *whether biological, psychological or social.*
>> *World Health Forum*, Vol. 5, 1984

Sample D
>> BACKGROUND
> Children in Circumstances of Armed Conflict and other Disasters
> *Whether they involve armed violence or natural phenomena*, disasters are growing both in number and in the severity of their impact. They are occurring more frequently . . . They may now directly threaten the lives, health or development of millions of children . . .
>> From a United Nations Policy Review

The particular structure selected for analysis here actually involves both grammar and lexis; it is the *whether* correlative subordinator used to indicate 'equality of options'. A similar formally and substantively isomorphic structure is available in Arabic to relay a similar function:

Sample C (Arabic)
> *sawaa'un 'a biyuuluujiyyatan kaanat haadhihi al-'awaamilu am nafsiyyatan am ijtimaa'iyya*

Sample D (Arabic)
> *sawaa'un 'a naajimatun 'anil 'unfil musallahi awil Zawahiril*

*Tabiʻiyyati fa ʻinnaal kawaaritha tashhadu ziyaadatan fii ʻadadiha
wa fii khuTuurati nataaʼijiha ʻalaa Haddin sawaaʼ*

But failing to discriminate between the rhetorical force of the *whether-*subordinate clause in C and that in D by slavishly adhering to the surface manifestations in the source text, and opting for the same surface form in Arabic when handling the two text types, reflects a basically flawed appreciation of text function. Text (C) is intended to be a through-argument in which a thesis is cited and then argued out. Here, the *whether*-element occupies a prominent place in the realization of this argumentative procedure. Given the overall text strategy, it is important to recognize that a set of alternatives is put forward, and that opting for either one or the other is not meant to be taken seriously. In this kind of text, the text producer is seeking to relay some rhetorical effect through sensationalization. In text-type terms, the *whether-* structure in question here is what we shall label '+evaluative'.

The expository text (D), on the other hand, is performing an entirely different function. It is intended simply to review a series of events, starting with a 'scene-setter', and moving on to tackle the various aspects of the scene. Here, the *whether*-element is not used merely to juxtapose two variants of a given situation. As far as the overall text function is concerned, 'disasters cannot simply be just disasters' and it is not immaterial to distinguish between those involving 'armed violence' and those involving 'natural phenomena'. In this type of text, the text producer is not trying to get rhetorical mileage out of an off-handed listing of alternatives. The *whether-* structure in question here is what we shall call, in text-type terms, '–evaluative'.

Thus, it is the distinction '+–evaluative', which English expresses by using one and the same structure, that must somehow be reflected more explicitly in Arabic. The use or absence of the correlative is strictly governed by text-type considerations. The *whether-* structure in Arabic is appropriate only in evaluative contexts such as that of sample C. An alternative rendering which strips this structure of its evaluativeness, however, will have to be found in dealing with sample D. This would simply be opting for the bare *or-* structure:

Sample D (Arabic)
> *tashhadul kawaarithu al naajimatu ʻanil ʻunfil musallahi awil
> Zawahiril tabiʻiyati ziyaadatan fii ʻadadihaa wa fii khuTuurati
> nataaʼijiha ʻalaa Haddin sawaaʼ* . . .

Back-translation
> Disasters involving armed violence or natural phenomena are
> growing both in number and in the severity of their impact...

It is interesting to note that a proper appreciation of the function of text D would entail the non-evaluative handling not only of the *whether*-structure, but also of the structure of the clause (opting for the Verbal clause type) and the 'cataphora' (which is embedded in this text).

Handling More Opaque Structures

As far as English as a source language is concerned, then, dealing with text samples such as C and D above is fairly problematic, and retaining the *whether*-structure indiscriminately is a difficulty specifically encountered in working into Arabic. But a more serious hurdle is when evaluativeness in English happens to be far more implicit and the +evaluative surface form *whether-* is actually suppressed. In Arabic, this 'correlative' signal will have to be reactivated. To illustrate this textual phenomenon, let us consider sample E below, and compare this with the relatively more explicit sample C above:

Sample E
> To the Arab intellectual versed in international law or the peasant
> whose orchards were bulldozed, there seemed no justification in
> Israel's maneuvers to make Jerusalem the de facto Jewish capital
> of Israel.
> (from Kate Maguire's *The Israelisation of Jerusalem*)

This argumentative text adopts a similar structure format to that of sample C: a thesis is cited to be extensively defended. The *or-* structure cited here states such a thesis. Essentially, a set of alternatives, the marking of which is crucial for the rhetorical development of the argument, is put forward. The function of *or* must thus be seen as +evaluative. The success of the text's rhetorical strategy depends to a great extent on appreciating that 'it does not in the least matter whether the person one was talking to happened to be a peasant or a professor of political science, this feeling is shared by everyone, repeat, everyone'.

Thus, while *or* can have the dual function of +–evaluative in English, Arabic, as we have seen, reserves this particular device to the –evaluative function only. Opting for a straightforward *or* in Arabic would thus strip the element in question of its essentially evaluative nature and therefore mar the flow of the argument as this unfolds. Here, translators must make the choice of activating a latent *whether-* structure in the following manner:

Sample E (Arabic)
> saawa'un 'a muthaqafan Dalii'an fil qanuun al dawlii kaanal
> 'arabiiyu am falaaHan sahaqat al jarraaratul israa'iliyatu
> basaatinahu, fa'innahu laa yaraa mubarriran . . .

Back-translation
> whether an intellectual, well-versed in international law the Arab is
> or a peasant whose orchards were bulldozed by the Israelis, he sees
> no justification . . .

'Literal' v. 'Free' Translation

Problems like those discussed above open up the age-old debate concerning whether translation should be free or literal. Some translation theorists present these two aspects of the translation process as though they were alternatives, one or the other of which is to be opted for at one time, depending on the translator's own brand of theory or the prevailing orthodoxy. But, as Hatim and Mason (1990, 1997) make abundantly clear, 'literalness' or 'freedom' are intrinsic properties of the relevant part of the text being translated. That is, it would be misleading to refer to a literal or a free translation of, say, an entire genre such as an editorial or a news report. Instead, it is more appropriate to talk of a less literal translation of a certain part of an editorial, or a more literal translation of a certain part of a news report. Text type, at both the micro- and the macro-levels, is thus the last court of appeal in determining what forms of expression are to be retained or discarded, and how these may be modified to be contextually appropriate.

In conclusion, it may be helpful to put the explicit texture hypothesis to the test by considering the following two examples. Sample F1 is taken from an expository text, F2 from an argumentative text. It is perhaps worth noting that, while in both texts *as a consequence* means 'as a result', the focus in F1 is on the 'temporal' and that of F2 is on the 'logical'.

Sample F1
> As a consequence, a WHO Regional Seminar on School Health
> Education was held in Kuwait in 1966 . . .

105

Sample F2
    As a consequence, fewer people were eligible for government
    aid . . .

An indiscriminate, literal approach to these samples would distort the true force of the utterance in context. But more seriously than these problems of 'comprehension' are the more concrete choices of 'texture' which have to be made in a language such as Arabic. The following is the translation into Arabic of samples F1 and F2:

Sample F1 (Arabic)
    wa qad 'aqadat munazamatul SiHatil 'aalamiyya 'alaa 'ithri dhaalik
    fiil kuwait 'aama 1966 Halaqatan diraasiya iqliimiiya 'anil tarbiyatil
    Sihiya fiil madaaris

Back-translation
    The WHO, in the period following that, convened . . .

Sample F2 (Arabic)
    wa natijatan li dhaalik, fa'ina 'adada . . .

Back-translation
    As a result, the number of . . .

Thus, the explicative nature of texture in Arabic demands that the focus on the 'temporal' or the 'logical' be thrown into sharper relief, actually using a different wording to produce this or that effect.

Regarding the issue of explicitness, I feel I must stress one particular point. This relates to the need not to confuse 'explicitness' with absence of subtlety. In explicative languages such as Arabic, intentions can be and often are expressed as opaquely as in any of the more implicative languages. Within a given range of expressions, the choices made could themselves contain deeper levels of indirect meaning. True, by not opting for cataphora or the use of an explicit correlative construction, for example, the text producer would indeed be signalling that he or she means business, engaging in detached exposition or whatever. But, the text receiver will still have to look beneath this or that choice for the motivation behind particular modes of expression. Take irony, for example. As Chapter 16 will make clear, the very explicitness of saying more than one needs (as opposed to being deliberately cryptic) could relay sarcasm in Arabic and quite a number of other languages. That is, intentionality remains to be a matter open for negotiation beyond a given wording or the particular specifications of a given text type. This does not in the least make having two separate expressions for two separate intentions any more accessible and therefore less subtle than having one particular form for the expression of two separate intentions.

Summary

In this chapter, I have tried to demonstrate that texture is almost causally determined by contextual specifications relating to higher-order contextual categories such as text type. Elements of both grammar and lexis are shown to yield a number of readings, only one of which is appropriate for a given text type. The problem arises when the various readings are expressed by one and the same surface element in the source language text (e.g. English), while various alternative formulations are available in the target language (e.g. Arabic). Decisions regarding what a given item is actually 'doing' and which alternative form of expression is the most appropriate are regulated by the notion of text type.

11

Emotiveness in Texts

We now come to the concluding part of our discussion of texture, a subject with which we have been concerned in the last three chapters. Having tackled the various devices used in making texts both cohesive and coherent, we can now examine more closely how texture responds to extra-textual factors such as power and ideology. In this chapter, the specific topic addressed is emotiveness and its linguistic realization in texts.

Like all other facets of texture, the expression of emotiveness is closely bound up with semiotic categories such as text type, discourse and genre, as well as with the hierarchical organization of texts or the way they are put together. But, perhaps rather uniquely, emotiveness is first and foremost a textural phenomenon whose primary domain is the set of relationships obtaining between ideological meaning and the lexico-grammar. In the course of discussing such inter-relationships, I shall briefly broach the issue of the intrinsic multi-functionality, and consequently the variable and hybrid nature, of all texts. My aim here is not to reiterate arguments already presented in earlier chapters, but rather to present more concrete proposals for the assessment of the degree of emotiveness present in evaluative texts.

My proposals owe their main theoretical thrust both to modern text linguistics and to notions developed over the centuries by classical rhetoricians. To introduce a contrastive slant, I focus on the work of Arab rhetoricians in this field. As we have seen in Chapter 5, the Arab rhetoricians' concern with text in context gave rise to what may be regarded, even by today's standards, as pioneering theories of text reception. Of immediate relevance for our purpose here is the specific issue of the assessment by the text producer of the likely reactions of the receiver and how this is used in motivating decisions regarding the appropriate degree of evaluativeness with which the utterance/text is imbued.

A combination of insights from both Eastern and Western traditions will thus yield a set of criteria that can inform the decisions of the language user regarding textual appropriateness. Such an approach will enable us to describe texts not only as belonging to one of two major types (exposition and argumentation) but also as displaying various degrees of 'detachment' within exposition or 'involvement' within argumentation. These subtle shifts in text function are elusive yet highly significant elements of text meaning. They are often overlooked to the extreme detriment of communicative effectiveness.

Macro- and Micro-processing

As I have already pointed out, the various contextual values accruing from the various domains of context combine to yield what may be termed a 'dominant contextual focus'. This is defined by Werlich (1976: 19) in the following way:

> Texts distinctively correlate with contextual factors in a communicative situation. They conventionally focus the addressee's attention only on specific factors and circumstances from the whole set of factors.

In the text-type model developed here, however, this 'focus' will initially be viewed at a 'micro' level, as accounting for the ways a given 'element' (i.e. clause, sentence, etc.) correlates with context. Only when this initial stage is completed (to varying degrees of success, of course) can the various elements together establish an orientation or a text slant towards a particular 'macro' text function. As will be argued shortly, the degree of evaluativeness displayed by this macro function can be rigorously determined on the basis of the contribution which the various elements make to the overall 'rhetorical purpose' of the text. Consider, for example, sentence (1) below. It is a statement by the British Foreign Secretary, made just before the execution of one British national and the 15-year imprisonment of another, both accused by the Iraqis of spying. This utterance is seen to display a particular rhetorical force, let us call it 'notification':

1 *The death and imprisonment sentences, if carried out, are bound to have a far-reaching effect on bilateral relations between the two countries.*

COMMUNICATION ACROSS CULTURES

But this reading, which is not definitive and may at a later stage be retained, modified or even discarded in the light of unfolding textual evidence, could only be reached through a cumulative process of information gathering. This involves negotiating pragmatic intentions within a particular social semiotics and other domains of textual activity such as register membership. The escalation of 'notification' to 'warning', and even to 'threat', is perceived as complete only when utterance (1) is seen against the background provided by the preceding discourse:

2 *Our objective now is to concentrate on the immediate future, the immediate next few hours, to try to get the death sentence lifted.*

Some languages would make the relationship between the two speech acts even more explicit. In Arabic, for example, the initial sentence (2 above) would be introduced by the verb of saying: *SarraHa* (Literally 'he stated') and would be linked to the sentence which follows (sentence 1 above) by an explicit adversative (e.g. 'but'), together with a 'warning' verb of saying: *illa annahu hadhdhara qaa'ilan anna* . . . (Lit. 'But he warned by saying that . . .').

Multi-functionality

Thus, for a given text to emerge and be recognized as a successful realization of a given type, a number of elements are singly and collectively made to function in such a way as to ensure the smooth implementation of an overall rhetorical purpose. It may be true that evaluativeness is an all-pervasive phenomenon in all texts and that, ultimately, no text is free from a certain amount of involvement. Yet, inevitable hybridization should not provide license for an 'everything goes' attitude. Texts must ultimately be made to address a single predominant purpose, and the question becomes not one of 'either this or that type' but rather of which type is predominant and which is subsidiary. Here, text processing would be specifically aimed at discovering (a) what motivates a given pattern of predominance and (b) where, when and how texts cease to be effective, efficient and appropriate as a result of employing this or that degree of evaluativeness. That is, when do news reports lapse into editorializing by becoming too involved, or editorials fail to achieve the desired goal by becoming too detached? The following, seemingly detached 'background' note (together with the highlighted phrase in inverted commas) which follows segments (1) and (2) cited above, is surely not inserted in the news report without ulterior motives:

3 *Under the present system there is no legal appeal, though the President can commute sentences 'for humanitarian reasons'.*

This shift in rhetorical purpose from detachment to involvement is not unmotivated and must therefore be preserved in translation. To pursue this point further, we might recall a point made in Chapter 7 that, in Arabic, 'background' notes like (3) are usually introduced by the phrase 'it is noteworthy that': *wa jadiirun bi al-dhikr* . . . A pragmatic meaning worth preserving may or may not be present in uses of this kind, however. That is, in Arabic, this signal has a dual function, depending on the degree of text emotiveness: it can either be void of evaluativeness, an empty cliché which competent translators into English, for example, always watch out for and normally discard, or it can be fully evaluative, as it would be in the case of sentence (3) above.

Thus, the degree of evaluativeness admitted is usually motivated by a variety of factors surrounding the text. However, functional shifts can never be determined with absolute certainty. After all, interaction makes its own rules, albeit within limits that are discoverable and describable. In this connection, I maintain that, while hybridization is the rule rather than the exception in executing the design of a given text as a realization of a given type, this should not be used as an argument against the need for more refined procedures of text classification (cf. Emery 1991). As Hatim and Mason (1990: 148) have pointed out:

> Hybridization, then, is a fact of life and the very fact that it exists lends credence to the notion that we do indeed perceive texts as belonging to recognizable types.

Put differently, how could deviations be at all determined if norms never existed? It is to this dynamic and variable nature of texts that we shall now turn our attention. For the purpose of this analysis, two text samples are subjected to an assessment not so much of their text-type membership (they are both predominantly expository news reports), but of the degree of evaluativeness which is displayed by each of them. The two samples cover the news of a British journalist's conviction for spying in Iraq. Sample A is from *The Observer*, sample B from *The Independent*. It should be pointed out that *The Observer* is the newspaper for which the journalist in question worked and which engaged in an intensive campaign to secure his release. The following are relevant extracts from both texts.

Sample A: *The Observer* 11 March, 1990

An *Observer* journalist, Farzad Bazoft, was yesterday sentenced to death by an Iraqi military court after being found guilty of espionage. A British nurse, Mrs Daphne Parish, accused of helping him, was given 15 years' imprisonment and an Iraqi co-defendant 10 years. There is no appeal and only the Iraqi President Saddam Hussein can commute them.

The evidence presented in the military court against Mr Bazoft, aged 31, and Mrs Parish, who is 52, failed to substantiate the charges against them. When the verdicts were handed down at about 10 a.m., London time, there was no translation and the defendants were still confused about their fate as they were led away.

The spying charge relates to Mr Bazoft's inquiries into a major explosion at a military complex south of Baghdad, where up to 700 people are reported to have been killed. Mrs Parish's offence was to give the reporter a lift to the area in her car last September.

The lawyer would not confirm whether, at his trial, Mr Bazoft repeated his defence that a videotaped admission to being a spy – produced by the Iraqi authorities after he had been in isolation for seven weeks – was made after intensive interrogation and threats of violence.

Sample B: *The Independent* 11 March 1990

The British government last night sent an urgent appeal for clemency to President Saddam Hussein of Iraq after a Baghdad court sentenced Farzad Bazoft, a journalist working for *The Observer*, to death on spying charges.

Mr Bazoft, 31, born in Iran, went to Iraq on British travel documents. A British nursing officer, Daphne Parish, who drove Mr Bazoft to a secret military complex near Baghdad, was sentenced with him to 15 years in prison.

Mr Bazoft and Mrs Parish were arrested last September, and in November Mr Bazoft was shown on Iraqi television confessing to spying for Israel. At the time the editor of *The Observer*, Donald Trelford, said he was certain the 'confession' was made under duress. Yesterday, Mr Trelford pointed out that he had been denied permission to attend the trial, *The Observer* was not allowed to give evidence, and an application for a British lawyer to be present was refused. The trial was attended by the British Consul-general in Baghdad.

112

The hypothesis advanced here regarding the degree of evaluativeness in the two texts is a simple one: we react to the two texts differently since sample B strikes us as more detached and far less emotive than sample A. The question now is: what is the textual evidence for the way we react and how does this reflect higher-level contextual specifications? That is, what criteria can we devise for confirming or refuting such first impressions? In the following, I will try to answer some of these questions by reviewing proposals from both modern text linguistics and classical Arab rhetoric put forward for the identification and description of evaluativeness. In the process, I shall embark on an analysis of the two texts and illustrate the various categories of the evaluative use of language.

A Text-linguistic Model of Evaluative Texture

As I have argued so far, the way texts are put together is primarily determined by contextual factors surrounding the text. As a contextual variable, evaluativeness is analysable in terms of the various manifestations of texture as this is manipulated to accommodate a variety of emotive values. The degree of evaluativeness is therefore bound to vary in response to whether and how far the text is intended to 'manage' or to 'monitor' a given situation (cf. Farghal 1991). In the analysis of texture in this way, a number of categories may be identified within an eclectic model of evaluativeness that draws heavily on proposals put forward by Fowler (1985) and Martin (1985).

Lexical Processes
(1) Overlexicalization is an evaluative device used to underline the prominence of a given concept in the thinking of a particular individual or community. For example, the term *nurse* and the network of semantic relations which it conjures up, is an overlexicalization intended by *The Observer* (sample A) to stress values such as 'compassion', 'self-denial', etc., with which the British reader is bound to identify. Compare this with *British nursing officer*, the more official title used by *The Independent* (sample B) for Mrs Parish.

(2) Referentiality determines whether concepts are abstract and general or concrete and specific. Abstract and general concepts are intrinsically more evaluative as they show intellectual superiority and institutional power. For example, *espionage*, the abstract term used in sample A, may be compared with *spying*, the more specific and thus less forceful term used in sample B.

Ideation
Ideation is realized by the lexico-grammatical system of transitivity. Here, different world views are relayed by the different patterns of participants (designated by nouns performing specific roles) and predicates (designated by verbs or adjectives communicating specific actions, processes or states). For example, interesting distinctions may be discerned at the level of transitivity between *Mrs Parish's offence was to give the reporter a lift to the area* . . . in sample A, and *Daphne Parish, who drove Mr Bazoft to a secret military complex* . . . in sample B. While the former manages to belittle the action by nominalizing it (*offence*) and by relegating it to 'state or process undergone', the latter *Independent* rendering categorically states that an agent has deliberately performed an action. Given the thematic arrangement of the two utterances, the former is by far a more evaluative (i.e. slanted) structure.

Deletion
(1) Ellipsis is used for the expression of brusqueness, emphasis, shared knowledge, etc. Such attitudes emanate from the fact that an ellipted second sentence relies for its interpretation on a preceding sentence. For example, in sample A, the meaning of the truncated *and an Iraqi co-defendant 10 years* is recoverable only when reference is made to the preceding utterance *Parish was given 15 years' imprisonment*. The element of 'brusqueness' emphasizes the ad hoc nature of the trial procedures.

(2) Nominalization involves rendering the meaning of a verb in the form of a noun, thus dispensing with both 'agency' and 'modality'. This evaluative device is very effective in masking real intentions, as we have seen in the use of *offence* (under 'ideation'). Another example of this in sample A is *admission to being a spy*. This packages experience in a way that deflects attention from who, if at all, admits what, and one that is better suited here for propaganda purposes.

Sequencing
This involves the order in which information is presented to the addressee. The choices made can reflect various degrees of evaluativeness as they selectively determine what objects are to be the focus of attention:

(1) Passivization evaluates by suppressing or de-emphasizing certain elements of the sentence for a particular purpose. For example, in terms of the order of elements and their informational value, *An Observer*

114

journalist was yesterday sentenced to death by an Iraqi military court in sample A is far more evaluative than *a Baghdad court sentenced Farzad Bazoft to death on spying charges* in sample B. The evaluativeness of the passive structure emanates from, among other things, the marked status of the sentence structure and the deliberate fronting of certain elements and not others. In languages such as Arabic, passivization of the evaluative type discussed here becomes particularly significant. Stylistically, Arabic has a preference for rendering the by-agent passive as active. In dealing with evaluative uses of the passive, the translator into Arabic should therefore opt for either:

(a) altogether abandoning the 'active' stylistic preference in the interest of preserving the evaluative rhetorical function, or

(b) manipulating word order and other syntactic and semantic possibilities in such a way as to ensure that any loss incurred by the non-permissibility of the passive construction is compensated for.

(2) Word order subsumes the various devices used in manipulating texture and in the process underlining topic salience within the sentence. A noun phrase, for example, may be taken out of its normal, unmarked position and placed in an unusual and therefore marked position. Consider, for instance, the position of adverbials in English news reporting. True, this is fairly flexible and adverbials could be sentence-initial, sentence-medial or sentence–final. Within this variability, however, norms develop which may be either upheld or flouted (see Enkvist 1991). In sample A, preserving initial position for an element other than the adverbial, particularly when one is somehow expected, is not insignificant. The sentence is worded in the following way: *An Observer journalist was yesterday sentenced . . .*, leaving the reader to react to and interact with an adverbial element here con- spicuous by its absence from initial position.

(3) Interruptions of a sequence evaluate discourse by the use of parenthetically-inserted linguistic elements. Of a number of parenthetical constructions used in a single paragraph in sample A, one is highly significant:—*produced by the Iraqi authorities after he had been in isolation for seven weeks*—. This is an interruption which is intended to cast serious doubt on the authenticity of 'the videotaped admission'.

(4) Order of paragraphs or of any other chunks of information beyond the boundaries of a single sentence can relay an element of

COMMUNICATION ACROSS CULTURES

evaluativeness. The decision in sample A to have the 'court sentence' as the initial chunk of information is revealing when compared with the more sedate choice in sample B of the 'British government reaction' theme for initial position.

Complexity of syntax

Complex syntax is essentially evaluative in that it normally relays attitudes of knowledgeability and authority. For example, as sample A goes on to relate: *the confusion which arose from the Iraqi lawyer's reluctance to confirm whether Bazoft repeated his defence that the videotaped admission produced by the Iraqis was made after intensive interrogation* is, perhaps not unintentionally, a highly complex structure. To break the sentence up into more manageable units when, say, translating into languages that do not readily accept this degree of complexity is to lose an important element of evaluativeness.

(1) Subordination of clauses implies complexity of logical relationships and thus acts as an evaluative device. Coordination, on the other hand, relays a more passive attitude to the sequencing of ideas, a naive or primitive mode of discourse. Sample A is highly subordinative to avoid relaying a smooth, detached progression of events (see Chapter 14 for a discussion of orality and the predominance of the paratactic style).

(2) Complexity of noun phrases in terms of what and how many premodifiers and postmodifiers there are may in itself be significant for the perception of evaluativeness. Compare, for example, *aged 31* and *who is 52* in sample A with the unmodified *31* in sample B. In the latter instance, the phrase is for information only and carries no evaluative weight whatsoever.

Modality

This includes a variety of intrinsically evaluative devices which indicate the speaker's attitude both to the utterance and to the addressee. For example, the highly-charged use of modality in *The lawyer would not confirm* in sample A is effective in relaying the feeling of a terrified judiciary. In Arabic, *wa lam yakun bistiTa'ati al-muHaamii an yu'akkida* ... (which may be glossed as 'he was somehow impeded'), will get round this subtle use of the modal 'would' and thus relay the meaning of inhibition.

Speech acts

Utterances do not only communicate propositional content but also

116

perform actions. The degree of opacity which the meaning of these actions normally exhibits will obviously vary from text type to text type. In this respect, intentionality in evaluative texts tends to be far more opaque than that encountered in non-evaluative texts. This confronts the translator with added levels of meaning whose subtlety must somehow be preserved in the target text.

The distinction 'opaque' v. 'transparent' may be illustrated by the degree of indirectness which a given utterance may exhibit. Evaluative discourse tends to favour indirectness as a way of capturing the attention of the text receiver (e.g. *was given 15 years' imprisonment* [sample A]). More direct utterances, on the other hand, predominate in non-evaluative contexts as they are generally easier to process and are thus more compatible with the air of detachment characteristic of expository texts (e.g. *was sentenced to 15 years* [sample B]).

Implicature
Implicatures are unstated propositions which lurk between the lines of discourse. This highly evaluative way of speaking is not accidental, but the product of an intentional act: there is a right to implicate, as it were. Also, the propositions that are implied may be consistent with one another and add up to a semantic system, a set of ideological commitments. Note, for example, the use of 'irony' in sample A: *There is no appeal and only the Iraqi President Saddam Hussein can commute [these sentences]; Mrs Parish's offence was to give the reporter a lift.* The implicatures in both these utterances enhance the ideological stance being propounded.

Address, naming, and personal reference
In the discussion of evaluativeness, a feature worth noting in sample A is the mention of Bazoft's and Mrs Parish's professions (*journalist, nurse*) before citing their names. This relays a specific attitudinal stance and thus carries ideological meaning.

The checklist above is by no means intended to be exhaustive of all the evaluative devices with which language users in general and translators in particular work in dealing with texts. What the list underlines, however, is the need to bear in mind that, on the one hand, evaluativeness is in fact an all-pervasive phenomenon and not restricted to aspects of text constitution such as emphasis or word order, and that, on the other hand, awareness of these subtle aspects of texture, which are crucial to an appreciation of discoursal meanings in texts, goes beyond basic, primary meanings of utterances.

The Text Receiver in Rhetoric

In the discussion by Arab rhetoricians of the inter-relationships between purpose and means of expression, the addressee consistently acquired supreme importance. But the text producer was not lost sight of altogether. In the producer's judgement, the receiver's state of preparedness to accept or reject propositions put forward was the focal point of rhetorical analysis. In fact, what is referred to in Arabic rhetoric as 'the science of meanings' is entirely devoted to tracking down those patterns of correspondence between speech and contextual factors such as the degree of the receiver's certainty regarding the validity of propositions.

As I have explained in Chapter 5, there are three 'states' in which the text receiver may be found and which motivate choices made by the text producer concerning the degree of evaluativeness which utterances are made to carry. These are the state of the 'denier', of the 'uncertain' and of the 'open-minded'. But, for the Arab rhetorician, a far more important issue than these 'unmarked' situations of receiver attitude was perhaps that of 'motivated violation' of what the norm dictates. In a purposeful manner, text producers can flout the rules and still keep within the bounds of rhetorical appropriateness. For example, the text producer may survey a situation unevaluatively while in fact addressing a denier, or manipulate language evaluatively while the person addressed is actually open-minded. Let us re-consider the 'background' segment taken from *The Observer* text (sample A) which is highly evaluative:

3 *Under the present system there is no legal appeal, though the President can commute sentences for humanitarian reasons.*

This sentence functions as a 'managing' device and can only be envisaged to cater for a high degree of denial on the part of the addressee. However, given the essential function of the utterance (background information), norms dictate that receivers should be entirely open-minded and minimal evaluativeness should therefore be required. But, to be thought-provoking and emotion-arousing, sample A seems deliberately to flout the 'evaluation' maxim and assume an element of 'doubt' on the part of the receiver when, in theory at least, none is to be expected.

The Translator at Work

In this final section, an attempt will be made to highlight a number of features from sample A and sample B and discuss these from the perspective of the translation task. While Arabic will obviously be the focus of my attention, it is hoped that my remarks will also be of interest to those working with other languages. Subjected to this kind of selective analysis will be the initial paragraph of sample A only, with sample B providing back-up material as appropriate. But, as will become apparent shortly, the guiding principles suggested, together with the illustrations in the above checklist of evaluative devices, should prove helpful in tackling the rest of the text. Furthermore, it is the initial 'scene-setter' which normally encapsulates the gist of the ideological stance that will unfold as the text develops.

Sentence 1, The Observer

> *An Observer journalist, Farzad Bazoft, was yesterday sentenced to death by an Iraqi military court after being found guilty of espionage.*

Given that this is the initial sentence of an expository text (news report), neutral style is normally called for in Arabic (e.g. the use of the detached Verbal sentence structure and not the evaluative Nominal sentence structure). However, another important contextual factor at work here is the highly marked discourse of the source text which is to be read not for its informational value only, but for the ideological stance being negotiated throughout: *The Observer* is trying hard to shake its Sunday morning readers out of their slumber and alert them to the plight of the journalist in question.

To resolve the tension between the requirements of the text (detached expository news report) and those of the discourse (highly evaluative and committed plea), the translator could opt for a compromise: choose the format of the Verbal sentence structure (verb first) and at the same time manipulate the order in which the information is presented. This conflation of rhetorical functions would ensure that the required degree of evaluativeness is generated. Within word order manipulation:

(i) one could highlight the adverb of time *yesterday = yawma ams* by using it anywhere except at the first possible opportunity immediately after the verb-subject sequence, a slot strictly reserved in Arabic for 'unmarked' adverbial elements. Manipulating the position of the adverbial in this way ensures that the marking of the source text element is preserved.

(ii) one could also choose an additional 'verb of beginning' which will prop up the verb *sentenced = Hakama* by nominalizing it thus, *aSdarat Hukmaha* = 'issued its judgement'. This would relay an effect intended

119

in the source text, namely drawing attention to the 'harshness' of the sentence.

(iii) another evaluative device would be a circumlocution to get round the compound in English *An Observer journalist* thus, *SaHafiyyun ya'malu fii SaHifatil observer* = 'a journalist who works for the Observer newspaper'. This sentence is linked to the preceding name of the journalist by *wa huwa* = 'and he is . . .' which underlines the emotive element intended by the source text.

(iv) finally, appending the minor sentence *after being found guilty of espionage,* with the emotive device *wa dhaalika ba'da an* = 'and that was after . . .'. Strictly speaking, the phrase signals 'logical consequence', which if used here could misrepresent the text producer's intention. But, when immediately followed by *being found guilty* rendered in terms which preserve as much of the semantics of 'whim' as is required by the source text, the overall effect would be more in line with the text producer's intention. With the implicit meaning of 'only after' already present, one way of rendering the element of 'whim' could be to select 'the court' as the agent of the passive construction, thus *wa dhaalika ba'da an athbatat al maHkama idaanatahu bi al- tajassus* = 'only after the court found him guilty of spying'.

In full, sentence 1 would read as follows in Arabic:

> *yawma ams ASDarat maHkamatun 'askariyyatun 'iraaqiyya Hukmahaa bi al- 'i'daami 'alaa farzad bazoft wa huwa SaHafiyyun ya'malu fii SaHiifat al observer, wa dhaalika ba'da an athbatat al maHkama idaanatahu bi al- tajassus.*

In back-translation, the Arabic rendering reads as follows:

> Yesterday, an Iraqi military court issued a judgement on Farzad Bazoft, a journalist working for The Observer, and this was only after the court found him guilty of espionage.

Sentence 1, The Independentd
> *The British government last night sent an urgent appeal for clemency to President Saddam Hussein of Iraq after a Baghdad court sentenced Farzad Bazoft, a journalist working for the Observer, to death on spying charges.*

One striking feature of this text is its almost total consistency of texture:

120

an expository news report in harmony with detached discourse. While the narrative is not altogether indifferent and evaluativeness does creep in, the text is certainly not a passionate appeal to reader sensibilities. In translating the above-cited scene-setter into Arabic, using an un-manipulated Verbal sentence structure would thus be sufficient to relay the predominant element of detachment.

Thus, none of the co-textual problems encountered in translating sample A above is likely to arise in dealing with sample B. For example, the adverbial *last night* would be embedded immediately after the verb-noun sequence, an unmarked position in Arabic. There would be no need for a verb of beginning to precede *Hakamat*, as the sentence is straightforwardly descriptive. Though circumlocution ("working for *The Observer*") is resorted to, this is more to do with idiomaticity in the Arabic way of handling such compounds than with a functionally motivated choice. Also, given the context of 'appealing for clemency', the identity of the journalist would be more formally presented (an *Observer* journalist called X). Finally, though the linker *wa dhaalika ba'da an* can still used, it is here a logical connector which in any case is optional. When used, the linker would not be as indicting as it is in *The Observer* text since the sentence continues in a way which does revolve round the element of whim.

In full, *The Independent*'s initial sentence will read something like this in Arabic:

taqaddamat al-Hukuuma al-bariiTaniyya laylata ams bi Talabin 'aajil ilaa al- ra'iis al-'iraaqi Saddaam Husayn taltamisuhu al- ra'fa wadhaalika ba'da an Hakamat maHkamatun 'iraaqiyya bi al-'i'daami bi tuhmati al- tajassus 'alaa SaHafiyin yud'aa farzad bazoft wa ya'malu fii SaHiifati al- observer

Summary

In the evaluativeness scheme suggested in this chapter, features (i)–(iv) above would mark *The Observer* sentence under analysis as a highly evaluative utterance. Tabulating the various evaluative devices in use throughout the text would yield both a quantitative and a qualitative assessment of the degree of emotiveness which the text carries. These can then be taken as an objective set of criteria for assessing the state of the text receiver as envisaged by the text producer and for distinguishing this text from other comparable texts such as *The Independent*'s.

Audience assessment is very important here. It is immaterial whether, on that quiet Sunday morning, the majority of *The Observer*'s readers were up in arms, showing extreme resentment at what the Iraqi President had done or not done. What is of more significance is that someone envisaged them to be that agitated and that resentful of what had happened to Bazoft. To fulfill this communicative brief, that 'someone' visualized *The Observer*'s reader as a 'denier' (as opposed to the 'open-minded' receiver of an innocuous news report) and in effect provided him or her with what deniers normally require: a highly emotive run-down of a sequence of events.

There is nothing remarkable about stressing the role which the reaction of the text receiver plays in the way texts are put together. This has been the subject of discussion since the beginning of rhetorical enquiry. Moreover, as translators, we have also always done well in this respect, intuitively reacting to text nuance and subtleties. What is truly remarkable about a scheme such as the one suggested here, however, is that we are now nearer to being able to use a set of criteria with which to measure attitudinal response to texts fairly objectively. The elusive nature of 'what the text producer is getting at' can now, I hope, be made somewhat more accessible and open to closer scrutiny.

12

Translating Direct Speech and the Dynamics of News Reporting

The aim of this chapter is to re-examine the well-established distinction between direct and indirect speech and to suggest that the use of one or the other carries wider implications for the expression of rhetorical purpose in texts. Of immediate relevance in this respect are the findings of a survey of reporting modes adopted in newspaper Arabic in which we noted a distinct preference for indirect forms. Carefully examining the use of indirect speech, we further noted that a number of 'tones' or different 'harmonies' can be detected within this mode of reporting in Arabic. In translation, whether the source text is in the direct or indirect mode, the indirect form likely to be opted for when working into Arabic will thus have to be multi-functional, communicating the various subtle shades of meaning of the original and is therefore not as straightforward a matter as one might initially think.

Thus, when translating direct speech into Arabic from a language such as English, the translator faces a dilemma: the need to preserve the autonomy of the utterance precisely as it was expressed in its original direct mode, and at the same time work with linguistic/rhetorical conventions that encourage 'indirectness'. As will be argued in the course of the following discussion, in situations like these, a third form of reported speech, which may best be termed 'quasi-direct', may be distinguished. Though indirect in form, this would be direct in function. To relay the 'veiled' kind of discourse involved, a variety of syntactic and semantic means are employed which enable the discourse to derive its 'tone' from the direct speech of the original while inhabiting a predominantly indirect textual environment in the target language. The task of the translator, in other words, is to allow at least two distinct rhetorical functions to co-exist in one and the same stretch of textual material that ultimately serves a single rhetorical purpose.

Modes of Reporting: An Example

With modes of reporting in mind, let us consider discourse sample A, divided for ease of reference into five major parts. As a journalistic text, sample A is typical of the kind of material regularly translated from English into other languages, and can thus adequately illustrate the kind of problems faced in the translation of direct speech:

Sample A

I The Defence Minister, Yitzhak Rabin, has repeated Israel's denial of allegations that it has collaborated with South Africa in developing a long-range nuclear missile.

II He told the cabinet Israel had transferred no technology to South Africa, least of all technology acquired from the United States for the Lavi fighter-bomber project.

III However, the denials have not stopped Israel feeling diplomatic fallout from the allegations on relations with the US.

IV Israeli papers reported prominently President Bush's comment on Saturday that such a project, if true, could 'complicate' US-Israeli ties.

V 'I hope our position is clear on transfer of any military technology that should not be transferred. If that's taken place, it would not enhance relations between us . . . It would complicate things. There's no question about that.'

The Guardian

It should be noted at the outset that, while translators of this text into other European languages face no particular problem with the direct and indirect modes of reporting, the translator into Arabic is considerably more constrained. Of course, like any other language, Arabic has the formal means of using either mode of reporting as a distinct form. Indeed, one only has to cite the Quranic text which abounds with examples of direct speech. However, in dealing with the kind of text illustrated by sample A above, the translator into Arabic has to work within parameters set by the news report as a genre, which imposes its own set of constraints that are different from those set by, say, the Quran or classical story-telling as generic structures. To complicate matters further, the news report as a genre structure is often not of the 'pure', but of a hybrid, variety. That is, in addition to news reporting as a major function, other more subsidiary communicative goals are also in

124

evidence. The translator has thus to deal with the co-existence of opposing contextual values in one and the same text:

(a) 'report' v. 'comment' (genre);

(b) 'detachment' v. 'involvement' (discourse);

(c) 'narration' v. 'argumentation' (text).

In Arabic such hybridization exists alongside a linguistic-stylistic pre-dilection for one form of speech reporting—the indirect. The preference for the indirect form is partly due to the intrinsic 'orality/aurality' of Arabic (texts must be heard as well as seen; see Chapter 14) which has rendered ancillary systems of representation such as punctuation and the usual diacritical marks almost redundant. These devices, though outside the language system proper in most other languages, help a great deal in shifting the burden of marking the various 'tones' (e.g. detach-ment v. involvement) away from the 'textural' to the 'visual' level in texts. In Arabic, such marking continues to be primarily a matter of wording or texture manipulation. For example, the meanings normally relayed by quotation marks, say, in English have to be made more explicit through verbalization in the Arabic text.

When working into Arabic, translators must therefore distinguish the kind of indirect speech which is direct in the source language (e.g. V in sample A) from

(1) the indirect which is also indirect in the source language (e.g. II in sample A), and

(2) the indirect which is not 'reported' speech in the source language but either 'authorial' intervention (e.g. III in sample A) or 'genuinely' indirect news reporting (I in sample A).

Given this discoursal diversity, the concern of this study is to discern precisely:

(a) how, in the absence of conventional signals such as quotation marks, meanings of distinct contextual values such as evaluativeness (normally more compatible with direct speech), and non-evaluativeness (best relayed through the indirect) are transposed into a single indirect text in the target language, and

(b) how the distinguishing marks of each set of contextual values (evaluative vs. non-evaluative) are kept virtually intact in the process.

This is precisely what happens when rendering speech such as that reported in sample A into Arabic. Capturing the intricacy of this context-switching requires skill and sensitivity to text in context. It is here that these issues become relevant points of discussion particularly in the training of contrastive linguists in general and of translators in particular.

Contextualizing Reporting

The definition of context adopted in this study rests on two basic premises. Firstly, lexical and syntactic choices are dictated by variables such as 'field of discourse' (including social processes and institutions), 'tenor of discourse' (including relations of power and solidarity) and 'mode of discourse' (including channel or physical distance separating text production from reception)—which we have collectively labelled as the 'institutional-communicative' dimension of context. These register membership variables are ultimately determined by 'pragmatic' considerations to do with the purposes of utterances, real-world conditions, and so on. For example, consider the following elements from sample A:

1 'If that's taken place, it would not enhance relations between us . . .'
2 'It would complicate things . . .'

In terms of register membership, these display the following contextual profile:

Field   journalistic account of international politics (e.g. *relations*)
Tenor   semi-formal (e.g. *us, enhance, complicate, that's*)
Mode   written to be read as if heard as an off-the-cuff remark (e.g. *things*)

Figure 12.1 Contextual profile of sample A

This way of defining the 'register' membership of a given text is an essential part of the translator's work. Problems involved in translating sample A, for example, include locating equivalent terms in the appropriate field and achieving target language expression in the appropriate mode and tenor. Much more than this, however, is involved in reconstructing context and in tracing the ways in which it is reflected in actual texts. The meanings of utterances 1 and 2 are ultimately determined by the pragmatic action involved, namely, 'warning' in the two examples. It is only when this pragmatic reading is invoked that intentionality is properly perceived and meaning appropriately relayed. The translation of direct and indirect speech is certain to benefit from such perceptions.

The second premise we adopt in the definition of context is that, in order to appreciate the full communicative thrust of an utterance, we need to appreciate not only the so-called illocutionary force of the utterance (e.g. to warn), but also its status as a token of a given type of sign. This 'semiotic' dimension of context regulates the interaction of the various discoursal elements within a socio-cultural system of meanings. For example,

3 *such a project, if true, could 'complicate' US-Israeli ties*

is a speech act that may be labelled 'warning'. But this has taken on the meaning it has only by virtue of the interaction between this particular utterance as a sign and the surrounding utterances/signs, e.g.

4 *Israel feeling diplomatic fallout . . .*

5 *'I hope our position is clear on transfer of any military technology'*

Semiotic interaction also takes place between the various signs and between the producer and the intended receiver of these signs. Though belonging to the same sign type (warning), utterances 3 and 5 are different semiotic tokens, while 5, 1 and 2 are similar. Part of the meaning of utterance 3 accrues from the relationship between the utterance in question, the journalist as producer and the newspaper reader as text receiver, while the meaning of utterances 5, 1 and 2 is a function of the intricate relationships obtaining between Bush and a possibly sceptical audience as text receivers, and between Bush and the journalist quoting him. As will be made clear later in the discussion of direct/indirect speech, these various semiotic readings have a bearing on the intersemiotic transfer which translation necessarily involves.

Mode and Register Membership

Of immediate relevance to the problem of reported speech discussed in this chapter is the variable 'mode'. Essentially, this refers to the 'physical distance' between text producer and receiver, on the one hand, and between producer/receiver and the actual message, on the other. This manifests itself as a vehicle for the interaction or the medium in use through which the language activity in question is represented. Mode is thus the linguistic manifestation of the language code in use. The basic distinction here is that between speech and writing and the various permutations on such a distinction (written to be spoken, etc.). Over-lapping considerably with mode are, of course, both the field and tenor of discourse. As I have pointed out in an earlier discussion (p. 26), these collectively relay the level of technicality and formality which characterizes the relationship between the addresser and the addressee.

In sample A above, the shift from the authorial (journalist's) speech (I, III) to the 'reported' speech (II, IV), and finally to the 'direct' speech signalled in English by quotation marks (V), involves a shift in field, tenor and, most importantly, in mode. In attempting to relay this shift in a language such as Arabic, the translator must learn to cope with the following kinds of constraint. Firstly, while the English text tends to be syntactically and semantically 'implicit' in marking the mode 'written to be read as if heard or overheard' (IV), a tendency which creates difficulties for text comprehension, Arabic is much more 'vocal' in articulating subtle distinctions in meaning, a tendency which, in turn, creates difficulties for text production.

The second kind of problem which the shift in mode may cause is that the translator into Arabic will have to mark the text for mode 'twice' as it were: to overcome the problem of stylistic implicitness of the English source text and to capture the tone of the direct speech. As an illustration, let us consider sample A, Part IV, reproduced here for easier reference:

IV *Israeli papers reported prominently President Bush's comment on Saturday that such a project, if true, could 'complicate' US-Israeli ties.*

The opaque use of *could complicate* is spelt out in Arabic to read something like 'likely to make the situation worse' (*min sha'nihi ann yufaaqima al- wad'* . . .). The modal element 'likely to' properly signals that the journalist has shifted onto Bush the responsibility for his own words.

Speech Act Sequence and Intentionality

Particularly in the translation of linguistic forms such as direct and

128

indirect speech, the problems faced by the translator into Arabic transcend mode to include a pragmatic component. In the analysis of sample A, for example, the fundamental question is: What is the difference between I and III, on the one hand, and, II and IV, on the other? The two sets would be lumped together by mode analysis simply as authorial intervention and reporting, respectively. But this captures the difference only partially. For the purpose of the present study and to answer the question just posed, we may single out 'speech act sequence' as one of the more important pragmatic variables. As an important indicator of overall intentionality, this is the cumulative effect of a series of speech acts leading to the perception of a predominant pragmatic force in a given stretch of discourse.

We have distinguished two basic strategies for the processing of speech act sequences. One is situation monitoring, the other situation managing. For example, in sample A, Part I:

6 *The Defence Minister . . . has repeated Israel's denial of allegations that it has collaborated with . . .*

is a clear example of 'monitoring' by the journalist, while:

7 *However, the denials have not stopped Israel feeling diplomatic fallout . . .*

in sample A, Part III, is an example of 'managing' to steer the situation into a direction favoured by the text producer. This manipulation of discourse, which is fairly 'innocuous' when attempted by the journalist, lapses into more 'tendentious' forms of managing as in sample A, Part V,

8 *'There's no question about that', said Bush.*

Transposing into the indirect form the force of the direct speech in utterance (8), as Arabic is prone to do, and allowing this 'quasi-direct' speech to co- exist with a genuinely indirect authorial context as in (6), and a 'less' genuinely indirect context as in (7), involves perceiving and relaying pragmatic values of monitoring and managing, which tend to be generally implicit in English. The translation of sample A, Part V may be taken as an example which illustrates the role of pragmatics in dealing with direct speech in English. The speech act sequence involved is reproduced as a series of speech acts.

(a) 'I hope our position is clear on transfer of any military technology that should not be transferred.

(b) 'If that's taken place, it would not enhance relations between us.

(c) 'It would complicate things.

(d) 'There is no question about that'.

Figure 12.2 Speech act sequence for Part V sample A

The choice of the reporting verbs which are used to introduce indirect speech in Arabic will be determined by the need to capture the very pragmatic import of the sequence in question. Here, it is "He signalled, confirming that . . .". This incorporates the 'warning' which cumulatively emanates from *hope, is clear, that should not, if, would not enhance, complicate things, no question.* Once introduced in this way, the sequence will undergo two basic modifications within and between the various speech acts, one semantic and the other syntactic. The Arabic translation will read something like this:

Sample B. Back-translation from Arabic

> and President Bush in his statement signalled, confirming that he hopes that the position of his government is clear regarding the transfer of any military technology, a transfer which is banned. And he added that, if that were actually to happen, he has no doubt it would not strengthen the relations between the two countries but would undermine them.

Notice how, in addition to the slightly more emotive lexical and syntactic choices made throughout the text, the Arabic text manipulates the speech act sequence in two ways: (1) conflating (b) and (c) and turning the additive relation into an adversative one; and (2) paraphrasing (d) and using it to introduce this adversative relation.

Intertextuality and Signification

To impose order on this seemingly unmanageable situation of discoursal diversity, we need a framework within which the various communicative and pragmatic values may be processed in both socio-cultural and socio-textual terms as 'signs'. An important principle to be focused on in the analysis of this semiotic dimension of context is the way we relate textual occurrences to each other and recognize them as signals which evoke in the text user whole areas of his or her previous textual experiences. This is 'intertextuality', a mechanism through which textual occurrences are recognized in terms of their dependence on other relevant prior texts. To illustrate this phenomenon of dealing with signs, let us compare an utterance from Part IV of sample A with one from Part V in the same sample. Both instances are reproduced here for easier reference:

IV (a) *Israeli papers reported prominently President Bush's comment on Saturday*
   (b) *that such a project, if true, could 'complicate' US-Israeli ties.*
V (a) *If that's taken place, it would not enhance relations between us.*
   (b) *It would complicate things.*

Segment (a) Part IV is an intertextual signal evoking our previous textual experience of news reporting, of journalistic neutrality and of the narrative as a text form. Segment (a) or (b) Part V, however, conjures up a different image—that of a public statement delivered with a maximal sense of commitment. Translation equivalence is achieved by evoking in the target language reader similar experiences stored and retrieved by language users as a series of signs which are in constant interaction with each other.

In the segments of discourse under consideration (Part IV and Part V), perhaps a more interesting phenomenon is the semiotic difference between Part IV (b) and Part V (a). The two utterances express the same propositional content and they are both 'warnings'. In semiotic terms, however, the two tokens are different from each other. The difference lies in the intertextual potential which they are bound to display as signs. Token (b) Part IV refers us to a 'polemic as reported neutrally in a narrative'. Token (a) Part V, on the other hand, intertextually refers the reader to a 'polemic as created subjectively in an argument'. The striking nature of the difference may be clearly illustrated by a comparison of *complicate* (IVb) with *complicate* (Vb). These two propositionally identical utterances which belong to the same sign type 'warning' are nevertheless different tokens. The grounds for establishing the difference are the same as for the previous two examples: the two occurrences of *complicate* are used by different people for different purposes (a journalist reporting v. the President of the United States arguing).

Here, it may be helpful to note that, in the analysis of intertextuality, the term 'textual occurrence' is used fairly generically. It is not restricted to 'texts' (e.g. narrative), but also covers the two other basic categories—'discourse' (e.g. journalistic neutrality) and 'genre' (e.g. the news report). All of these semiotic structures are capable of displaying intertextual potential, imposing their own constraints on the inter- semiotic transfer entailed by translation.

As has already been made clear, genres are conventionalized forms of texts which reflect the functions and goals involved in particular social occasions as well as the purposes of the participants in them (Kress 1985b). These semiotic structures impose their own constraints on the process of translation. In this respect, it is perhaps useful to point out that generic constraints emanate not only from a single genre seen to predominate on a given communicative occasion (e.g. the news report), but from a number of minor ones usually deployed to make the master-genre operational. This is most relevant in translating direct/indirect speech. In sample A, for example, there is the predominant genre of news reporting, within which we have a periodic switching from the authorial/journalist's contribution (an interventionist sub-genre), to the reported speech (a straightforward reporting sub-genre) and to the direct speech (a polemical sub-genre). Through intertextuality, the wording of the message will have to reflect the subtle differences which exist between the various generic structures. That is, lexical and syntactic choices are made in the light of considerations of genre-membership. In the case of Arabic, noted for its explicitness, this manipulation of texture in the service of higher semiotic (e.g. generic) considerations is of crucial importance. As has been shown above (in samples B, C1 and C2) the reader of the translation will be guided from 'tone' to 'tone' by different genres highlighting the various contours of the text.

The participants in the social events which are reflected in genres are bound to be involved in attitudinally determined expression characteristic of these events. For example, the news report as a genre involves journalists in the expression of typical attitudes towards their subject. In this case, the mode of expression is 'non-evaluative'. But the journalist is not tied to one and only one mode of operation. He or she may at times find it more appropriate to engage in evaluating the news as well as reporting it. Journalists may also sometimes rely on an 'invited' speaker (e.g. an authority on the subject) who may engage in an objective review of events or in a polemic or comment (i.e. altogether different sub-genres to that of the 'dominant' news report). A different attitudinal expression emerges with each of these fluctuations. Two basic shifts may be distinguished. The journalist yields the floor either to a different persona (himself as a commentator) or a different person (the invited speaker).

In a language such as English, the former shift to a different persona is relayed subtly (e.g. through understatement), while the latter shift to a different person is signalled by quotation marks. In Arabic, however, the various sets of attitudinal expression are conflated, and it is the task of the translator to make sure that different intertextual signals are faithfully relayed through all kinds of syntactic or semantic means. These will sometimes have to point to the discourse of detachment (the journalist's), at other times to the committed discourse of the polemicist/ commentator from within or from outside. Skill and sensitivity to discoursal expression are called for in handling intricate situations like these.

Finally, within discourse and genre there are fluctuations which have to be accounted for in the reworking of any text. In the genre of the news report, for example, differences arise when the discourse of 'objective reporting' gives way to that of 'subjective evaluation'. The latter varies in intensity from the mildly evaluative sections of the journalist's own mainly objective discourse to the highly evaluative argumentation likely to dominate in, say, the committed discourse of the 'comment' as an intruding genre. Here, there could always be a subjective 'element' set against the background of an objective exposition. These differences give rise to rhetorical intents such as 'to counter-argue' or 'to narrate'. Counter-arguments, narratives, etc. are what we have been calling 'texts'.

In dealing with the problem faced by the translator in rendering direct speech, the textual dimension is of crucial importance. So-called journalese (which is a misleading cover term for what may be more rigorously defined in terms of genre and discourse) is nothing but a body of mutually relevant texts, each with its own specific rhetorical purpose. It is this sense of purpose which the translator must make sure to convey when the news report slides from objective narrative (the journalist's) to subjective evaluation (which could also be the journalist's or that of the 'invited speaker') to even more extreme forms of evaluation (which are most probably the invited speaker's but could also be the journalist's). In fact, viewing sample A in terms of the relative degree of evaluativeness as distributed among the various parts of the text, we can see a systematic build-up from least to most evaluative, beginning with Part I through to Part V. That is, the direct speech quoted in Part V, functioning as the 'substantiator' of the 'opposition' to a 'cited thesis' in the unfolding argument, marks the highest point of evaluativeness.

This switch from one rhetorical intention to another may distinguish one text from another (rhetorical intention would then equal rhetorical purpose) or one part of a given text from another part (rhetorical intention would be the same as discourse function). The direct speech cited in sample A is an example of one such discourse function. Figure 12.3 represents the discourse functions in sample A:

Thesis Cited	The Defence Minister Yitzhak Rabin has repeated
To be	Israel's . . . denial of allegations . . .
Countered	He told Cabinet . . .
Opposition	However, the denials have not stopped Israel feeling diplomatic fallout . . .
Substantiation	Israeli papers reported prominently President Bush's comment on Saturday . . .
Substantiation Enhancer	I hope our position is clear . . .'

Figure 12.3 Text structure of sample A

While quotation marks play an important role in English, setting off the various texts and text segments one from the other, the translator into Arabic has to rely solely on his ability to tap the appropriate intertextual resources as and when appropriate for text development. All of this will ultimately have to be reflected through actual wording as opposed to punctuation that is formally available but functionally redundant. Within the text strategy illustrated in Figure 12.3 above, Bush's comment takes on the textual value 'enhancer of a substantiation'. In Arabic, the substantiation and the enhancer, which are more appropriately rendered as indirect speech, are respectively marked with a substantiation particle (*fa*) ('thus') and an additive particle (*wa*) ('and').

The Interaction of Text, Discourse and Genre

Genre and discourse strategy, then, informs textual strategy. But texts, in turn, modify the specification of the genre and, consequently, of the discourse within a given communicative transaction. This may be illustrated schematically in figure 12.4 for sample A above:

GENRE	DISCOURSE	TEXT	
Newsreport	Neutral	Narrative	VIRTUAL
Investigative	Semi-evaluative	Juxtaposotory Report	ACTUAL

Figure 12.4 Text–discourse–genre chain

Thus, the type of juxtaposition displayed by the semi-evaluative discourse of this investigative news report may be distinguished from the counter-argumentative text format found, for example, in the highly evaluative discourse of the genre Letter to the Editor. That is, the opposition, signalled by *however* in sample A, is different from a similar opposition in sample B below.

Sample B
> KENNETH CLARKE, Health Secretary, is reported (Guardian, November 14, 1989) as saying that the inclusion of a question on ethnic origin in the 1991 census 'would yield valuable information in the fight against racial discrimination.' The census will not, however, yield any information about the discrimination faced by Irish people in Britain.
> The Irish community is the largest ethnic minority in Britain . . .
> *The Guardian*

In sample A, the opposition is somehow veiled. It is, as it were, held at some remove from the author. In sample B, on the other hand, it is more 'up front'. These distinctions have a bearing on the way we perceive the wider implications which the direct speech has for the structure of the entire text.

Direct, Indirect and Quasi-direct Speech

I have thus far presented the difficulties faced by the translator in rendering direct and indirect speech into Arabic. I have also made clear that such difficulties are not normally encountered by translators of texts into, or, for that matter, producers of texts in, English or the majority of European languages. In these languages, a conventionally sanctioned, time-tested system of punctuation and quotation marks carries the responsibility of presenting as distinct the various modes of speech reporting in text. Here, within each mode of reporting, aspects of genre, discourse and text, while present as they would be in any language, are

135

nevertheless realized implicitly. Context, tight text structure and a fairly opaque texture together relay subtle pragmatic, semiotic and other kinds of meaning.

If one were to embark on an analysis of Arabic textual conventions, one would find almost all of these aspects of text constitution equally present. But such an analysis would only be formal, rarely delving sufficiently deeply into the underlying functional significance of surface realizations. True, the choice between direct and indirect speech is available in Arabic. A system of punctuation has been 'imported' by certain Arab neo-rhetoricians from English and other European languages. And, as I have made amply clear, generic, discoursal and textual constraints operate in Arabic in more or less the same way as they do in other languages. A closer examination of these phenomena in actual use, however, would reveal that the analogy between Arabic and these other languages is far from complete. First, while the means of expressing direct and indirect speech is no doubt formally available, this is not unconstrained. A number of factors render the use of the direct in a genre such as news reporting in Arabic rare indeed. This is borne out by my initial survey of modes of reporting in newspaper Arabic which conclusively points to the remarkable frequency of the indirect form (almost 98 per cent).

The second area in which the comparability between Arabic and western European languages in this respect is likely to be partial relates to the fact that the system of punctuation outlined in modern manuals of Arabic style has been wished on Arabic by those intent on imposing a Europeanized system of punctuation on this language. In surveying a number of these manuals (e.g. Nu'aimi and Kayyal 1984), even when the so-called punctuation marks are removed from the various textual elements cited, those textually well-formed examples are found to stand up to scrutiny for cohesiveness. With or without punctuation, on the other hand, those cited examples which are ill-formed simply do not work. That is, when standards of textuality are met, these marks become redundant, if not meaningless, serving decorative purposes only. Cohesion in Arabic is maintained through text syntax and semantics, and not by the use of marks that artificially set off parentheses or unnaturally separate the various elements of the clause, the sentence or the text. In the final analysis, the test of a cohesive text in Arabic is that it should display continuity of sense (coherence) when heard as well as when seen.

Finally, while generic, discoursal and textual considerations are no doubt as important in Arabic as they are in other languages, the relationship between, say, the contextual level of a given generic

136

specification and the textural level of the linguistic realization of that particular specification is much more explicit in Arabic than it is in other less 'oral/aural' languages. In fact, it is this very explicit and almost causal relationship between text and context that may help us explain 'why' users of Arabic opt for indirect speech in texts such as the ones analysed in this study, despite the formal availability of the choice of direct/ indirect speech, as well as punctuation.

The Grammarian's Position

Typically, Arabic grammarians, classical and modern, take a system-oriented stance towards aspects of language use such as the choice of direct/indirect speech under consideration. Hasan (1975), for example, fully discusses the phenomenon under *al-Hikaaya* (narration) and points to the availability of the choice alluded to earlier. However, like all system-oriented grammarians, he restricts the description to the 'what' and to the 'how' but does not deal with the 'why'. Moreover, the description is restricted to the level of the sentence and below, in total obliviousness to considerations of genre, discourse and text.

Inspired by valuable insights into the relationship between text and context provided by Arabic rhetoric (*balaagha*), I would for my part submit that the constraints on the use of direct speech are primarily regulated by certain modes of expression, such as that which is referred to in Arabic rhetoric as *iltifaat* (reference-switching from journalist to direct quote, for example). This will explain the predominance of the indirect in Arabic texts such as sample A in translation. The genre of news reporting does not permit the reference-shift allowed by other genres (e.g. the Quran as a unique genre, the traditions of the Prophet Mohammed (*Hadiith*) as a rare genre, storytelling as a more mundane genre, etc.). This shift is appropriate only when the context is generically, discoursally and textually more 'turbulent' and 'restless', performing a managing act of persuading and not a monitoring act of informing.

Summary

In this chapter, I have shown that the stylistic conventions of Arabic tend to favour the use of indirect speech in genres such as news reporting. This is partially due to genre, discourse and text constraints which are related to certain rhetorical modes of expression such as 'reference-switching'. For example, the shift of reference from, say, the third person to the first person which would be entailed by the use of direct speech within reporting, is reserved for loftier forms of expression and not, say, the more pedestrian occasions such as that of reporting the news. But whatever the cause, the translator's responsibility when working into Arabic is to preserve the 'immediacy' of direct speech in the source text while at the same time operating with textual conventions which generally encourage the use of indirect forms. The way to reconcile these seemingly conflicting goals resides in tapping the resources of the semiotics of genre, discourse and textual strategy which play an important part in making maximally interactive the pragmatic purport of the direct quote when this is used in a predominantly indirect reporting situation in the source text. Pragmatic action, in turn, motivates the use of a particular mode of discourse for direct speech. When the direct is turned into indirect in Arabic, preserving these pragma-semiotic properties ensures that the direct speech of the source text does not necessarily lose its tone when it will most certainly lose its original form.

13

The Pragmatics of Politeness

A general aim of this chapter is to extend the basic theory of 'politeness' as developed by Brown and Levinson (e.g. 1978, 1987) and to apply it to the analysis of non-dyadic discourse. Like a number of other studies (e.g. Myers 1989), my primary intention is not so much to evaluate or drastically modify the basic theory as to test, and I hope demonstrate, the degree of its flexibility in handling entire stretches of monologic discourse. Unlike the majority of these studies, however, I will be concerned with both written and spoken texts, and will define text rather more stringently in terms of rhetorical purpose.

A more specific aim of this study is to examine the hypothesis that politeness *of*, and not simply *in*, texts (Sell 1993) is closely bound up with text-type variation. It will be argued that the choice between exposition and argumentation, or between one form of argumentation and another, is regulated by a combination of contextual factors relating to the communicative act as a 'sign' intended to perform a given rhetorical function as part of achieving an overall rhetorical purpose. It will be further argued that this pragmatic and semiotic specification of the utterance or of the text could be usefully explained in terms of politeness strategies.

To take scientific communication as an example, it is my contention that the scientist, just like the civil servant or the cookery writer or any text user one cares to name, has available to him or her the same wide range of choices between wanting to engage in exposition, in argumentation, or in neither text type. Within, say, argumentation, the choice is also wide open as to which form to use (explicit or implicit counter-argument, through-argument, etc.). What is important, then, is to be able to identify and work within those conditions under which a particular form of argumentation, for example, may or may not be appropriate.

Text Typology: A Recapitulation

In the present study, spoken or written communication is seen in terms of the way text users utilize a number of different genres, each with its own characteristic discourse and particular text types. In the 'academic article' as a macro-genre, for instance, the committed and involved discourse of the 'discussion' part (a micro-genre) is distinct from the detached discourse of the 'review' part (another micro-genre). Given this complexity, what is of immediate relevance to us both as language users and as analysts is the set of constraints within which our scientist or politician operates and which regulates the acceptability or otherwise of a given mode of speaking or writing (for a comparable view of genre in contexts like academic writing, see Swales 1990).

But as we have seen throughout this book, the characterization of discourse and, perhaps to a lesser extent, of genre, is diffuse and the boundaries almost seamless. For this essentially open-ended nature of interaction to be brought under control and made more accessible, some other more concrete system of meaning-making must be relied on. That is, for discoursal statements and generic structures to be perceived as coherent wholes, relatively less intangible units of communication must be employed to perform the various rhetorical tasks. These 'sites' in which rhetorical purposes are negotiated are what we have been referring to as 'texts'.

Thus, the detached discourse of the scientist in the 'review' part of the academic article, for example, finds concrete expression in the text type 'exposition'. Exposition is in turn realized by sub-types such as 'conceptual exposition', text forms such as the 'summary' or the 'abstract' and ultimately by text tokens such as the text samples we have been working with in this book. Diagrammatically, this chain of realization may be illustrated as in Figure 13.1.

Genre (e.g. the review)
Discourse (detached)
Text type (exposition)
Sub-type (conceptual exposition)
Text form (the summary)
Text token (actual text samples)

Fig. 13.1 The type-token relationship in texts

The choices which are exercised by one and the same text producer and which normally run the entire gamut of text type, sub-type, forms and tokens seem to be closely bound up with the text user's 'power' and 'distance' and ultimately with the set of do's and don'ts that is regulated by pragmatic politeness. Therefore, any assumption indiscriminately entertained about sub-cultures like those of the scientists, the civil servants or whatever, as if these were self- contained, monolithic entities, is essentially ill-conceived and unsustainable. Variables such as 'power' will fluctuate as the language user switches from one rhetorical purpose (i.e. text) to another. Genre- and discourse-switching is also heavily involved in the process, and, given this multi-faceted activity of doing things with texts, the question of 'face' is bound to figure significantly. To pursue this line of enquiry and to try to substantiate some of these hypothetical statements, I will in this chapter address a question not substantially dissimilar to the one originally raised in relation to politeness strategies by Brown and Levinson themselves in their classic work on politeness (1978: 62): 'What sort of assumptions, and what sort of reasoning are utilized by participants to produce such universal strategies of verbal interaction?'

Politeness of Texts—An Example

Before presenting a detailed account of the implications which text typologies can have for a pragmatic theory of politeness, it may be helpful to illustrate the main issue of text-type politeness by means of a simple example used earlier for a slightly different purpose:

Sample A
   The University of X and Y University have a proven track record
   . . . which this collaborative venture *can only* enhance.

Sample B
   The University of X and Y University have a proven track record
   . . . which this collaborative venture *is intended to* enhance.

In considering these sample texts, what is particularly relevant for the present discussion is the communicative privilege of using 'emphasis' (*can only*), which is enjoyed by the speaker in sample A and denied to the speaker in sample B. Of immediate interest is also the fact that one could not envisage the producer of sample B as engaging in anything approximating to the kind of evaluativeness which is almost part and parcel of the discourse associated with the language of sample A.

141

For rhetorical goals such as 'persuading' (e.g. sample A above) or 'informing' (e.g. sample B) to be properly pursued, and for role relationships to stabilize, language users must negotiate meanings in texts and thus react to context in an interactive manner. In the desire merely to inform, the producer of sample B remains a spectator among spectators of the way a sequence of events unfolds. The producer of sample A, on the other hand, seeks to persuade and basically wants to invite everyone to take part in the construction of a universe of discourse of which he himself approves. The two activities of being a participant or a spectator (Britton 1963: 37) are kept somehow distinct in the socio-textual practices of language users, and it is the intriguing question of what regulates such practices in the life of a linguistic community that will occupy us in the remainder of this chapter.

Politeness Recast

I adopt the position that argumentation and exposition are distinguished one from the other by the relative presence or absence of the element evaluativeness. Argumentative texts are taken to be intrinsically evaluative, an orientation which manifests itself in either one of two basic text formats:

(1) Through-argumentation, characterized by extensive substantiation of an initial thesis (for an example, see sample G below)

(2) Counter-argumentation, involving the rebuttal of a cited thesis (e.g. sample F below).

In terms of politeness theory, a text user (producer or receiver) may be seen as a *Model Person* (MP), one who is 'a willful fluent speaker of a natural language' (Brown and Levinson 1978: 63).* MPs have at their disposal, 'a precisely definable mode of reasoning from ends to the means that will achieve those ends' (p. 63), that is, they exhibit *rationality*. For example, producers like that of sample B usually respond to a context such as the 'event review' in a manner which may be described in the following terms. They first negotiate a text-initial element which 'sets the scene', then they cover, in as much detail as is deemed appropriate, the various aspects of the scene. The process is

*Unless otherwise specified, bracketed page numbers in this chapter refer to Brown and Levinson 1978

continued until a threshold of termination is reached, i.e. a point where text reception or production is seen to be complete.

But the same text user of the review, on the same or on a different occasion of text production, could also perceive a claim which is open to negotiation. In order to rebut or defend such a claim, he or she needs to operate in a different capacity—that of an arguer. In situations like these, text users switch to a different mode of reasoning but only by first discharging current responsibilities and signalling their new intentions. The latter task of relaying intentionality can be achieved in a number of ways, one of which may be by first 'citing the opponent's contentious claim', then 'opposing' it and finally 'substantiating' the claim put forward, a text form we have labelled 'counter-argumentation'.

Alternatively, as in sample A above, a claim may be put forward and extensively defended or argued through, a text form we have called 'through-argumentation'. Whether responding to the expository context of, say, a review, to the counter-argumentative context of a rebuttal, or to yet another kind of context which calls for through-argumentation, text users are all the time trying out various plans. They would assess the different means by which to reach a given end, eventually opting for a particular path considered optimally effective and efficient in reaching the desired communicative goal. In all of this 'practical reasoning', text users are constantly guided by 'relevance' as a basic principle: 'not to waste effort to no avail' (p. 70).

These goals and the means to achieve them as illustrated by sample A and sample B above, for example, relate to two different types of focus which cater for different kinds of context and involve different kinds of producer-receiver relationship. As I have shown earlier, any transgression involving an unsanctioned move from one contextual domain to another (e.g. when news reports lapse into editorializing totally gratuitously) is deemed textually inappropriate. To avoid what can and does at times amount to a breakdown in communication, text users are endowed with another property, namely *face*. They have 'two particular wants—roughly—the want to be unimpeded and the want to be approved of in certain respects' (p. 66). The desire on the part of an MP to be left alone and free to do as he wants is 'negative face'; the desire that others actually approve of him is 'positive face'.

That is, as text users, we seem to have textual rights and obligations. Unless motivated by context, news reports displaying a degree of evaluation which goes beyond the expected limits are condemned as being 'over the top'. Conversely, editorials which sound too measured and factual are condemned as being 'coy'. In effect, what seems to be happening in either case is that a particular text receiver is being somewhat thwarted (the dreaded reaction of writer and reader alike: 'so what!') or, alternatively, disregarded (a comment all too familiar here is: 'this is an insult to my intelligence'). At stake is 'the basic claim to freedom of action and freedom from imposition' (negative face) and/or 'the positive consistent self-image or "personality"' (positive face) (p. 66). The textual stance adopted by the producers of sample A and sample B above is a case in point. These texts demonstrate how smoother interaction entails that text users behave as cooperative, rational face-possessing agents.

Our proposals have thus far re-examined rationality and face and recast these in terms of textual competence, viewing the mechanisms in use within the perspective of being able to 'do things with texts'. But, face (and rationality) will differ in different cultures. Within the framework adopted here, moreover, culture is meant to include the limits to personal territories, the mutual knowledge of members' self-image, and the social necessity to orient oneself to current norms of interaction. All these facets are ultimately made to relate to individuals in their capacity as competent users of texts. The kind of community of text producers and receivers which emerges will thus be multi-cultural as well as multi-lingual. However, these terms are to be understood not in their traditional, purely socio-cultural sense, but rather in the sense of an individual both well-versed in a variety of modes of speaking and writing, and also willing and able to cooperate in upholding the text conventions sanctioned by the culture in question. It is this orientation which we have labelled 'socio-textual' that will inform the following discussion.

Text-type Controls

The kind of community we have portrayed is not always harmonious, and there is bound to be the odd upset. To return to our example briefly, had the speaker in sample A (the dean of a faculty) violated the norms of argumentation, he would have only managed a weak-kneed, faint-hearted comment on the future of the new venture. Similarly, had the writer of sample B (a PR office journalist) been too emotive, trying to whip up support for the joint venture and all that it stands for, he would have been ticked off for 'speaking out of turn', for being linguistically cocky, for having the cheek to tell his readers 'how they ought to think'.

As I hinted above, these and similar misdemeanours can and often do happen, particularly in cross-cultural communication. In terms of polite-ness theory, the acts committed will belong to the class of acts which 'intrinsically threaten face, namely those acts that by their very nature run contrary to the face wants of the addressee and/or the speaker'

(p. 70). These acts which can threaten both negative face and positive face are called *Face Threatening Acts* (FTAs). The orator or the reporter not operating by the rules of customary communicative practice could be seen as implicated in a similar damage to face. In unnecessarily flouting the norm, they would leave an audience of receivers feeling somewhat disoriented, even frustrated, with the text producer in either case likely to be considered indifferent to the addressees' wants and feelings.

Thus, text-type controls provide us with the first set of tools for policing this linguistic community of 'model text users'. The seriousness of an FTA is assessed in the light of upholding or violating generic, discoursal or textual conventions, which directly or indirectly relate to the context, structure and texture of a communicative occurrence. Cohesion, coherence, the linguistic manifestations of attitudinal meaning and the various rules and principles which regulate the membership of a given text within a particular type of language event, are some of the areas which could be at risk and are therefore heavily implicated.

Distance, Power and Imposition

At a slightly higher level of contextual negotiation, text-type criteria will involve the observance of another set of instructions. These specifically regulate the process of assessing the seriousness of an FTA from three points of view: distance, power and imposition.

Social Distance
The social distance (D) between the text producer and the text receiver is 'a symmetric social dimension of similarity/difference within which [co-communicants] stand for the purpose of the act, based on the frequency of interaction, the kinds of material and non-material goods exchanged . . . and [a number of other, more] stable social attributes' (p. 82). Although for fundamentally different reasons, both producers of sample A and sample B above could under this definition be assumed to display great distance with their respective audiences. Status as a stable social attribute (e.g. dean of faculty) and the kind of goods exchanged (news dis- semination) can have a bearing on the distance of the first and the second speakers respectively.

This kind of distance analysis, however, is too static and does not stand up to scrutiny when text type fluctuations have to be accounted for. In sample A, status is a minor factor and what is central to the question of distance is, paradoxically, the need on the part of the speaker to be more approachable, to be close to Mr and Mrs Average, to identify with the masses. In this way, the arguer can enhance his chances of success as an arguer, and distance can therefore be assumed to be lessened.

This would be the case particularly if we were to assume that the predominant mode of persuasion involved in sample A is actually one of counter-arguing. If, on the other hand, the context specified for sample A calls instead for through- argumentation, then the distance could safely be presumed to be greater, if only slightly so. It is hard to imagine that the through-arguers among the better-known orators on the present-day political scene in Britain, for example, are prepared to relinquish distance completely. But try as they might to hold on to a greater distance, the desire to succeed as arguers, which necessitates that distance be prevented from becoming forbiddingly great, remains to be fairly high on their list of priorities.

In the case of sample B, the kinds of 'goods exchanged' are no doubt a relevant factor. However, what is essentially at stake in the way the second speaker goes about his textual business is the fact that news reporting is ideally in the service of the truth. It is this received wisdom, conventionally enshrined in societal norms that regulate the acceptability of certain modes of writing (e.g. journalese), which may more helpfully account for distance being fairly great: the writer for a university bulletin does not ideally feel the urge to impress, nor is such an impression expected by his or her audience.

Thus, unlike those of the sociologist, these ratings of distance are purpose-related and have little or nothing to do with 'personalities'. That is, deans can and often do modify their assumptions of distance and adjust it accordingly. For example, distance would be lessened when deans deal, say, with the situation of having to win over their audience in speaking on issues such as cuts in higher education. By the same token, reporters attending to the business of news dissemination of a type not as institutionalized as that of covering a formal ceremony for a university bulletin may find themselves adjusting distance slightly by lessening it to allow a certain amount of evaluativeness to creep into their reporting.

Relative Power
The relative power (P) of the text producer and receiver is an 'asymmetric social dimension [which calibrates] the degree to which [the receiver] can impose his own plans and his own self-evaluation (face) at the expense of [the text producer's] plans and self-evaluation' (p. 82). Given the context of a formal address by a dean, for example, the producer of sample A, particularly when through-arguing, can be assumed to display greater power than that possessed by his audience of receivers. Reporters, in turn, also wield power, but of a different kind

146

to that of the arguer. In order to win over their audience, arguers tend (or pretend) to share power with the addressee, i.e. to empower him or her to become a participant in condoning or condemning the state of affairs being depicted. Reporters, however, assume an authoritative stance that is least concessive. Such authority derives its main thrust from similar factors to those which engendered distance. As servers of the truth (as they see it), they feel that they can afford to entertain a 'take it or leave it' attitude.

Once again I stress that while attributes to do with 'deanship' or 'news reporting' are no doubt in evidence, I take the real reason behind power, shared or latched on to in these specific contexts of language use, to be primarily text-typological. Whether they happen to be deans or cookery writers, arguers assume and share power by virtue of the rights and obligations provided by the argumentative context and type of text. Reporters, on the other hand, deal with a community of text receivers whose relationship with the producer of the texts they buy solely relies on the assumption that 'truth' (or the commodity offered by the text-type exposition) is more powerful than all.

As with distance, it is perhaps worth reiterating here that the two particular contexts of argumentation and exposition, and the power differences attached to them, are also purpose-specific. That is, they are in no way permanent attributes of deans or journalists. When deans perceive the need to engage in a detached review of a sequence of events, they immediately reverse roles and adjust the degree of power on display to be at a level acceptable to the larger and more powerful community of 'truth-seekers'. By the same token, when reporters feel that what is at stake is an issue which goes beyond the bounds of 'detachment', they too can switch over, this time to the 'inciting of emotions', adjusting their power accordingly and pitching it at a level which puts their audience in tune with the ensuing evaluative slant. In this latter case, the receiver will no longer be one who is to be informed, but one to be won over. For this role reversal to be sustainable, however, sufficient contextual motivation must be provided, otherwise each and every one of these new roles would be a monumental communicative disaster—an FTA.

Ranking of Imposition

The absolute ranking of impositions is 'a culturally and situationally defined ranking . . . by the degree to which [impositions] are considered to interfere with an agent's wants of self-determination or of approval (his negative and positive face wants)' (p. 82). Rephrased in terms of our text-type model, impositions will be ranked in a way which reflects the extent to which power and distance are effectively and justifiably used, by certain users, in certain contexts, and for certain rhetorical purposes. Ranking of this kind is, in a sense, a balance sheet showing the credits and debits accruing from the interface of text type with power and distance.

But it is not only considerations of text type or power/distance/ rank of imposition which determines the relative weighting of a Face Threatening Act (FTA). Avoiding the FTA altogether, or adopting strategies to minimize it, which are all courses of action open to any rational, face-possessing agent, may be seen in the light of 'the relative weightings of (at least) three wants' (p. 73): the want to communicate the content of the FTA, the want to be efficient or urgent, and the want to maintain receiver's face. We may illustrate these by an informal analysis of an extract from a news report which, in the words of Carter (1988: 10–13) 'offers no pretense to neutrality or objectivity . . ., [and] is generically more appropriate to the discourse conventions of an editorial . . .'. Seen from the text producer's point of view, however, the various lexical, syntactic and textual 'tricks' seem to be well worth the effort and the report is thus unashamedly one-sided:

Sample C

A soaking on the beach . . . a snub by the Left
CANUTE
KINNOCK
By GORDON GREIG, Political Editor

NEIL KINNOCK, just elected Labour's youngest leader at 41, saw an old party tide threaten to swamp his new beginning last night.

Once again, the night mare question came up. How far are you going to dismantle Britain's nuclear defence shield?

The answer helped Michael Foot lose the last election and from the way the argument was boiling at Brighton, it clearly threatened to help Mr Kinnock lose the next one.

His induction to the mantle of leadership began with a soaking on Brighton beach as he stumbled and fell at the sea's edge while posing for photographers. But the embarrassment of the Canute-like ducking was nothing to the problem of a backroom row between Labour's Left and Right over the rising tide of pacifism and one-sided nuclear disarmament in the party.

The Daily Mail, 8 October 1983

Let us now look at each of the above-listed wants in some detail:

(a) The want to communicate the content of the FTA. this may be illustrated by the use in a news report of evaluative text structure (say, a cleft sentence, an opaque metaphor or some subtle use of epistemic modality) which constitutes an FTA forced on the text receiver. However, the threat can be attenuated, as it probably is in sample C, by textual facts such as the event in question being the subject of a raging controversy at the time (e.g. the election of Neil Kinnock as leader of the Labour Party and the implications of this event for conservative aspirations).

(b) The want to be efficient or urgent, as is the case when a producer switches to a biased, slanted review of events. This is usually seen to have high 'informativity' and in the above sample is tantamount to saying that 'the election of Kinnock is an unmitigated disaster which leaves no room for an exchange of pleasantries'.

(c) The want to maintain receiver's face to any degree, a state of affairs which should be sought (i.e. FTA minimized or avoided altogether) unless (b) is greater than (c)'.

Of course, the key want in politeness is not to commit an FTA altogether. But, if such an act has to be committed, then a number of strategic orientations are available to the text producer. He may do it:

(1) On Record, when 'it is clear to participants what communicative intention led the actor to do the act' (p. 74), that is, when contextual and, to a greater extent, cotextual clues are clear for all to see as justifying the transgression. Explicit flouting (as opposed to breaking or violating) any of the Gricean maxims is a case of On Record FTAs. The ideological 'hobby horse' or 'an axe to grind' in the *Daily Mail* sample, if considered sufficiently motivated, is also an example of On Record FTAs.

(2) Off Record, when there is 'more than one unambiguously attributable intention so that the actor cannot be held to have committed himself to one particular intent' (p. 74). The more opaque the motivation is for flouting the Gricean maxims referred to above, for example, the more 'off record' it becomes: 'linguistic realizations of off-record strategies include metaphor and irony, rhetorical questions, understatement, tautologies, all kinds of hints as to what a speaker wants or means to communicate, without doing so directly so that the meaning is to some degree negotiable' (p. 74). Contextual and, to a lesser extent, cotextual clues are the key factor in the success of doing FTAs off record. In the *Daily Mail* sample, metaphoric expression abounds to represent the serious consequences of a Labour return to power; Kinnock is subtly

149

reduced to 'a frantically fluttering flag on the mast to which his colleagues inexorably nail him'—Carter (1988: 13).

On Record FTAs and Off Record FTAs may be placed on a continuum. Doing an FTA *On Record Boldly Without Redress* is the most extreme of On Record acts: an FTA is done 'in the most direct, clear, un-ambiguous manner' (p. 74). Doing an FTA *On Record With Redress*, on the other hand, is the least extreme of On Record FTAs: 'action that gives face to the addressee, that is, that attempts to counteract the potential face damage of the FTA by doing it in such a way, or with such modifications or additions, that . . . indicate clearly that no such face threat is indicated or desired' (p. 75).

Similar variation within Off Record acts may also be discerned. But the more significant point about all kinds of redressive and non-redressive off record and on record FTAs is that FTAs, wherever they emanate from, are regulated by the variables of power, distance and, consequently, rank of imposition, which are in turn themselves regulated by, on the one hand, text typological criteria to do with (non-)evaluation, and on the other, the set of basic kinds of 'wants' to communicate content efficiently and so on. (A text-type perspective on these and other issues specifically related to the notion of FTA is presented in Hatim, forth-coming).

Exposition and Politeness

Pragmatic notions such as politeness could thus be usefully invoked to make sure that text-type transgressions are kept under control. Face becomes a property of context, and face-threatening action the dividing line between textually competent and incompetent use of language. In exposition, rational and non-face-threatening action assumes that distance will be great. Readers of abstracts, for example, are essentially there to be informed, in as efficient a manner as possible, of the contents of, say, an entire annual report. This justifies the blandness, dullness and stereotypical nature which we invariably encounter in this text form. To illustrate distance as an aspect of politeness in exposition, consider sample D:

Sample D

INTRODUCTORY NOTE

Volume I contains the Final Act, the resolutions adopted by the Conference, and the Draft Additional Protocols prepared by the International Committee of the Red Cross. Volume II contains the rules of procedures, the list of participants, the report of the Drafting Committee and the reports of the Credentials Committee. Volumes III and IV contain the table of amendments. Volumes V to VII contain the summary records of the plenary meetings of the Conference. Volumes VIII to X contain the summary records and reports of Committee I. Volumes XI to XIII contain the summary records and reports of Committee II. Volumes XIV and XV contain the summary records and reports of Committee III, and volume XVI contains the summary records and reports of the Ad Hoc Committee on Conventional Weapons. Volume XVII contains the table of contents of the sixteen volumes.

From the UNs *Documents of the Diplomatic Conference* 1974

For the mechanisms of polite exposition to run smoothly, maximal distance must be accompanied by an equally high level of Power. Receivers of ultra-detached abstracts, for example, are hardly the kind of audience to impress with a quaint turn of phrase, emotive use of language or graphic metaphor. The content itself is invariably colourless, normally possessing a sense of urgency which demands to-the-point recount. Furthermore, the producer of the expository text rarely sets out to persuade or try to form future behaviour. Abstract writers are debarred from engaging in the business of manipulating language for effect.

Thus, to violate the normal pattern of lexical cohesion in this type of text unnecessarily by, for example, opting for lexical variation as opposed to the expected strict repetition is to compromise the distance and/or the power variables and ultimately to flout the conventions of the genre, the discourse and the text type in question. Such violations would, I maintain, be face-threatening and reader-disorienting acts which, in the absence of extenuating circumstances, will render the text in question utterly incoherent.

To illustrate such transgressions, consider sample E (a published translation of an academic Abstract from Arabic) which we cite here with two purposes in mind. Firstly to show that different cultures handle text-type politeness differently (that is, text forms not judged 'polite' in English could be tolerated and accepted as 'polite' in Arabic). And secondly to show that the expression of pragmatic politeness is an important aspect of text meaning which must therefore be heeded in translation. Politeness should be preserved and, if it must be adjusted, this would have to be done in such a way as to maintain compatibility with target-language conventions without compromising source-text 'difference' (Venuti 1995). Regrettably, such goals do not seem to be achieved in the following rather unidiomatic rendering:

151

Sample E
Patterning in Pre-Islamic Love Poetry
No doubt, the sentimental dialogue is one of the sources of aesthetic values which portray the similarity of the human intellect and its universality in the world of sensations. The paper attempts to observe the expressive methods of patterning these sensations through spiritual meanings and psychological and religious content as well as personal and non-personal experiences. This research also tries to establish a pattern for the world of sensations in pre- Islamic love poetry: a pattern that combines Arabic sentiment in the pre-Islamic period . . . with its counterpart in Babylonian love poetry . . . Moreover, this research tries to mark the beginnings of the love poetry of the Arabs . . . This is made possible owing to the similarity of the human, intellectual and religious content . . .

Given that contextual requirements to maximize both power and distance in relation to the text-type exposition were fulfilled, the rank of imposition is slight and face-threatening action thus avoided. This description of politeness, however, is idealized, portraying what could be considered as the 'unmarked' case. Subsidiary functions such as evaluativeness could in varying degrees be allowed to creep in. Only when motivated, however, would these transgressions be tolerated and the threat to face minimized. By motivation is meant purposeful manipulation of the levels of distance and power, but with the provisos that distance is not made lesser than, and power not made greater than, the levels allowed by the textual conventions of the genre and the discourse associated with the text-type exposition and with expository text forms such as the Abstract. If such violations do occur, a series of face-threatening acts will ensue and the identity of the text form Abstract will be obliterated, as is made clear by sample E.

As an example of how distance and power are manipulated to effect and within the limits suggested, consider sample F. This is an Abstract of the 'attention-getting' type, normally provided by editors to 'advertise' what is on offer:

Sample F
The Influence of Culture
[ABSTRACT]
A society's attitudes to health and disease are closely bound up with its culture. However, this culture is rarely static and can usually accommodate new ideas if they do not appear to threaten it.

Whatever changes health workers introduce, they should always harmonize their activities with the culture in which they find themselves.

World Health Forum Vol. 5, 1984

Sample D above may be considered to be typical of the text form Abstract. It is an example of unmarked exposition which relays an appropriate level of politeness through the display of maximal power and distance. Sample E, on the other hand, is flawed as an Abstract: the levels of power and distance are compromised in a manner not deemed appropriate for the text form in question. Finally, sample F handles politeness in more or less the same manner as E, but, I suggest, can nevertheless be tolerated and is deemed appropriate in its own context. Here, the FTAs in evidence are motivated (cf. the 'attention-getting' editorial intervention), and the text form in question is acceptable as a marked variety of expository Abstracts.

Counter-argumentation and Politeness

Sample F is interesting for yet another reason. It vividly illustrates the role of constraints imposed by genres on both the discourse and the text as units of semiotic interaction, and ultimately on what constitutes face-threatening action. In a motivated manner, both the discourse and the text of sample F are shifted away from their unmarked forms in the direction of more evaluativeness. But genre sets limits on how far the shift can go. Power and distance are minimized but not so much as to obliterate the identity of the genre in question. Had generic constraints not been heeded in this context, we would have ended up with a totally different genre (e.g. a rebuttal), and expository politeness would have been irreparably harmed. That is, had power been raised and distance lessened more noticeably than they are at present, the generic structure of the Abstract would have been irredeemably compromised due to the ensuing face-threatening action.

This brings us to a consideration of politeness in counter-argumentation, where power is normally maximized and distance minimized far beyond what is admitted by a text sample such as F. Within the unmarked form of this type, text producers try to accommodate counter-views but still hope to give due prominence to their own claims. This text type is a variety of argumentation which builds on the 'citation of the opposite view' before countering it. To achieve this in a way that does not threaten face, text users opt to part with distance and continue to hold on to the power of the arguer. Thus, while the power of the arguer is kept maximal, distance would be lessened to facilitate getting through to a sceptical audience assumed to entertain counter-beliefs which even the arguers themselves found worth citing. This is exactly the opposite of what actually happens in exposition. As an example of a through-the-back-door persuasive strategy, consider the counter-argumentative sample G and compare it with sample F and D above in terms of the gradience of both power and distance:

Sample G

The Influence of Culture

Asked to provide an example of the relationship between culture and health, many professional health workers would point to the persistence of certain time-honoured medical procedures in some simple rural society. But culture may shape and fashion attitudes and responses to health and sickness in any society, whatever the level of sophistication. An awareness of the ways in which it can do this is of the highest importance, not only in promoting health in the community but in understanding disease processes . . .

World Health Forum, Vol. 5, No. 1, 1984

Thus, through the appropriate use of power and distance, the producer of sample G has managed successfully to keep within the 'unmarked' form of the 'rebuttal' as a genre, with its own evaluative discourse and counter-argumentative text strategy. Had the text been envisaged within a lower level of power and a greater level of distance, it would have become essential that a different generic structure be used in order to maintain the appropriate level of politeness. Put differently, had sample G maintained the level of power (or raised it slightly, which is more likely) but raised the level of distance too, the result would have been a series of FTAs as far as the genre 'rebuttal' is concerned. But, as will be explained in the next section, displaying maximal power and a fairly high level of distance is a precondition for the success of another form of argumentation—through-argumentation.

Through-argumentation and Politeness

Texts which belong to the through-argumentative type, we recall, build on a premise which the text producer posits and extensively defends. Such texts derive their distance, which tends to be slightly higher than that in counter-argumentation, from the fact that they are 'masked expositions'. That is, these texts are expository in layout, which provides distance, and argumentative in tone, which neutralizes such distance.

This tension is manifested in the logical analysis which tends to be biased one way or another and which dominates the reasoning throughout. The maximal power in these texts, on the other hand, is derived from the authoritative air assumed by the text producer in his capacity as arguer/persuader. To illustrate this text type with its maximal power and fairly high level of distance, consider sample H and compare it with its expository counterpart (sample D) which also displays maximal power and distance.

Sample H

> Sickness introduces an entirely new dimension into any society. It is an unwelcome intruder, it threatens people, and it may lead to death. A society's attitudes and practices in respect of the sick reflect its understanding and interpretation of the causes of disease. In some societies, it has been the custom to isolate the sick and take no care of them. This practice probably originated with infections such as smallpox or pulmonary tuberculosis, which were often transmitted to members of the patient's family or others living in the same compound. In many places, a basic reluctance to go near the sick can still affect the behaviour of members of the health team, inclining them to neglect their patients. (. . .)
>
> *World Health Forum*, Vol. 5, No. 1, 1984

The hallmark of this kind of through-argumentation, then, is its reliance on a premise accepted and defended categorically by the text producer. The systems of evidentiality and modality in evidence in this kind of committed discourse which tends towards 'down-toning' and 'tentativeness' may at first give the impression of intimacy and weakness. This may be seen in a surface reading of *may lead to death, in some societies, this practice probably originated, often transmitted*, and so on. In reality, however, these are important linguistic characteristics of science as a discipline and do not in the least diminish the distance and the power which the producer has claimed for himself.

Summary

In this chapter, we have examined rational and face-saving (i.e. polite) message construction from the viewpoint of text types in actual language use. Politeness is shown to manifest itself through the appropriate handling of two variables: distance and power. Misperception of the relationship between distance and power, on the one hand, and type of text, on the other, is claimed to be an important source of 'face-threatening action' (FTA). Schematically, all other things being equal, politeness interrelationships may be represented as follows:

Exposition: max. D; fairly high level of P
Counter-Argumentation: min. D; fairly high level of P
Through-argumentation: fairly high level of D; max. P

Figure 13.2 Text-type, Power and Distance

Within this 'idealized' matrix, it is argued that any transgression, unless motivated by factors such as genre and discourse or the need to be communicatively efficient, would constitute an FTA.

In conclusion, it is perhaps worth noting that the proposals put forward here are not intended to be a prescriptive set of rules, nor indeed a descriptive statement of what actually happens. We simply do not know enough at this stage. But there are sufficient indications which enable us to present our scheme as a set of hypotheses to be confirmed, modified or discarded, once tested against authentic data. If shown to be sustainable, these insights into textuality should prove helpful to users of language in fields as disparate as translating/interpreting, academic writing, and the general field of foreign language teaching.

14

Cultures in Contact

It is a daunting task to discuss the notion of culture *per se*, let alone when it involves contact and perhaps even conflict. This chapter will therefore be restricted in a number of ways. Firstly, primary concern will be accorded to what members of two particular cultures (to be loosely referred to here as Western and Islamic-Arab) do with their own texts and those of each other. Secondly, the focus will be on how literate members representative of either socio-linguistic grouping actually engage in handling one particular rhetorical purpose—that of arguing for or against a stated position.

The basic assumption underlying the present study is that it is only when they are in contact, actually using texts, that peoples from different cultures can reach and understand one another properly. In the regrettable but not uncommon situation of cross-cultural misunderstandings, which often result in or from a breakdown in communication, what is at the root of the problem is invariably a set of misconceptions held by one party about how the other rhetorically visualizes and linguistically realizes a variety of communicative objectives. Such notions would then be paraded as truisms about the nature of the language of those on the other side, its textual norms and its rhetorical tradition.

In discussing this aspect of 'doing things with texts' within and across cultural boundaries, my ultimate aim is to arrive at a number of conclusions that will enable the language user from either of the two cultures in question to operate felicitously within the rhetorical conventions not only of the target culture but those of his or her own. On a more specific level, the scope of my analysis is restricted to the interaction which takes place between advanced users of language in the context of academic writing.

In the following discussion, a textual example from English is presented which illustrates the kind of reception problems often experienced

157

by Arab readers of English. This is immediately followed by a textual example from Arabic which demonstrates the way an Arab would typically handle the situation depicted by the problematic English text. In fact, when presented in English, the Arabic example will illustrate the kind of production problems which Arab writers of English often encounter.

The two example texts are both argumentative. However, two different contexts, structure formats and sets of texture patterns are in evidence. As we have seen in Chapter 4, this difference between the counter-argument and the through-argument reflects deeper differences in persuasive strategy, with two basic argumentative procedures emerging (counter- and through-argumentation), and with each language displaying a particular preference for the use of one over the other.

Both classical rhetoric and modern text linguistics are referred to for a plausible explanation of why Arabs or Westerners tend to argue the way they do, understandably finding the other way alien if not utterly misleading. For a likely explanation, particular focus will be placed on the contextual element 'audience', as this seems to have a great deal to do with the way we go about our textual business. In the case of Arabic, a number of interesting factors further complicate the issues involved. These include the status enjoyed by the classical language and the position of the vernacular, with the so-called Modern Standard Arabic hovering in between; literacy and methods of teaching the mother tongue; the nature of hierarchical society; societal mores such as politeness; religious values such as the attitude to truth; political pressures and a host of similar facts of Arab society in the modern age. These will be discussed and illustrated in an attempt to answer the original question hinted at earlier, namely, how viable are textual conventions as transmitters of cultural values?

A Problem of Language Use

Working for some time with Arabic-speaking students in fields as varied as purpose-specific ELT, interpreting and translation into and out of English and Arabic, I have always been struck by one particular problem of text comprehension. This is the general inability to appreciate the rather subtle rhetorical function involved in counter-arguing in English. Broadly, a counter-argument is a text type which is typically characterized by a fairly opaque statement or endorsement of the opponent's position, followed by a rebuttal. An example of this rhetorical strategy may be drawn from a group of texts which in English typically open with what rhetoricians call a 'straw man gambit':

158

Sample A

Tomorrow's meeting of OPEC is a different affair. Certainly it is formally about prices and about Saudi Arabia's determination to keep them down. Certainly it will also have immediate implications for the price of petrol, especially for Britain, which recently lowered its price of North Sea oil and may now have to raise it again. But this meeting, called at short notice and confirmed only after the most intensive round of preliminary discussions between the parties concerned, is not primarily about selling arrangements between producer and consumer. It is primarily about the future cohesion of the organization itself.

From a *Times* editorial

This kind of text has always proved to be a blind spot for my Arab students, particularly in classes of translation. Sample B, for example, is an approximation to what happened to sample A above in a test given to a group of translator-trainees prior to embarking on a postgraduate course in English-Arabic translation. Consider this rendering and note the italicized differences and the absence of 'but':

Sample B

Back-translation from Arabic

Tomorrow's meeting of OPEC is a different affair *since/because* (Arabic *idh*) *it is certainly about* prices and about Saudi Arabia's determination to keep them down, *and because it is also certain* that it will have immediate implications for the price of petrol, especially for Britain, which recently lowered its price of North Sea oil and may now have to raise it again. This meeting, called at short notice . . .

Turning the thrust of the initial comment from one which only pays lip-service to concerns such as pricing and selling arrangements, to one genuinely advocating that these are OPEC's primary concerns at the moment, and, perhaps more important, losing sight of the opposition signalled by *But* . . ., are serious discourse errors which have always left me intrigued as to why they should be so regularly committed. In search of a remedy, the first thing I did was to look for similar discourse signals (say, the text-initial *certainly*) in authentic Arabic texts. Having ascertained that something like these text-initial elements does exist in Arabic too, in form if not in function, the first question I then asked myself was: What do Arab writers actually do with such text-initial elements when they go on to develop their texts? Let us consider the following English translation of an Arabic text which illustrates the use of this initial device:

Sample C1
> No doubt, the distinction has to be made between the Iraqi People and the Iraqi Government, and Security Council Resolution 661, in permitting the provision of Iraq with medical and food supplies, reflects how seriously the world views this distinction.

But, the answer to the above question comes when we also consider how sample C1 continues:

Sample C2
> Thus, if the decision-makers in Iraq have committed a heinous crime in the snuffing out of Kuwait and driving out its Muslim-Arab population, the world should not allow itself to use the same methods as those of the Iraqi regime.
>
> From an Arab newspaper editorial

The problem will no doubt be immediately spotted as one of text production by a good number of those who have taught advanced English academic writing to Arab students. As used in sample C1 and C2, this text-initial element sets off the kind of expectations which are totally defied by the way the text continues. That is, the English reader is in a sense thwarted, since he or she could typically see the relevance of the initial citation only in terms of some kind of a subsequent rebuttal. But, alas, this is not the case in Arabic, where, as it stands, the text is both cohesive and coherent.

At this point, I feel I must emphasize once more that rhetorical strategies such as that illustrated by sample A above are not entirely alien to the Arabs. As I have pointed out in Chapter 5, the counter-argumentative strategy was not only known, but was exhaustively studied and widely practised during socially and intellectually more enlightened periods in the development of Arabic rhetoric. Furthermore, such a strategy is still practised in Modern Standard Arabic with felicity and utmost effectiveness, but almost exclusively by a minority of Western-educated Arabs and those well-versed in classical Arabic rhetoric. This leaves us with quite a substantial percentage of users of Arabic today for whom the strategy in question is virtually non-existent in mother-tongue text production and is often overlooked in both the reception and the production of texts in the foreign languages with which they come into contact. In Modern Standard Arabic, we thus find a tendency

160

towards, indeed a strong preference for, a through-argumentative format which is illustrated by sample C above and may be defined as the statement of a given position followed by an extensive defence.

Contrastive Rhetoric

Problems of Arabic rhetoric have attracted the attention of a number of scholars from fields as diverse as the ethnography of speaking, political theory, psychology and applied linguistics. However, before offering insights from Arabic rhetoric proper and from more recent trends within Arabic text linguistics, it may perhaps be helpful to summarize what some of these Arabists, both native and non-native, have to say about the kind of problem illustrated above.

Let us start with some of the pre-theoretical pronouncements often made regarding the so-called 'mentality' of the Arabs as viewed from a 'psychological' point of view by writers like Shouby (1951). Arabic, we are told, is characterized by a general vagueness of thought which stems from over-emphasis on the symbol at the expense of its meaning. This, the argument continues, leads to overassertion and exaggeration in the form of stereotypical and highly emotive responses. As Shouby puts it:

> [Arabs tend] to fit the thought to the word . . . rather than the word to the thought . . ., the words becoming the substitutes of thought, and not their representative. (p. 295)

Rich on rhetoric, but with meagre corroborative evidence, statements like these have nevertheless proved somehow attractive and have had a considerable impact on a large body of research in this area of contrastive rhetoric. Judging by the kind of conclusions they reached, quite a number of researchers—linguists, applied linguists and social anthropologists—seem to have uncritically accepted generalizations like Shouby's. Thus, as I will show in greater detail shortly, we have the organization of Arabic described as 'circular and non-cumulative', Arabic logic as defying even the rudiments of simple Platonic-Aristotelian paradigms, Arabic writers as confused, coming to the same point two or three times from different angles, and so on. (For a detailed critique of some of these views, see Sa'adeddin 1989.)

Statements like these, which at best focus on the 'what', and never venture, except perhaps subjectively and anecdotally, into the 'why', have impeded attempts to understand as complex an issue as language in social life across cultural boundaries. That is, unless they are subjected to a critical examination which, as it were, separates the wheat from the

161

chaff and salvages parts that are usable, such conclusions remain unfalsifiable and therefore practically meaningless. It is precisely such an assessment that I intend to carry out in the following discussion.

Orality vs. Literacy

Most promising in this maze of activity is an interesting dichotomy (that of oral v. literate) offered as one way of explaining differences in rhetorical conventions which govern the preference of the Arab for a number of textual strategies alluded to by the above writers and, more pertinently from our point of view, for something like the strategy opted for in sample C. The non-periodic, additive style (commonly attributed to Arabic) is claimed by some to be typically associated with oral composition (e.g. Ong 1971). The high degree of parallelism, the loose, paratactic sentence structure, the predominance of co-ordination and the paucity of subordination (features which could all be correlated with oral style and thus be taken as features of Arabic by the 'oralists') are found by others to be characteristic of unplanned, spoken discourse, and early and popular writing in any country (Ochs 1979; Turner 1973). (For a review of these views see Koch 1983).

Thus, the notion of 'orality', viewed suspiciously by many a native Arab, and understandably so, particularly when exclusively and often pejoratively applied to Arabic, is a potentially useful one. To begin with, the framework of orality, used appropriately to describe an important element in the context of the historical development of Arabic, contributes most positively to the overall picture of Arabic rhetoricity which we are attempting to put together. It tackles head on the question of the different status accorded both to language and to the power of the word by different cultures.

In fact, it is in this spirit that Bauman (1977) explains the function of rhetorical aspects of text such as the predominance of paratactic structures and parallelism. These, Bauman argues, have been found to 'key' (i.e. establish the meta-communicative frame for) artistic verbal performance. While by no means endorsing a reading of this statement which promotes distinctions such as poetic v. non-poetic or literate v. non-literate as the basis of the difference between English and Arabic (taken as though languages could ever be so monolithically labelled), I feel that Bauman highlights an important fact which places languages such as Arabic within their proper rhetorical and historical context. This relates to the capacity of any linguistic system of communication to evolve in a way which responds to and copes with the ways its community of users evolves through time.

Viewed in this light, however, orality cannot be exclusively a designation of Arabic or of any other language for that matter. By the above definitions of orality, no English text could conceivably be void of oral features. Equally, not all Arabic texts display these features to the extremes depicted. Perhaps more importantly, indiscriminate dichotomization such as this ignores the crucial distinction of 'formal' vis-à-vis 'functional'. That is, while a text may formally exhibit an absence of, say, subordination, the functions of backgrounding, projecting, etc. are nevertheless very much present. For example, in this paragraph-final sentence,

And in Lebanon, at whose citizens' hands the massacres were committed, the parallel enquiry has turned into a charade.

the function of *and*, although seemingly one of coordination, is in fact highlighting through 'conceptual subordination' an implicit element which may be glossed by something like: 'Finally, and perhaps most importantly, one simply cannot deny that in Lebanon . . .'.

The second point regarding orality, then, is this: having accommodated orality within the general context of the development of Arabic rhetoric, we should have no problem in accepting the notion of orality in the case of Modern Standard Arabic (and indeed that of current English) but only if seen on a scale of some kind: some texts are bound to be more oral than others. To make such a statement more meaningful, I suggest that more or less orality is a function of text type first and the specificities of a given language second, as we shall see in the subsequent discussion of sample A and sample C.

Presentation v. Proof

Orality has been the back-drop against which another distinction is made in identifying the differences between Arab and Western rhetorical preferences. This relates to persuasion by 'presentation' v. persuasion by 'proof'. Koch (1983: 55) introduces these terms in the following manner:

Arabic argumentation is clearly argumentation by presentation. An arguer presents his truths by making them present in discourse, by repeating them, paraphrasing them, doubling them, calling attention to them with external particles.

163

This mode of argumentation which, according to Koch, is essentially paratactic (characterized by heavy coordination), abductive (displaying horizontal reasoning) and analogical (essentially figurative and hyperbolic), is contrasted with Western modes of argumentation which are:

> based on a syllogistic model of proof and made linguistically cohesive via subordination and hypotaxis. (p. 47)

To try and make sense of what this dichotomy (presentation v. proof) actually involves, let us briefly cast our minds back to the English-source sample A and the Arabic-source sample C. Doesn't A exhibit interesting characteristics of so-called presentation (e.g. *Certainly it is formally about . . ., Certainly it will also have . . .*)? Given that the sequence of elements in the entire first paragraph is highly horizontal, one would surely say that the text is not particularly hypotactic or paratactic, nor is it particularly deductive/inductive or abductive. As to persuasion by analogy, the reader is invited to browse through any issue of Hansard (the verbatim record of debates in the British Parliament) for interesting examples of extended metaphor.

Equally pertinently, it could be asked whether sample C does not have a logic of its own which, while by no means corresponding to Koch's Aristotelian model, is nevertheless one that is sustainable in its own right. To illustrate what we mean by logic and proof, let us consider the following use of *Thus, if . . .*, an information chunk which follows that initiated by *No doubt . . .* in sample C. Of course the connection is nebulous, but only if assessed in terms of the counter-argumentative text format in English. As this and numerous other instances clearly show, claiming universality for rhetorical structures which are only valid for given languages is a failing to which many of those working in this field of contrastive rhetoric are particularly prone. In Arabic, given that the *No doubt* is the equivalent of an English text-initial element such as 'There is absolutely no doubt that', there would be no problem accommodating the *Thus, if* element as a conclusion. Within the text conventions of Arabic, therefore, the text is both cohesive and coherent, and the argument is logically sustainable with the element of proof very much in evidence.

Koch often cites the phenomenon of repetition as evidence of persuasion by presentation in Arabic. In Arabic, however, there are two types of repetition which often seem to be conflated and dealt with indiscriminately. One we shall call non-functional, the other functional. Non-functional repetition is that necessitated by the rules of the linguistic system (*langue*), not necessarily motivated and thus not necessarily serving a particular rhetorical purpose. When used in this capacity, a given structure would be serving no particular logical function and what is involved would be mere presentation. Functional repetition, on the other hand, can indeed subsume categories of non- functional repetition, but extends the repertoire to include a variety of forms that are essentially non-systemic (*parole*). This is of course assuming that there is sufficient rhetorical motivation.

The basic difference between the two kinds of repetition, then, is that functional repetition is motivated, serving important rhetorical functions and thus has a place in the overall plan of developing a text. Consider, for example, the textual function of one of the structures which Koch generally cites to illustrate repetition in Arabic, that of the cognate accusative:

1 *wa nafaa waziiru al-khaarijiyyati al-suurii nafyan qaaTi'an an takuuna li- suuriiyaa ayyata 'alaaqatin bi . . .* (from a news report)

The Syrian Foreign Minister categorically denied that Syria had anything to do with . . .

2 *innanaa narfuDu rafDaan qaaTi'an rabTa mas'alati al-kuwayt bil-Halli al- silmii . . .* (from a political speech)

We absolutely and utterly reject any linkage between . . .

Given the genre of the news report, the discourse of detachment and the narrative text type which characterize (1), the repetition involved in the use of the cognate accusative is non-functional. It is a feature of the system whose role is merely to relay the grammatical function 'adverbiality' and, If preferred to something like *bi shaklin qaaTi'*, this is only because it is perhaps more idiomatic or collocates better. Example (2), on the other hand, is from the genre 'political speech' where the discourse is one of 'commitment' and the text type is argumentative. These features render the repetition involved in the use of the cognate accusative highly functional. When occurring text-initially, as it does here, it signals a 'step' in the argumentative procedure: it makes a commitment to which a response is required as part of the logic of interaction.

The upshot of this discussion is that, while argumentative texts such as sample C above can be heavy on presentation, though only slightly more so than the inherently less emotive prose of English texts belonging to the same type, presentation is bound to be functional, motivated and always there for a rhetorical purpose. That is, while they do not directly display a syllogistic kind of reasoning which the English eye finds familiar, Arabic through-argumentation nevertheless strikes the Arab ear with 'recurring structural cadences' that not only please but persuade. There are two points worth underlining in this discussion:

(1) Although Arabic texts tend to be heavy on presentation, they are no less logical (i.e. proof-oriented) than texts which explicitly observe time-honoured Aristotelian models of logic;

(2) The important criteria for effectiveness are text type and audience. Regardless of the source language, counter-argumentation, for example, will no doubt settle for the minimum of presentation, but, to sustain text coherence, other more universal systems of logic are bound to be present, perhaps acquiring prominence and even becoming conspicuously more apparent.

Here again, we may resort to the notion of the continuum regarding presentation and proof, restricting the scope of the latter category to subsume 'a conventional logical text structure' rather than 'logic' *per se*. Some texts are more presentation-oriented than others, a statement which is equally applicable to both English and Arabic. To limit the scope of what such a statement entails and thus make it generally more relevant, I suggest once again that greater or lesser presentation or proof is a function of text type first and the specificities of a given language second, as we shall see in the subsequent discussion of sample A and sample C.

The Aural v. Visual Distinction

In the search for features distinctive of each of the two forms of argumentation (e.g. sample A and sample C), a more productive line to pursue may be that of 'cultures playing to different kinds of audience'. In this respect, another dichotomy, which is potentially useful but does not significantly depart from the traditional position on orality, presentation, etc., is that of 'aural' v. 'visual' texts offered by Sa'adeddin (1989). Here, a visual text is one which would ideally be 'a surface ortho-graphic representation of a linearly-developed, logically coherent and syntactically cohesive unit of sense' (p. 39). An aural text, on the other hand, is one which would typically be utilized 'to establish a relationship of informality and solidarity with the receivers of the text' (p. 39). This aural focus on the audience, which Sa'adeddin associates with Arabic, is said to be realized through the preservation of:

the artifacts of speech (while ensuring that [the texts] are gram-
matically well-formed) . . . on the assumption that these are
universally accepted markers of truthfulness, self-confidence and
linguistic competence, as well as intimacy and solidarity.

However, in closely examining the proposed definition of visual texts of
which sample A could conceivably be taken as an instance, every term
seems to beg a question: 'linearity', 'logically', 'coherent', 'cohesive',
'sense' and so on. Is linearity a sufficient precondition for logicality? Is
cohesion a sufficient precondition for coherence? What is non-linear
(and hence by implication non-logical) about aural texts (of which sample
C could conceivably be taken as an instance)?

An assessment along similar lines could also be carried out on the use
of most key terms in the definition offered for aural texts. But two
important questions may help us make better sense of the present model
of Arabic rhetoric. Is aurality tantamount to orality and presentation as
redefined in the terms above? Can sample C be said to be more aural
than, say, sample A? If the answer to both questions is in the affirmative,
the categories visual-aural can be accepted and included in the catalogue
of the other revised distinctions adopted so far. But this is also to be
envisaged on a scale: some texts are more aural than others, a statement
which is equally applicable to both English and Arabic. To delimit what
such a statement could indicate, it is suggested (as with the other
dichotomies) that greater or lesser aurality is a function of text type first
and the specificities of a given language second, as will be shown in
the subsequent discussion of sample A and sample C.

A Text-type Continuum

To sum up and bring together the various strands which have emerged
in the discussion of orality, presentation and aurality, the idea of a
continuum may be generally represented in the following manner:

*Regardless of the specific language involved, some texts are bound to
be more oral, more presentation-oriented and more aural than others.
Placed within a text type framework, this hypothesis could be reform-
ulated to suggest that, within argumentation, and regardless of the
source language, through-arguments tend to be more oral, more
presentation-oriented and more aural than counter-arguments. Here,
it may be recalled that Arabic has a particular preference for
through-arguments, a statement which can now be taken as tantamount to saying that, on a continuum, Arabic texts tend to swing
more towards the +oral, +presentation and +aural end. But this does*

not rule out the possibility that an Arabic counter-argument, albeit less common, would nevertheless be less oral, less presentation-oriented and less aural than an English through-argument (which is, again, not as common as counter-arguments in this particular language).

Schematically, with reference to sample A (a counter-argument in English) and sample C (a through-argument in Arabic), for example, the orality-, presentation- and aurality-scales may be represented as follows:

+Oral	–Oral
+presentation	–presentation
+aurality	–aurality
Sample C or	Sample A or
an English equivalent	an Arabic equivalent

Figure 14.1 The text-type continuum

But, to concentrate on the task at hand, namely finding out more about not only what is happening in texts but why it is happening, the question of audience raised in the discussion of oral, presentation-oriented and aural texts deserves a more detailed treatment. As will be most strongly argued shortly, it is the type of status assigned by a given language and a given culture to the type of audience generally assumed that is the crucial factor in accounting for the way context is negotiated and texts developed.

Audience of Receivers and Rhetorical Choice

In most of the discussion of the rhetoric of orality, presentation and aurality summarized above, reference is constantly made to 'audience' as a contextual factor which determines rhetorical choice. In claiming that Arabic argumentation is argumentation by presentation where, in the words of Bateson (1976: 80–1) 'the elegant expression of an idea may be taken as evidence of its validity', Koch (1983) views 'audience' in the general context of a number of factors including the nature of a hierarchical society, power and authority, even religion and politics:

Argument by presentation has its roots in the history of Arab society, in the ultimate, universal truths of the Quran, and in hierarchical societies autocratically ruled by Caliphs who were not only secular rulers but also the leaders of the faith, and later and until recently, by colonial powers. (p. 55)

Sa'deddin (1989) takes a more pragmatic view of 'audience', relating it to level of formality, solidarity, etc. as determinants of the aural features which he finds pervasive in the Arabic text:

The native Arabic producer intends, by exploiting the informal and casual mode of text development, to establish such relations of solidarity as friendliness, intimacy, warmth, self-confidence, linguistic competence, etc. (p. 43)

Both statements contain a great deal of truth about the nature of persuasion in Arabic and thus take us some considerable way towards answering the question why a text such as C above, for example, strikes, say, an English reader as somewhat awkward. This awkwardness stems, among other things, from the text producer making his or her argumentative claims linguistically present, by repeating them, calling attention to them, rather than by appealing to some logical proof (Koch, p. 47). By the same token, Sa'deddin's English reader would feel no less awkward, regarding the text producer as 'trespassing, presumptive, illiterate, haranguing and breathing down the neck of the audience' (p. 44)

However, two questions could legitimately be posed at this juncture. Firstly, how would an Arab audience react to such 'awkward, haranguing' texts? And, if variables of tenor such as the informality of the occasion were invoked, the next question would have to be: irrespective of what the particular audience happened to be, how would an Arab approach his audience and what kind of assumptions would he be making regarding their likely reaction? Such a line of questioning inevitably leads to the following conclusion: for our statements to be ethno-semiotically valid, they have to transcend the immediate here-and-now and generalize on the basis of reactions and assumptions that form an integral part of the discourse of a culture. The receiver must thus be viewed in the abstract, which allows us to pin-point:

(a) socio-culturally motivated attitudes (semiotic concerns);

(b) the way norms can be maintained or flouted in the expression of these attitudes (pragmatic concerns); and

169

(c) the way categories such as formality/informality are upheld or manipulated to relay particular effects entailed by such attitudes (institutional-communicative concerns).

To put this differently, the receiver may be viewed in terms of general discoursal values promoted by a given socio-cultural milieu (e.g. the Arab-Islamic society). This has a significant bearing on the way texts are negotiated and text norms established. For example, to initiate a text with the utterance 'It is correct to say that . . .' is to an Arab text producer an attitudinal expression of commitment to the truth value of the statement. Now, in the persuasive context I have in mind, the last thing an Arab will think of when uttering this is an audience which is in any way sceptical. He may be totally wrong in this, but, nevertheless, this is how he would approach his text receivers.

Our Arab speaker may very well be haranguing his Western audience, but to be sure the same could not be said of what he takes his audience to be—one with whom the establishment of intimacy is an overriding factor. Similarly, intimacy sought and reciprocated will probably be the most likely option entertained by the Arab text-receiver. This is the case, if not in reality, then at least in the kind of assumptions which text producers make and which ultimately is all that matters. Given appropriate contextual signals, the Western text-receiver would have warmed to the argument initiated by 'It is correct to say that . . .', only if the text had proceeded in something like the following way:

> However, the Golan Heights were nothing but a launching pad for Syrian missiles on the State of Israel.

That is, the item 'correct' would be intended to serve a lip-service function and thus imply the expression of a certain attitude that, among other things, always assumes a sceptical audience. To an Arab, by contrast, this argumentative strategy is likely to be shunned on the grounds that the means employed are devious. Ultimately, both the Western speaker and the Arab speaker are perhaps seeking the same objective, namely that of conveying the truth, as they see it. But the Arab's notion of truth is to reveal all, 'to make a potentially available truth actually available to the hearer' (Koch 1983: 53). After all, the communicative contract established between an Arab arguer and his audience is qualitatively different from that upheld by the rhetorical conventions of English. Particularly when the written record is involved, it seems that the onus on the Arab arguer is to be 'truthful' in return for the trust which his audience is assumed to have placed in him as arguer, a different kind of demand to that made by a Western audience or responded to by a Western arguer.

Regarding the two modes of argumentation exemplified by sample A and sample C above and said to be typical of English and Arabic respectively, two important points emerge from the discussion of the view which an Arab typically takes of his audience. The first relates to the kind of audience envisaged, the second to the kind of text opted for as most suitable for such an assumed audience. For social, political, religious and other kinds of reasons to do with language in the social life of the Arabs, which are simply too complicated to go into here, the Arabic language and culture appears to have promoted a unique vision of who is assumed to be the typical addressee. This vision may be summed up by the following rhetorical maxim:

> *On a given occasion, assume that the world is divided into those who vehemently oppose your views and those who whole-heartedly endorse them, but when it comes to whom your contribution is designed to address, talk only to your supporters and ignore the opposition.*

In short, no sceptics to be entertained, no adversaries to be recognized. Sample C above admirably illustrates this strategy, which brings us to the second important point of the above discussion of audience—the one which relates to text type. Two basic rhetorical purposes are distinguished within argumentation—to counter-argue and to through-argue. But the entire argumentative text is originally viewed as one macro-rhetorical purpose in contradistinction to that of 'exposition', a text type which sets a particular scene and presents it through formats such as description, narration or exposition by induction or deduction, all done with varying degrees of detachment.

The reason why the issue of 'exposition' is raised here is basically to point to a problem inherent in the Arab view of audience as depicted above, namely that of exclusively talking to one's supporters. This kind of audience assessment seems to be most compatible with the way exposition is normally pursued. In its purer forms, this text type would involve addressing an audience of non- sceptical, non-adversarial, open-minded receivers. But, as I pointed out earlier, expository texts are not intended to persuade. The question now becomes: how can we introduce a manageable dose of involvement into an otherwise detached use of language? The Arab rhetorician steps in here with an important insight. Expectations regarding audience reactions can be defied: for maximal effect, the good orator would be addressing the open-minded as though they were deniers, for example. This text-type shift from expected exposition to unexpected argumentation must, of course, be motivated and functional in context.

Through-argumentation seems to provide us with this kind of half-way house. Here, as in sample C, we have an expository text in form gradually shifting to serve an argumentative function. On the face of it, what we are given is an almost indifferent expounding of one's own ideas addressed to a supportive audience whose support is taken for granted. This exposition, however, is clothed in the kind of texture that only befits a denier. Part of the success of such a shift with an Arab audience lies in the ability of the text to lure them into feeling, through some process of cathartic identification, that they are deniers.

Within this orientation, text types such as the counter-argument (sample A) and the through-argument (sample C) may be distinguished one from the other in the following way. In counter-arguments, the variable +sceptical –supportive audience would be involved. One would be assuming that the addressee is simply too discerning to accept a text-initial set of sentences such as 'Europe is dying, Europe is dying, Europe is practically dead' as a report on the demise of Europe. Given the constraints of a genre such as the Editorial and those of a critical kind of discourse such as that of the quality paper, an utterance like this would simply be too irrelevant to sustain a text which continues with more of the same. A change of gear is thus essential; some opposition is expressed ('but, Europe is alive and well'), followed by substantiation ('look at this achievement, and look at that achievement.') and there you have a robust argument.

Through-arguments, on the other hand, would require that the audience is envisaged to be –sceptical +supportive. In Arabic, this time, a through-argument initiated by a statement such as 'Certainly, the Madrid Conference was a historic event', all meant absolutely sincerely, would to the English ear sound as nothing but reams of sycophantic discourse. Such a text would assume total endorsement on the part of the audience of the views expressed, an assumption which is most likely to be resented by, say an English text receiver.

The mode of reasoning illustrated by sample C helps us to appreciate the function of texture phenomena such as repetition, parallelism and paraphrase, the intimacy involved in the liberal use of metaphoric expression, hyperbole, even exaggeration, and the 'fantastic' worlds which emerge from listening to a piece of oratory in Arabic. But, in conclusion, it must be stressed that the Western reader ignores these seemingly superfluous features of the Arabic text at his peril. They are all there for a purpose and while the means of expressing the attitudinal meanings involved may differ from one language to another, the ends are universal values which are globally recognizable. As such, these values are not impossible to relay whatever the language and should therefore not be lost sight of.

Summary

We are now in a slightly better position to account for the differences between the two modes of argumentation illustrated by sample A and sample C above. We have identified the two kinds of audience that the producers of the two texts assume: counter-arguments would be typically addressed to the sceptical (the 'uncertain' in Arabic rhetorical terminology), while through-arguments typically assume a supportive audience turned into temporary 'deniers' for the purposes of the current persuasive exercise. Within this text-type orientation, variables such as orality, presentation-orientedness or aurality, used as exclusive labels for rhetorical strategy in particular languages, may now have to be reconsidered as they are universal features of all texts.

Of course, some texts are going to be more oral than others. While this can certainly implicate text type, it does not necessarily make orality an exclusive property of Arabic, English or any other language. Furthermore, some languages would tend to display a particular preference for this or that strategy, but this does not make the tendency in question an exclusive feature of the rhetoric of that language. These are merely preferences, tendencies, trends. For example, Arabic prefers through-argumentation whereas English orients its rhetorical strategy the other way, towards counter-argumentation. But these are no more than general tendencies which may well hold good but should not be taken as more than rough indications in need of further evidence.

15

The Discourse of the Alienated

The relationship of language to discourse and ideology is one of the more promising developments which linguistic stylistics has recently begun to address. While the social implications of semiotic structures such as genre and text are no doubt obvious, these are seen in more meaningful socio-textual terms only when considered within discursive practice. Discourse or the attitudinally determined mode of expression (e.g. feminist discourse, racist discourse) is thus particularly privileged as a carrier of ideological meanings. As Martin (1985) points out, when ideology is challenged, discourse becomes implicated in a number of ways: which discourse a group is able to use and which discourse a group chooses to use, where, when and how, are all matters of immense ideological significance.

In this chapter, the aim is to examine the role of language in the expression of ideology and to discuss a number of micro-level aspects of this kind of semiotic analysis. Semiotics is a dimension of context which subsumes the assumptions, presuppositions and conventions surrounding a given utterance and ultimately represents them as signs in constant interaction. For example, in a speech on immigration into Britain, it was interesting to observe how a politician, obviously operating within the dictates of a particular kind of discourse, constantly referred to 'immigrants and their children' as *immigrants and their offspring*. The utterance *offspring* has thus become a sign (a semiotic entity) in that it no longer simply means 'children' but has in addition taken on discourse values such as 'legalistic', or even 'de-humanizing' (Sykes 1985).

This orientation within which language is viewed as a vehicle for the expression of discoursal meanings is essentially prompted by a feeling shared by many in stylistics that a narrower focus on the language of literary discourse would perhaps shed better light on the nature of literary meaning and thus help to assess it more adequately. Ideology seems to be one of the more salient features of discoursal expression, and the analysis of ideological structures and their modes of linguistic expression would therefore not only enrich the analysis of linguistic forms but would also enhance appreciation of linguistic function. In lexicography, for example, an attempt is often made to capture contextual values by 'usage labels' such as 'derogatory', 'offensive', etc. But will lexicographers go the whole hog one day and include in the entry of words such as 'offspring' some of the pragmatic and semiotic values with which utterances are imbued?

To illustrate this socio-cultural angle on literary communication, short extracts from *Qindiil Um Haashim* ('The Saint's Lamp'), an Arabic novella by the Egyptian writer Yahya Haqqi, will be subjected to a semiotic analysis of the kind introduced above. The novella is regarded as one of the most successful examples of prose writing in modern Arabic fiction. In the preface to his English translation (which we shall use throughout to represent the Arabic original), Badawi (1973: ix) observes that the novella is particularly:

> rich in sociological significance . . . It traces the spiritual development of [Ismail, the main character], and the development of his social, moral and mental attitudes. In so doing the story illustrates the tension and dramatic clash between two sets of values . . .

In a similar vein, Siddiq (1986: 126), who embarks on a most valuable 'deconstructionist' analysis of the novella, maintains that:

> few works of fiction in Arabic or any other language can boast of artistic economy and craftsmanship superior to Haqqi's novella.

By way of introducing the conceptual framework within which the analysis proper is carried out in this study, let us consider the following extract from the novella:

> At these words *silence fell* on the house, the oppressive silence of the tomb—that house where *dwelt only the Koran* recitations and echoes of the Muezzin announcing prayers. It was as if *they all awoke and grew attentive, then were crestfallen and finally put out.* In their place *reigned darkness and awe—they could not live* in the same house with that *strange spirit that came* to them from across the seas.
> (*The Saint's Lamp*, pp. 26–27, italics added)

In general, what seems to happen in literary communication is a

175

deliberate and systematic effort to confront, challenge and at times dismantle well-established socio-conceptual structures, to imbue expression with the unexpected and the unfamiliar, to turn the ordinary into the unusual and to foreground the unforeseen. In the extract cited above, the feeling of powerlessness finds its own discourse, a world-view expressed through limiting the action to agents who are not human and directing it at no one; inanimate non-doers producing only virtual events: *silence fell, dwelt only the Koran, they all awoke, then were crestfallen, reigned darkness, they could not live, strange spirit that came.* It is this kind of artistic manipulation of linguistic structure to relay a variety of discourse functions (e.g. alienation) which will primarily occupy us in this study.

Literary Context

Within the text-linguistic model outlined in this book, literary context (the relevant extra-textual factors and circumstances surrounding a piece of creative writing) is defined in more or less the same terms as those used for other kinds of contexts (e.g. scientific or legal communication):

(1) The communicative values of register membership. These define the context of situation in terms of the use and user of language seen within relevant social processes and institutions. In the above-cited extract from *The Saint's Lamp*, socio-cultural vocabulary (field), the awesome formality (tenor) and the rhetorical echoes characteristic of the narrative (mode) are all communicative aspects of context to which text users, producers and receivers alike, constantly refer.

(2) The pragmatics of intentionality. This subsumes the rules of use governing the appropriateness of utterances, the systems of presupposition and inference at work, and the real-world conditions under which utterances achieve a purpose and become speech acts through which we do things with words. At one of many levels of analysis, the intention of the author in the above-cited extract is to establish 'silence' as the answer to 'words' originally intended to 'defile', to underline a contrast, to underscore a conflict. Knowledge of the world in question, among other things, is vital in order to appreciate, accept or reject these intended meanings.

(3) The semiotics of intertextuality. This regulates interaction, or its absence as in the 'silence' scene above, within a system of socio-cultural as well as socio-textual assumptions and conventions that define an utterance or a sequence of utterances as a 'sign' among signs. In the

above extract, the familiarity of the scene depicted is a function of language users' internalization of similar signs making up our knowledge of the 'genre', which is part of our textual-discursive competence. By the same token, the conflict resulting from the juxtaposition of signs like 'the Koran' and 'the muezzin', on the one hand, and, on the other, 'strange spirits coming from across the seas', represents our awareness of different modes of talking (i.e. different 'discourses'). Finally, at a very basic level of semiotic analysis, our knowledge of 'texts', existing in the present, the past or the future, helps in recognizing signs such as the narrative which threads its way in the extract under discussion.

But, as I have argued elsewhere in this book, semiotics and discursive practice must be singled out as particularly relevant to an understanding of the creative act. Certainly, aspects of the communicative or the pragmatic dimensions of context and the ways categories like register or intentionality find expression in texts are worthwhile angles from which literary text may be viewed. The same may be said of the analysis of genre and text, as the implications of these semiotic categories for a definition of 'literariness' are only too obvious. But pride of place must go to the social semiotic and, within this, to the category 'discourse'.

To start with, it is the perception of the utterance as a 'sign', and the appreciation of discourse as 'a mode of talking' characteristic of a given institution (Kress 1985), which in the final analysis enable us as language users to communicate our intentions. The Joycean discourse of alienation, of his 'dear, dirty Dublin', which finds interesting echoes in *The Saint's Lamp*, runs through the novella and turns both genre and texts into ideological statements on behalf of the 'alienated'. That is, through the discourse in question, the genre materializes as a mega-statement of inner struggle and texts emerge to serve this higher-level purpose in the same way, enhancing the narrative with a particular slant on reality that is unique to the inner struggle being depicted.

The second reason for the primacy of discourse relates to our own intuitive feeling that text users usually take a particular stance on reality and can articulate attitudinal meanings only through their discourses. The alienation theme in parts of *The Saint's Lamp* is a statement of (i.e. a discourse of) inner conflict which the anti-hero Isma'il experiences well before his entanglement with the wider, exterior conflict of East and West. This colours the lenses through which we are invited to view the various staging posts on the journey to self-redemption.

Finally, discourse is particularly conducive to the expression of attitudinal meanings in general and ideology in particular. As distinct from genre and text, which are essentially mere sites for the expression of what can at times be a number of competing discourses, it is only through our discourse that our attitudes to class structure and class conflict, and consequently our perception of reality and our view of the world, fully come into their own. Alienation is but one among many essentially conflicting attitudinal meanings dispersed throughout *The Saint's Lamp* as signs in disarray, searching for resolution. It is with this crucial relationship between discourse and ideology that I will now be primarily concerned.

Discourse and Ideology

In a penetrating study of ideological structures in discourse, Kress (1985: 27–28) defines 'discourse' as

> 'a mode of talking' . . . In essence it points to the fact that social institutions produce specific ways or modes of talking about certain areas of social life . . . That is, in relation to certain areas of social life that are of particular significance to a social institution, it will produce a set of statements about that area that will define, describe, delimit, and circumscribe what it is possible and impossible to say with respect to it, and how it is to be talked about.

But social institutions are rarely static. Institutional expression is always imbued with attitudinal meanings. For example, alienation and utter powerlessness are the hallmarks of the discoursal theme relayed through the portrayal of characters like Isma'il in *The Saint's Lamp*. For this ideological structure to make its presence felt within a socio-cultural system of signs, however, the ideological significance must be made more transparent. That is, we must be able to 'read off' the ideology in question from the linguistic expression encountered in the text. Language is inevitably implicated when socio-cultural values are involved, as they always are in any work of art.

Thus, both within and across semiotic boundaries, it seems that cultures sanction attitudinally-determined statements of a given ideological stance which themselves become filters through which institutions find expression. In other words, ideologies are best viewed as 'systems of ideas' or 'world views' which relate material conditions to linguistic structure. It is small wonder then that all good literature, being *par excellence* a faithful mirror of society, is saturated with ideological meaning, concerning itself with all forms of knowledge, dominant or oppositional.

One way of examining ideological structure, then, would be through an examination of language. This relationship may be identified at a number of levels: at the lexical/semantic level or the grammatical/ syntactic level. A pioneering study of linguistic function as reflected in the syntax of literary discourse is Halliday's analysis of William Golding's *The Inheritors*. The realm is one of 'syntactic imagery' which Halliday (1971: 360), in the context of the novel, explains thus:

> In *The Inheritors*, the syntax is part of the story. As readers, we are reacting to the whole of the writer's creative use of 'meaning potential'; and the nature of language is such that he can convey, in a line of print, a complex of simultaneous themes, reflecting the variety of functions that language is required to serve . . . In *The Inheritors*, it is the linguistic representation of experience, through the syntactic resources of transitivity, that is especially brought into relief.

The Experiential Meaning of Transitivity

A basic property of language is that it enables its users to formulate a mental picture of reality and to make sense of and express what goes on around and inside them. The system of transitivity has evolved to cater for the expression of this kind of experiential meaning. By transitivity is meant the different types of process that are recognized in the language, and the structures by which they are expressed. Essentially, this system consists of (i) the process itself , (ii) the participants in the process, and (iii) the circumstances associated with the process. These may be illustrated from the beginning of *The Saint's Lamp*:

Later my grandfather set up a grain shop in the Square,

where *set up* is a process, *my grandfather* and *a grain shop* are participants, and *later* and *in the Square* are circumstances.

Predicates like the one illustrated in the above example divide into several types:

(i) Action predicates, concerned with deliberate action and its consequences which are under the control of the principal noun, e.g.

Ismail set up a clinic in Al-Baghalla district;

(ii) State predicates, which simply attribute properties, mental or material, to objects, e.g.

Though he was not smartly dressed, his clothes were always clean;

(iii) Process predicates, or events or changes, mental or material, which happen to things without their control, e.g.

her eye would water.

In proposing the 'mind-style' hypothesis, which will be adopted in this study, Fowler (1986: 157) has this to say about these distinctions within the transitivity system:

> [These] convey different pictures of what is going on in the world. It is easy to imagine the types of mind-styles associated with a dominance of one sort of pattern: predominant action predicates may go with strong physical activity, foregrounded mental processes with an introspective mind-style, and so on.

In the kind of analysis envisaged in this chapter, however, it is the following types of relations that would seem to be of more immediate relevance:

(1) Transitive action predicates in which a noun referring to an inanimate object serves as the subject, e.g.

the destructive axe of the town-planning department demolished it together with other old landmarks of Cairo;

(2) Intransitive process predicates in which, although people act or move, they do not act on things and they move only themselves, e.g.

he would pause and smile, thinking: if only those girls knew how empty-headed they were!;

(3) Intransitive process predicates with an inanimate actor, where not only is the action directed at no-one, but it is also done by no-one animate, e.g.

Gradually the square fills anew with people.

This 'mind-style' hypothesis has had a considerable influence in setting the parameters for a view of linguistic stylistics which basically holds that language is not neutral with respect to discourse and that, therefore, certain syntactic forms will necessarily correlate with certain discourses. In his analysis of *The Inheritors*, Halliday finds intransitive structures to be particularly productive in relaying an atmosphere of 'helplessness': 'people act but not on things; they move but only themselves'. In this kind of 'no-cause-no-effect' discourse, moreover, a high proportion of the subjects are not people; they are either parts of the body or inanimate objects. For example,

The bushes twitched again.

What this and other analyses carried out in this domain demonstrate is that the kind of processes, participants and circumstances opted for by a given text producer ultimately and cumulatively point to an attempt to relay a variety of added textual values. As Halliday shows, these could be related to feelings of cognitive limitation, a diminished sense of causation and an unexpectedly vigorous objective world.

The Language of Alienation

For the purpose of the analysis attempted here, I have selected as an ideological structure the alienation theme to which Badawi (1973: x) aptly refers in the following terms:

> The problem, therefore, is set in social terms. It is not the eternal silence of the infinite spaces that terrifies Ismail, but the silence of the people around him, the absence of communication with his own family, the discovery that he has become *dracin*, an outsider among his kith and kin.

This sense of alienation includes the trials and tribulations of Isma'il, the main character, on his spiritual journey from beginning to end. This motif, I submit, is bound to find its own discourse and consequently select the appropriate syntactic and semantic imagery in order to facilitate the emergence of this discourse. With this in mind, the square is selected as the vantage point from which to observe Isma'il's inner-world unfolding.

The square is first introduced into the novella in the following way:

Extract A
> *Later my grandfather set up a grain shop in the Square. Thus our family lived within the precincts of the Saint's mosque and under her*

181

protection. The Saint's feasts and calendar became ours and the calls of the Muezzin our only clock. (pp. 1–2)

Notice how, apart from the first clause, the subjects are not people and the predicates are not of the 'action' type: *lived* is an intransitive process, and *became* a transitive process. It is also worth noting that both verbs are 'ellipted' when a second event comes along: *and lived under her protection; and the calls of the Muezzin became our only clock.* The ellipsis here seems to further highlight the prevalent atmosphere of ineffectual activity.

Initially, however, the square is presented to us as a haven of peace:

Extract B

> *. . . his greatest pleasure was to stroll by the river, or stand on the bridge. At nightfall, when the heat of the sun had gone and the sharply-etched lines and reflected light changed to curves and vague shadows, the square came into its own, ridding itself of strangers and visitors.* (p. 5)

But, this peace is short-lived. For one thing, although Isma'il's 'strolling' or 'standing on the bridge' are movements, they lack the status of 'transitive action' and therefore seem to affect the mover only. For another, more compelling reason, the 'going' of the heat of the sun, and the square 'ridding' itself, through the intransitive and the reflexive respectively, ensure that nothing else changes: a combination of activity and helplessness.

It is the square 'coming into its own', however, which is perhaps a more significant development. It introduces the necessary element of doubt and foreboding and, through the reflexive, signals the ultimate in combining activity with powerlessness and displaying inner strife:

Extract C

> *Gradually the square fills anew with people, weary figures, pale of face and bleary-eyed. They are dressed in what clothes they can afford, or if you prefer it, in whatever they have been able to lay their hands on. There is a note of sadness in the cries of the street-hawkers . . .* (p. 5)

Here, subjects are not people, even when 'they' are dressed; conceptually *they* refers to the 'weary figures'. Again none of the subjects is engaged in actions with consequences. In fact, nothing seems to be under the control of the principal subject, which is inanimate in any case: even the clothes are 'whatever they have been able to lay their hands on'. The inactive 'state' is finally ushered in as one of 'sadness'. But conflict escalates and is at its highest in:

Extract D
> *What hidden tyranny have they suffered from and what heavy load weighs upon their hearts? And yet their faces express a kind of content and acceptance of things. How easily these people forget! There are so many hands to receive so few piasters and milliemes. Here there are no laws . . . No one really seems to mind much.* (pp. 5–6)

There is a large number of clauses in which nouns referring to inanimate objects are used as subjects: 'no one' is in control of his environment, let alone interacting with it:

Extract E
> *Rows of people sit on the ground leaning against the wall of the mosque. Some of them lie asleep on the pavement, a mixed crowd of men, women and children. No one knows where they come from or where they will go. They are like fruit dropping from the tree of life to rot and wither away beneath its boughs.* (p. 6)

The peculiar transitivity which imbues this and other passages has cumulatively contributed to what Fowler (1986) labels an 'estranged mind-style'. Throughout, the feeling has been one of total powerlessness. The following extracts make this point clearly:

Extract F
> *When Isma'il came to the square he found it as usual crowded with people, all looking poor and wretched and their feet heavy with the chains of oppression. They could not possibly be human beings living in an age in which even the inanimate was endowed with life. They were like vacant and shattered remains, pieces of stone from ruined pillars in a waste land: they had no aim other than standing in the way . . .* (pp. 27–8)

The weight is too heavy for words:

Extract G
> *The crowd, like a mass of dead and disfigured bodies, weighed heavily on Isma'il's chest, making his breathing difficult, and straining his nerves. Some of the passers-by collided with him as if they were blind.* (p. 29)

And so on. To sum up, in examining the language of Extracts A–G, one particular feature is most prominent. This is the predominance of intransitive process predicates which reflects the limitation on people's actions and their world-view. In an intransitive structure, the roles of 'affected' and 'agent' are combined. This clearly indicates total absence of cause and effect: people do not act on things around them, they act within the limitations imposed by these things. The frustration of the struggle with the environment is embodied in the syntax.

This pervasive reading may be contrasted with the world of 'cause and effect' outside the square, particularly in the very beginning and towards the end of the novella, including most importantly the period which Isma'il spent in England. As a sample of the 'intruder' theme of 'self-sufficiency', 'total satisfaction', etc. (cf. Siddiq 1986), let us consider the following extract from the very end of the novella:

Extract H

> Isma'il set up a clinic in Al-Baghalla district, near the hills, in a house that was fit for anything but receiving eye patients. His fee never exceeded a piastre per consultation. Among his patients there were no elegant men and women, but they were all poor and bare-footed. Oddly enough, he became more famous in the villages surrounding Cairo . . .
>
> He performed many a difficult operation successfully using means which would make a European doctor gasp in amazement . . .
>
> Isma'il married Fatima and she bore him five sons and six daughters.

(p. 38)

Gone is the world of total powerlessness which allowed for only the momentary hints of potency. This potency, by contrast, dominates Isma'il's world later when he recovers his faith and regains the lost light. As Extract H clearly shows, the majority of the clauses are transitive actions with a human subject. The world is organized in a way we can recognize as 'normal'. People may be bare-footed, but they are not hopeless or powerless.

In conclusion, it must be acknowledged that the uniqueness of this text as a statement of an ideological position does not lie merely in the foregrounding of inanimate agents or a predominantly intransitive clause structure. These patterns interact with other structures intended to relay alienation. Lexis also encodes this idea. This, in turn, interacts with other estranging structures, including a constant disturbance of sentence structure and sentence sequence. Cumulatively, these features contribute

184

to a topsy-turvy world which is far from neutral or straightforward. An analysis which brings out these elements in their interaction within the text would be extremely useful and future work on literary discourse, particularly in a language like Arabic, would do well to attend to these and other matters within the framework of ideology and language.

Summary

In this chapter, the aim has been to subject *The Saint's Lamp*, a modern Arabic novella, to a semiotic analysis. This took the form of matching form with function, socio-cultural values with linguistic expression, ideology with discourse. The discourse of alienation, expressing the ideology of inner conflict is found to be pervasive throughout the novella. Intransitive structures, mostly with an inanimate agent, relay an atmosphere of total absence of 'cause and effect', of total alienation.

16

The Translation of Irony:
A Discourse Perspective

The aim of this chapter is to pursue further the theme that, in terms of underlying textual strategy, the distinction between literary and non-literary discourse becomes of lesser importance than all those features which the two forms have in common (Hatim and Mason 1997). In the previous chapter, I used our discourse processing model in the analysis of a literary sample in the same way as we would do when analysing other non-literary varieties of language use. In the present chapter, irony, a theme that has traditionally tended to be of interest, sometimes almost exclusively, to the literary critic or the stylistician, is tackled as an area of language use in non-fictional texts.

In the following discussion, I will continue to argue for the primacy of semiotics. To demonstrate this, I will offer a discourse-oriented framework for the analysis and description of irony. The specific aim of this exercise is to search for a possible solution to problems encountered in translating ironical use of language from English into Arabic. Irony is shown to impinge not only on the institutional-communicative aspects of register and on pragmatic meaning, but also, and much more significantly, on the three semiotic categories—text, genre and discourse. Texts embody rhetorical purpose (e.g. to report 'tongue-in- cheek'), discourse expresses attitudinal meanings (e.g. to be disparaging) and genre conventionally establishes the appropriateness of particular forms of expression for particular social occasions (e.g. the 'send-up'). The problem for the translator arises when different pragmatic and institutional-communicative procedures are employed by different languages in the expression of almost universally recognized attitudinal values which are essentially discoursal and semiotic. That is, while almost all languages have at their disposal the potential ultimately to relay, say, a disparaging attitude (a semiotic concern), what constitutes this in terms of rules of politeness, types of implicature, etc. (which are pragmatic concerns) and those of register appropriateness, level of formality, etc. (institutional-communicative concerns) can and does vary from one language to another. Given obvious socio-cultural and text-linguistic dissimilarities, English and Arabic are a language pair ideally suited to demonstrate how problematical these contrastive text-linguistic processes can be.

Perceiving Irony

Let us consider the following text sample taken from Edward Said's *Orientalism*, a book noted for its superb polemical style. (For the sake of clarity, the sample is presented element by element and these are numbered.)

Sample A
[Following an initial presentation of Balfour's basic stance on the issue of the West v. the Orient, Edward Said continues . . .]

1 Since these facts are facts,
2 Balfour must then go on to the next part of his argument.
3 Balfour produces no evidence that Egyptians and 'races with whom we deal' appreciate or even understand the good that is being done them by colonial occupation.
4 It does not occur to Balfour, however, to let the Egyptian speak for himself,
5 since presumably any Egyptian who would speak out is more likely to be 'the agitator [who] wishes to raise difficulties' than the good native who overlooks the 'difficulties' of foreign domination.
6 And so, having settled the ethical problems,
7 Balfour turns at last to the practical ones.
8 'If it is our business to govern, with or without gratitude, with or without the real and genuine memory of all the loss of which we have relieved the population;
9 [Balfour by no means implies, as part of that loss, the loss or at least the indefinite postponement of Egyptian independence]
10 'If that is our duty, how is it to be performed?'
11 England exports 'our very best' to these countries.
12 These selfless administrators do their work 'amidst tens of thousands of persons belonging to a different creed, a different race, a different discipline, different conditions of life.'

Orientalism, pp. 33–34

A number of renderings attempted by a group of postgraduate Arab translator trainees were used in obtaining a profile of how the above sample is generally perceived, processed and rendered when translated into Arabic. The specific issue which the exercise of acquiring this data was meant to address is the following: Sample A seems to confront the translator with a serious problem of both understanding and re-producing a crucial aspect of text meaning, namely that of the use of irony around which the entire text revolves. To ensure optimally realistic conditions within which to operate, the students were first given a brief overview of the background to the text, the ideology of the protagonists, and so on.

My expectations regarding the degree of difficulty posed by such a text were confirmed by the fact that almost all of those who participated in the experiment were unable to appreciate and properly handle the ironical meaning involved. The questions I shall therefore ask and attempt to answer in the following discussion are: What went wrong for such an important omission to occur? How could these and similar receivers of such texts be helped? Could the appreciation of irony be made more systematic? Can text linguistics contribute to this effort? How could insights from a contrastive linguistic view of text in context be used to enrich translator training programmes in this and similar areas of language use?

But, before embarking on the details of what constitutes irony pragmatically and how this is processed from a discourse perspective, a comparative statement of what is actually rendered vis-à-vis what should ideally have been rendered in the translation test referred to above may perhaps be helpful. A representative student version is presented here in back-translation from Arabic. In itself, the chosen rendering will not be very revealing of the use of irony under analysis. I have therefore indicated the linguistic means of ironical use and appended a gloss of attitudinal meaning. The glosses (in square brackets) are more like a commentary on the limits of discoursal expression (i.e. on the attitudes relayed) than anything which could qualify as equivalent meanings of source text items. Finally, to appreciate fully the erratic nature of the students' rendering, the following back-translation and the glossing appended must be read in the way it was intended by the students, i.e. as if the text producer were utterly genuine and optimally sincere in what he said:

Sample B

1 Since these facts are facts	(Source text)	
Lexical repetition	(Means of irony)	

Since these are indeed facts   (Back-translation)

[Since what we have been
presented with so far is a factual
account of events]   (Attitudinal gloss)

2 Balfour must then go on to the next part of his argument
Modality/Lexical

Balfour feels it is incumbent on him to proceed to the next
part of his argument

[Balfour feels a logical necessity to proceed . . .]

3 Balfour produces no evidence that the Egyptians and 'the races with
whom we deal appreciate or even understand the good that is being
done them by colonial occupation'
Text-type/ Syntactic reference-switching/Lexical

Balfour has no evidence that the Egyptians or the races with whom
the British deal appreciate or even understand the good that is being
done them by colonial powers

[It is a pity that no evidence was forthcoming of the gratitude of the
natives, as gratitude on the part of these peoples for the great deal
of good done them by the colonizer is expected and wouldn't have
gone amiss]

4 It does not occur to Balfour, however, to let the Egyptian speak for
himself
Lexical/ Text-type

Balfour did not think it was necessary to let the Egyptian speak for
himself

[Simply did not feel that he should have done]

5 since presumably any Egyptian who would speak out is more likely
to be 'the agitator [who] wishes to raise difficulties' than the good native
who overlooks the 'difficulties' of foreign domination
Textual-conjunctive/Lexical

Since it can be safely assumed that those who will speak out are likely to be agitators bent on causing trouble rather than good citizens who constructively circumvent difficulties

[On the grounds that those who will speak out more often than not turn out to be resentful, trouble-making agitators and not responsible, upright citizens who think positively, taking the difficulties in their stride]

6 And so, having settled the ethical problems,
Textual-conjunctive/Lexical

Thus, having solved the ethical problems,

[Thus, having attended as exhaustively as possible to the ethical problems]

7 Balfour turns at last to the practical ones
Lexical/Textual-elliptic

Balfour finally turns his attention to the practical problems.

[Balfour finally turns to a discussion of the practical problems] (. . .)

8 If it is our business to govern, with or without gratitude, with or without the real or genuine memory of all the loss of which we have relieved the population
Lexical/ repetition and parallelism

If we have to govern, with or without gratitude or a genuine memory of the loss which we have spared the people

If government is what we have been called upon to carry out, then we must fulfill the task with which we have been entrusted

9 Balfour by no means implies, as part of that loss, the loss or at least the indefinite postponement of Egyptian independence
Textual-informativity (of the unexpected)

Balfour does not of course imply as part of that loss the loss of Egyptian independence

[In talking about the loss of which the colonized population have been relieved, Balfour implies nothing as sinister as the loss of independence which the Egyptians suffered]

10 If that is our duty, how is it to be performed?
Lexical/formality

If that is the duty assigned to us, how are we to carry it out?

If it is our destiny to govern, the question that has to be addressed urgently is how to go about this?

11 England exports our very best to these countries.
Syntactic reference-switching/Lexical

England sends her very best people to these countries

[The best brains, the best expertise are all sent to help these countries—total commitment and self-denial]

12 These selfless administrators do their work 'amidst tens of thousands of persons belonging to a different creed, a different race, a different discipline, different conditions of life.'
Lexical/ Lexical repetition

These unselfish administrators carry out their duties amidst tens of thousands of persons belonging to a different creed, a different race, a different discipline, and different conditions of life

[The ultimate in self-denial is having to work with people who do not only belong to a different creed but also to a different race, discipline and conditions of life.]

Ironical Meaning

Now that the main cause of the problem encountered by most of our students in the translation of sample A above has been identified as an inability to appreciate and handle ironical meaning, it is perhaps useful at this stage to review some of the major approaches to the analysis of irony and to try and present a synthesis of views regarding what actually constitutes this kind of non-literal meaning. In developing this framework, primary concern is given to the kind of analysis that could

191

sufficiently account for both inter- and intra-lingual differences in what successfully counts as ironical.

Irony has traditionally been defined as saying one thing literally and meaning the opposite figuratively. Quintilian is quoted as saying that the use of irony involves us in understanding 'something which is the opposite of what is actually said' (IX. II: 44). This 'semantic' account of irony begs several questions, however: What is figurative meaning? How is figurative meaning derived from literal meaning? And, as Sperber and Wilson (1981: 295) remark, 'Why [should] a speaker . . . prefer the ironical utterance . . . to its literal counterpart?'

As an alternative to the traditional view, Grice proposes a pragmatic approach to irony: figurative meaning is analysed in terms of conversational implicature. Basically, implicatures tell us how it is possible to convey information without putting this into words:

> A: Is John back yet?
> B: The pubs are still open.
>
> (Johanesson 1985: 205)

Since, as with all implicatures, B's negative answer together with the reason why John is not back are unsaid, the speaker expects the hearer to be able to work out the implied meanings through knowledge of the world or of the topic of conversation, etc. Grice bases his theory of implicature on a general rule which he calls the Cooperative Principle:

> Make your contribution such as is required by the present direction of the conversation.

He then lists four sets of rules which he calls 'maxims' and which are said to enable the speaker to achieve cooperativeness:

> Quantity: (1) Make your contribution as informative as is required (for the current purpose of the exchange).
> (2) Do not make your contribution more informative than is required.

> Quality: (1) Do not say what you believe to be false.
> (2) Do not say that for which you lack adequate evidence

> Relation: Be relevant.

> Manner: Be perspicuous

But the tremendous appeal which Grice's theory has had for applied pragmaticians is not in the maxims themselves, but rather in the ways in which speakers can break these, fail to observe them, or blatantly flout them. In a summary of the Gricean theory, Johanesson (1985: 208) explains the distinction between the different ways of infringing the rules:

> A speaker may accidentally break a rule (this is FAILURE to observe a given maxim).
> More interesting than failure is what happens when a speaker intentionally breaks a rule. This is done in two fundamentally different ways: either the speaker breaks the rule in a COVERT manner, never intending the hearer to realize that a rule is being broken, or s/he can break the rule in an OVERT manner, intending the hearer to understand that a particular rule is being broken. In the first case we may say that the speaker VIOLATES a maxim, in the second that s/he FLOUTS a maxim.

Irony is presented by Grice as a case of flouting the first maxim of Quality (namely, do not say what you believe to be false) and cites the following example (1975: 53):

> X, with whom A has been on close terms until now, has betrayed a secret of A's to a business rival. A and his audience both know this. A says 'X is a fine friend' . . .

Crediting Grice with relieving 'semantic theory of the problem of defining figurative meaning and deriving the figurative meaning of an utterance', Sperber and Wilson (1986: 240) nevertheless take the implicature theory to task on the grounds that it is unable to account for why a speaker should opt for an ironical utterance and not its literal counterpart. However, in examining the alternative theories put forward by Sperber and Wilson, it is difficult to see how the authors' new proposals fill this particular gap, if indeed a gap it is. From the translator's point of view, and that of contrastive linguistics, it may be useful here to reiterate what Hatim and Mason (1990: 98) say on the matter:

> Sperber and Wilson's view of . . . irony is not inconsistent with an essentially Gricean view. Thus, ironic understatement, while it may not flout the maxim of quality, does involve apparent flouting of the maxim of quantity ('make your contribution as informative as required').

At this point, a brief account of the Sperber and Wilson model of irony should be given. My aim is not to add more of the same to what Grice has already said, but rather to underline those valuable insights which specifically argue for the semiotic status of irony.

An important distinction which Sperber and Wilson draw is one between first-order interpretation and second-order interpretation, the latter being exemplifiable by irony. In irony, it is maintained, 'the thought of the speaker which is interpreted by the utterance [i.e. Said's in sample A] is itself an interpretation. It is an interpretation of a thought of someone other than the speaker (or of the speaker in the past) [Balfour's in sample A]' (1986: 238). Another basic distinction the authors make is between 'use' (involving 'what an expression refers to') and 'mention' (involving 'reference to the expression itself') (1981: 303), with irony properly belonging to the latter category. With this in mind, irony comes to be seen as a case of echoic mention:

> By representing someone's utterance, or the opinions of a certain type of person, or popular wisdom, in a manifestly sceptical, amused, surprised, triumphant, approving or reproving way, the speaker can express her own attitude to the thought echoed, and the relevance of her utterance might depend largely on this expression of attitude.
>
> (1986: 239)

Two points emerge from this discussion, which, incidentally, enhances rather than conflicts with the Gricean account. First, the kind of attitudinal meanings listed, which are beyond a pragmatics of text to describe exhaustively or identify definitively, are in fact semiotic categories (i.e. they are sign systems). As such, pragmatics becomes an adjunct discipline which supplements semiotic description. This explains the many different and varied ways which pragmatic activity entails in attending to a given semiotic attitudinal meaning.

The second point which emerges from the Sperber and Wilson account relates to the intertextual potential of these various attitudinal meanings. This is made amply clear by subscribing to the notion of the echoic mention. Here it would be far more helpful for us to talk about 'intratextuality' (echoic mentions which span a single, currently evolving text), 'intertextuality' (mentions which echo other texts) and 'contratextuality' (echoes which conjure up earlier mentions only to cancel or contradict them) (Martin 1985; Lemke 1985).

What is being inter-, intra- or contra-textually echoed, then, is an attitude (a sign) held by someone other than the speaker. But the more important aspect of semiotic meaning is that which reveals the speaker's attitude to the opinion echoed. It is an attitude to an attitude, as it were, and it is commonly one of rejection or disapproval. Sample A provides us with a classic demonstration of both the Gricean and the Sperber and Wilson accounts. The overall disparaging attitude is relayed through a number of implicatures, each of which relays a particular attitude not unrelated to the macro-sign (disparagement). Although the maxim of Quality, predictably, is the one most at risk in English, other maxims are also being flouted. Here Sperber and Wilson (1986: 240) step in with a supplementary aid to the analyst:

> The recovery of these implicatures depends, first, on a recognition of the utterance as echoic; second, on an identification of the source of the opinion echoed; and third, on a recognition that the speaker's attitude to the opinion echoed is one of rejection or disapproval.

So far, I have been seeking to demonstrate that it is semiotic systems of signification which inform both the pragmatics and the register communicativeness of texts. That is, the latter domains of context could most profitably be viewed merely as sets of means which ultimately achieve semiotic ends (signs among signs). It is in this sense that attitudinal meanings can be approached and irony analysed as the implication by echoic mention of such meanings. But before moving on to a discussion of the multi-levelled nature of irony which views the manifestation of ironical use as text in context, the problem encountered by our students will be stated specifically in Gricean terms.

Flouting of Maxims and Cultural Norms

What to implicate and how, which maxim to flout and where, all these pragmatic considerations seem to be at the heart of the problem encountered in the translation of sample A above. Of course the problem is initially one of appreciating source text irony. But, from subsequent class discussion with the students tested, a repetition of the exercise, and after consulting a number of professional, published translations of the sample in question and similar texts, I was able to conclude that, even when the knowledge is made available regarding what is intended in a particular instance of irony, translators from English into Arabic (and I dare say into a number of other more explicative languages) tend to, rather persistently, opt for some literal rendering that simply defies the ultimate communicative objective of a given text in this regard. It is as though by inclination that the text receiver generally warms up to literal meaning, shunning the extra work involved in the contextual reconstruction necessary for the perception of ironical meaning. Thus, as pointed out earlier, preserving irony becomes a problem not only of reception but of production too. The question now becomes simply why the English source text remarkably succeeds whereas the Arabic target text utterly fails? Precisely what went wrong and why did this communicative breakdown happen?

For socio-cultural and linguistic reasons too complex to unravel in the present discussion, English has developed a particular preference for understatement and the cryptic. Irony seems to be one of those aspects of verbal behaviour which benefit considerably from this kind of attitude to language use. In context, the speaker can leave so much unsaid, yet express the attitude in question. But what is unsaid by no means leaves the utterance incomplete; on the contrary, the utterance will be 'pregnant' with meaning as a result. That is, English seems to allow some economy with the truth: one is basically telling a lie, or in Gricean terms, flouting the directive 'Do not say what you believe to be false' in as overt a manner as possible. Sample A optimally demonstrates this attitude to truth and the maximal effect which accrues as far as English is concerned.

For similarly complex reasons regarding this preference in English, Arabic tends to move in the opposite direction: one can simply do more by saying more. In the context of sample A, for example, it would be virtually impossible for the speaker to announce that 'these facts are facts' and only mean that they are mere humbug. The translators in our experiment went wrong when they underestimated how intolerant Arabic is to this kind of opaqueness. They assumed that a literal rendering of a straightforward statement such as *Since these facts are facts* would suffice, particularly if they preserved the repetition by something like an emphatic device ('indeed').

The expression of 'disparagement' successfully relayed through flouting the maxim of 'truth' (Quality) in English, must be somehow preserved in translation, however. And preserving this kind of attitude must not be done too transparently lest we lose the subtlety of the source text. These are the horns of the dilemma for the Arab translator which pragmatics could once again resolve. Arabic has a particular preference for what the Arab rhetoricians were fond of calling 'useful circumlocution' (i.e. motivated, functional redundancy). This could be the solution to our problem: motivated overstatement could relay as sarcastic an attitude as the most cryptic of English styles. Thus, element 1 of sample A:

Since these facts are facts

which was literally rendered by the students as 'since these are indeed facts', and could thus only relay the attitude 'since what we have been presented with so far is a factual account of events', would most effectively preserve the expression of disparagement were it to read in the Arabic something like:

wa lammaa kaanat haadhihi al-Haqaa'iq fii naZari balfor Haqaa'iqa laa ghubaara 'alayhaa

'Since in Balfour's eyes these facts are facts, totally unblemished'.

This relays the attitudinal meaning: 'since in the blinkered eye of Balfour these are facts (and the mind boggles to think what non-facts would sound like!)'.

That is, what would be at risk in relaying the ironical meaning involved is not Quality but Quantity—the maxim which in a normal world penalizes one for being over-informative, for unnecessarily overloading one's utterance. In a world of motivated use of language, however, this verbal excess would be highly communicative, telling the reader that there is more than meets the eye in a given circumlocution and thus ultimately pointing to a variety of attitudes over and above the literal meaning.

Implications for the Contrastive Linguist

Recast in terms particularly relevant to contrastive linguists in general and translators in particular, the hypothesis entertained in this study may be phrased as follows. Translation is a sign-for-sign act of transfer which does not necessarily entail the need to preserve the very same pragmatic or register values of the source text. Put slightly differently, translation is not necessarily the transposition of a given field, mode or tenor by identical register values, nor is it necessarily the transposition of a given speech act, implicature, etc. by an identical pragmatic manifestation. Translation could by all means be all these things but only if this one-for-one correlation adequately caters for, and ultimately keeps intact, the semiotic sign in question (e.g. a disparaging attitude).

To return to irony briefly, the English source sample A above expresses a disparaging attitude by the utterance of a series of ironical statements. The pragmatic procedure opted for is basically one of implicature through flouting the maxim of Quality. There are other register-related features exploited specifically to uphold this kind of pragmatic reading. But, as we have seen, although the preservation in

Arabic of the semiotics of 'disparagement' (the ultimate sign, and the ultimate goal of translating this text) can be achieved by an implicature (basically saying what you do not mean, etc.), this has to be of a different kind to that of the source text: Arabic flouts Quantity and not Quality. By the same token, although register considerations are also involved in translating this particular text (level of formality, etc.), 'implicating' in the way Arabic deems appropriate entails the exploitation of different register features from those originally and successfully employed in the source text. Semiotics may thus be considered as the last court of appeal in translation and it is to basic semiotic categories that we should now briefly turn our attention.

The translator working into Arabic could resort to the principle of 'least effort' and follow procedures similar to those adopted by the majority of those who took the test described above. However, what this has entailed is literally translating the text into admittedly a standard idiomatic variety of Arabic, but one which has simply failed to communicate crucial aspects of source text meaning. We cannot for certain judge whether this is done consciously or unconsciously, that is whether or not they saw the irony for what it was. However, what is produced is a reading which only reflects a wholesale and uncritical rendering of the same pragmatics and general communicativeness of the source text. The result has not been satisfactory. The transfer of the flouting of Quality and the register features of the source text cannot in this case relay the ironical, disparaging attitude focused on so crucially in the source text.

To end with a word on the likely reasons why Arabic seems to favour flouting a maxim like Quantity and not Quality, all one can say pending further research is that there seem to be deep-rooted socio-cultural and linguistic grounds as to why choosing to flout Quality is certain to fail from the outset. At the risk of oversimplifying what is essentially a complex argument regarding this point, one may tentatively conclude that the aversion to 'saying what one knows to be false' has to do with the Arab's attitude to truth and is no doubt related to aspects of the communicative act such as politeness, as well as to more general aspects of language in social life such as sociological and political norms. Generally, one might say that an Arab simply feels rather uncomfortable with appearing to commit an untruth particularly to the written record. Flouting Quality is most probably seen in this light.

But, as I argued in Chapter 4 and 5, this is not a permanent condition and rhetorical mores might change as time goes by. Diachronic criteria are helpful in attempting to account for the way languages evolve in dealing with aspects of use such as irony. English prose of the nineteenth century, for example, shows unmistakable tendencies to flout Quantity and not Quality in relaying irony, a trend which seems to have been on the wane in modern English.

Summary

In this chapter, we attempted a review of basic theories of ironical meaning and focused on the problems of translating ironical use of language into Arabic. Irony was shown to impinge not only on aspects of message construction such as register membership and intentionality, but also on semiotic categories such as genre and discourse. The latter is shown to be particularly privileged as home to attitudinal meanings. Discoursal meanings are almost universal and must therefore be heeded and constantly resorted to by the translator as it is in this domain of context that the last court of appeal for adequacy and equivalence would most certainly be found.

17

The 'Other' Texts: Implications for Liaison Interpreting

If one can separate theory from practice, and I believe one cannot except as a methodological convenience, then the more practical aim of this chapter is to introduce liaison interpreting as a translation-related skill and to call for its inclusion into programmes of translator training. Put simply, liaison interpreting involves the use of an interpreter as an intermediary in situations such as an informal discussion or a more formal interview/question-answer session between two speakers who do not understand each other's language, or do so only imperfectly.

Over the years, our own experience with translator and interpreter training has shown that providing the translator with basic interpreting skills such as liaison interpreting serves at least two objectives. First, interpreting helps translators acquire an added skill which will no doubt be professionally useful. The second objective relates to the fact that, albeit indirectly, interpreting skills make translators more aware of what the translation process actually involves, an awareness which will undoubtedly shed more light on the nature of translation itself.

With interpreting in mind, and assuming once again that the theory-practice distinction is valid for the moment, the more theoretical aim of this final chapter is to build on earlier proposals regarding the supremacy of semiotics in the construction of meaning and to argue that a useful way of modelling context is perhaps to see it in terms of: *all the other relevant prior texts which the various textual clues in a given utterance conjure up for a given language user on a given occasion of use.* The provenance of each of these prior texts thus becomes the site of some form of contextual activity, the locale which must be 'revisited', as it were, if the linguistic item in question is to be processed adequately. This highly interactive sense of intertextuality is all-pervasive and may be located on any level of linguistic description (phonology, morphology, syntax or semantics), and on any level of linguistic expression (word, phrase, clause, text, discourse, or genre).

Multi-level Intertextuality

To illustrate the proposal just put forward for the analysis of context, and before turning to the issue of text in context within liaison interpreting, let us by way of an example consider the following title of a *Guardian* editorial: *Vaanunu Vanishes*. The leading article was condemnatory of 'the act of piracy' committed by the Israeli agents from Mossad when, in broad daylight, they abducted Mr Vaanunu from a London street. Vaanunu, a nuclear technician previously employed at a nuclear site in Israel, had earlier talked to the *Sunday Times*, revealing important information about Israel's nuclear potential.

In the analysis of this utterance, and to avoid getting involved in the intricacies of the reading process and the question of individual differences, we will envisage a model reader and assume some form of idealized linguistic behaviour. The reaction of such a reader and the way he or she would go about gathering the relevant information and feeding this into the process of discovering text are bound to involve, among other things, attributing motivation to the salience of the alliterative repetition of *va*. Morpho-phonology would be involved here and reference would be made to actual or virtual texts (Beaugrande 1980) which have in one way or another codified the form and function of alliteration at the rank of entities below the word. On this occasion, what will immediately occur to the reader is the thought that 'I have seen this so-called embellishment device used somewhere before and I somehow intuitively know why it is used when it is used'. Involved in this intertextual retrieval exercise would be poetics (a feature of register) and the intention to go beyond the decorative effect of devices such as alliteration, into purposefully doing things with the colourful, the flowery, etc. (a pragmatic consideration).

But also involved, and perhaps far more significantly, is the expression of certain attitudinal meanings through the utterance of what on the surface strikes one as merely cosmetic. Here, we are in the domain of the sign, the socio-cultural, the semiotic, as the prime mover of pragmatic action and communicative interaction. To be 'comical' (which I take to be one of the socio-cultural meanings of the alliterative use under discussion) is a sign recognizable by a given community of text users in terms of the attitude relayed and the linguistic material signalling such an attitude. It is then and only then that the expression of this attitude begins to acquire purposefulness as intended by someone in speaking to someone, and as executed to best effect sometime, somewhere. Here, the universal attitudinal meaning becomes narrower and fairly more specific (i.e. pragmatic, which is by definition local and language-specific). This meaning becomes even narrower and more specific when, as a rebuttal, the 'comical' turns into a journalistic satirical weapon (the register's field, mode and tenor are involved here). Ultimately, of course, this particular use will have acquired socio-textual dimensions as a conventionally sanctioned mode of speaking or writing.

Thus, as we have just seen when morpho-phonology was invoked, the attitude 'comical' is appreciated only in terms of other relevant texts (other instances of the same register, other occurrences of the same intention, other tokens of the same sign). Staying with the same utterance for the moment (*Vaanunu Vanishes*), let us see how semantics is brought to bear on intertextual retrieval. At the rank of the word, appreciating the communicative potential of the verb *vanishes* would be that much richer if one were to build on some form of overall attitudinal meaning. This, I suggest, is still the 'comical' theme which somehow activates, in my mind at least, the image of the magician, adeptly conjuring up all kinds of tricks as part of the 'disappearing act': things 'vanish', 'just like that!' (in the memorable words of the late British comedian Tommy Cooper). Not in the real world of modern Britain, though, but only in a magician's world, the world of Alice in Wonderland! Intention and register specification will prop up this kind of analysis, and the utterance begins to act on the textual and extra-textual environment.

But perhaps even more intertextually potent here is 'other' texts, including, once again for me at least, that of an Agatha Christie's novel—*The Lady Vanishes*. The entire 'whodunit' genre, the entire 'brain-cells' discourse of Poirot, and the actual text of the title itself are somehow implicated in relaying the comical attitude in question and making it pragmatically active in a given register. This, together with the timelessness of the present tense used (thus involving text syntax), cumulatively adds to the effect of expressing an attitude of someone who, in utter disbelief, simply cannot take too seriously the whole business of someone disappearing in broad daylight from the middle of London.

In reality, the search for 'other' texts constitutive of the context of a given utterance continues unceasingly. The notion of intertextual retrieval as a way of modelling context may be represented diagrammatically as follows:

Vaanunu Vanishes

Phonology | Morphology | Semantics | Syntax

sub-word | word | phrase | clause | text | discourse | genre

actual | virtual

register transaction | pragmatic action

Semiotic Interaction

ideology | culture

Figure 17.1 Intertextual retrieval

In the maze of contextual activity taking place while a given utterance is being processed, intertextuality in both its active and passive senses (i.e. in both its long- and short-span forms) thus seems to be the moving force behind making sense of the unfolding text and restoring coherence. Under-pinning intertextual retrieval is a complex system of meaning-making that relies for its viability on a network of relations which are essentially semiotic. That is, it is a system of signs at work, engaging in some form of interaction that may be identified at the levels of:

(a) the interaction of speaker/writer with hearer/reader,

(b) the interaction of speaker/writer or hearer/reader with the text produced or received,

(c) the interaction of text with text.

Text as Macro-sign

Signs as units of interaction are at work at the three levels just listed. But, as I hope to have made clear throughout this book, privileged among the various domains of interaction is undoubtedly that which involves text with text. It is here that we need to be specific about text as a macro-sign within which various micro-signs are seen to be mutually relevant to the realization of an overall rhetorical purpose. For example, we cite an adversary's thesis, we then rebut it with one of our own and we follow this with some form of substantiation, hopefully ending with some cogent conclusion. These are the basic micro-signs with which we operate in realizing the rhetorical purpose 'to counter-argue' in English. Counter-argument is thus the macro-sign which embodies the statement of the rhetorical purpose involved. Let us consider the following text samples:

Sample A1
> Interviewee (English): Certainly, it is difficult to predict the effect of economic sanctions, when they will begin to bite. However, the sharpest pain has already started hitting exports. Before the invasion, Iraq earned 95% of its foreign exchange from oil. Now, its pipelines have been shut and its tankers are stuck in the Gulf. With this measure alone, the Alliance is depriving Iraq of some $80 million a day in oil revenues.

It is worth remarking that in a practical exercise in liaison interpreting, the text-type focus of this particular text was so drastically misperceived by one of the students taking the test that some serious loss of meaning ensued, as the transcript in sample A2 shows:

Sample A2
Back-translation from the interpreter's Arabic rendering
> Solving the problem in the current situation is certainly difficult. Iraq used to earn nearly 90% of its foreign exchange from oil, of course. But now that its pipelines have been shut and its tanks stuck in the Gulf, it is obvious that Iraq will lose nearly $80 million a day. It is this yardstick which the Alliance uses to gauge to what extent the economic sanctions have been effective.

Now let us compare counter-argumentation with a different kind of text as macro-sign. Here, we normally have no axe to grind and we only wish to report events in time, describe objects in space or expound on a series of concepts within the framework of analysis or synthesis. This expository rhetorical purpose as macro-sign requires a different set of micro-signs to those encountered in a counter-argumentative text. In exposition, we first set the scene to be covered, then single out the most salient and relevant aspects of the scene set for more detailed exposition which may or may not lead to an explicit concluding statement. This may be exemplified by sample B below:

Sample B
Journalist (English): How far did you get in your negotiations with Saddam Hussain?

Kurdish Leader (Arabic): We produced a paper to normalize the situation in Kurdistan. We also produced the new law for self-determination. Regarding the borders of the self-determined region, here there was disagreement.

There is no doubt that note-taking, a skill indispensable to summary writers in general and to liaison and consecutive interpreters in particular, would benefit from an approach to text which views overall organization in terms of problem- solving and means-ends analysis, as the text typology presented clearly does. Furthermore, albeit at a virtual level and not necessarily always at an actual level, it is to these macro/micro-signs (such as the 'thesis cited to be opposed', the 'scene-setter') that reference is constantly made by the language user. It is on 'sites' of textual activity such as these that context may be crucially reconstructed and negotiated. The schemata-like nature of these text signs indicates that they have a psychological reality, that they are internalized as part of our textual repertoire, and that they correlate with specific cognitive aspects of the way culture and the mind interact.

To illustrate the usefulness of text type as a grid which the language user intertextually uses to impose order on communication incongruities, let us consider sample C1 below. This text (discussed earlier to illustrate a slightly different point) is a literal translation of an answer offered in Arabic by a government minister in an attempt to dodge a question from an English journalist asking bluntly through a liaison interpreter: "Are you or are you not going to abolish passports and thus facilitate movement among the Gulf states?":

Sample C1
Journalist (English): Is it not now time, all these years after the establishment of the Gulf Cooperation Council, to abolish pass-ports . . . ?

Minister (back translated from Arabic): Travelling between the countries of the Cooperation Council is the easiest thing to do, and the Gulf citizen doesn't need a visa. *Then* [Ar. *thumma*], the passport is considered a proof of identity and as such is indispensable . . .

Regrettably, the minister's reply was rendered by the interpreter in more or less the form in which it appears in this back translation, which meant virtual loss of coherence. An interpreter more aware of text types would have produced something like the more context-sensitive rendering of sample **C2**

Sample C2
> Minister: Travelling between the countries of the Cooperation Council is the easiest thing to do, and the Gulf citizen doesn't need a visa. *But then, surely,* the passport is a proof of identity and as such is indispensable . . .

Discourse as Macro-sign

Texts do not occur in a vacuum, but within discourse, a macro-sign whose function it is to provide another kind of contextual input for semiotic analysis. As the mouthpiece of institutions, discourse becomes the vehicle of attitudinal expression, and the framework within which terms of reference pertaining to a given cultural code are established. Structurally, discoursal considerations determine the way texts concatenate (often in sequence, sometimes embedded within each other). Internally, on the other hand, discourse regulates the way the various patterns of texture (theme-rheme, lexical cohesion, etc.) ensure that a text is both cohesive and coherent. It is in the latter domain of internal connectivity that discourse may be usefully examined. Key concepts which represent a particular view of the world are inscribed in specific 'cultural codes' that serve a given ideological stance towards an issue or cumulatively function as a statement of some socio-cultural significance (Fairclough 1989).

Though essentially diffuse, discourse utilizes fairly concrete signals and relays definite statements which provide the text with a variety of 'voices'. At a general level, we may have undertones such as those of 'evaluative' discourse typical of 'managing' (as opposed to 'monitoring') as in persuasion, argumentation, etc. More specifically, we may encounter attitudes to text-worlds such as the didactic, the literary, the scientific. Even more specifically, we may come across committed ideological statements as in feminist discourse, racist discourse, monetarist discourse, etc. All such discoursal values may well be fuzzy and negotiable but they are certainly not seamless. As we have seen in the analysis of text as a macro-sign, discourse and the micro-signs subsumed within it are psychologically real, are internalizable as part of textual repertoires and are effective reference grids within which communication is ordered to best effect.

To illustrate the crucial role which discourse awareness plays in the pursuit of optimally effective communication, let us consider sample D, once again drawn from liaison interpreting. The English journalist's provocative libertarian discourse fell on deaf ears as far as his Arab interpreter and the government minister interviewed were concerned: the terms he used were pejorative, appropriate for the discourse of the Western critic of autocracy. In Arabic, however, those terms constituted a cultural code associated with the discourse of a stable petro-dollar economy, wealth and prosperity:

Sample D
> Journalist: Look at Tunisia, despite democratic trappings, power remains *concentrated* and *personalized*. But perhaps more to the point, look at Algeria. Some 180,000 well-schooled Algerians enter the job market every year. Yet a hobbled economy adds only 100,000 new jobs a year, and some 45% of these *involve working for the government.*

To the interpreter, who was from a country with a rich and viable economy, there is nothing pejorative about power being *concentrated* and *personalized*, and it is a privilege to be able *to work for the government.* But, had the interpreter been more aware of the discoursal thrust, which in this example is fused into the fabric of the other macro-sign—text ('Some 180,000 . . . Yet . . .'), he would have had no difficulty in establishing the connection. This would have meant retrieving the intertextuality which points to a body of communicative behaviour realized by a variety of discourses and texts as signs. We are constantly aware of these as they surround us all the time, as signs among signs. Sometimes they are manageable and easy to pin down, at other times they prove to be too slippery and elusive. But they are there, constituting an important layer of the context enveloping a given utterance.

Genre as Macro-sign

Texts, then, embody forms of expression appropriate to a given rhetorical purpose. Discoursal expression is that which is appropriate to a given ideological stance or a view of the world. The third macro-sign, genre, differs from both text and discourse only in that it subsumes forms of expression appropriate to a given social occasion. The notion of appropriateness in the semiotic analysis expounded here captures the way society and culture sanction particular generic, discoursal and textual structures. In terms of the mechanisms involved, such a conventional act of authorization is akin to what actually takes place in the process through which the Saussurean signifier-signified or even the Barthesian structure of the myth develops (Barthes 1957).

Like the categories of text and discourse, genre has been variously defined. A few of these orientations may be helpful to list as they are categories with which translators and interpreters normally work. At a very general level, it is useful to be aware of generic structures identified, say, within literary criticism, such as the sonnet, the ballad, the short story or the novel. It is also useful to be aware of the conventions governing other kinds of generic structures such as the academic article and the annual report.

But from the point of view of contrastive linguistics in general and that of translating/interpreting in particular, there seems to be ample justification for focusing on more specific notions of genre (James 1992). The grounds for doing this, and in effect relegating other more general approaches to secondary place, is simply to do with the fact that within the short story or the academic article, for example, we as translators or interpreters actually work with numerous kinds of generic structures and feel that these also qualify for the term 'genre'. Genre would equally appropriately be used here to cover all forms of language use con-ventionally sanctioned as expressive of what happens on a given social occasion. These 'genrelets', as I prefer to call them, and the smaller, the more useful and yet demanding they prove to be, are formulations such as 'the court will rise' or the auctioneer's rapid manner of bid acceptance ('going, going, gone').

Though not commonly recognized by mainstream interpreting theory, the fact is that interpreters do work with generic structures and, unlike translators, require an extremely agile mind to put their cultural awareness into words under pressure. Let us consider sample E1 drawn from an interview with an Egyptian ex-Foreign Minister and literally rendered here from the original Arabic:

Sample E1
> Interviewer (English): What line of poetry do you often remember?
>
> Riyad (Back-translated from the Arabic): A hemistich from a line in a poem by the great freedom fighter Shaykh Bashir al-Ibrahimi. I heard him recite the poem which was about the deteriorating situation the Arab nation finds itself in.
>
> Interviewer: What is this hemistich?
>
> Riyad: Their constitution is: Do not read, nor write, nor understand

208

[Arabic: *wa dustuuruhunna . . . la taqra'ana la taktubanna . . . la tafhamanna*]

As I pointed out above, awareness of the conventions governing literary genres is a useful asset in the training of interpreters who could find themselves in situations where this kind of knowledge is called upon, as the example of sample E shows regarding the structure of the poem, parts of the verse, etc. However, the problem in sample E is slightly more complex than this, requiring that the interpreter be more aware of the genrelet as a unit of semiotic analysis. A number of questions must cross the interpreter's mind in processing this text sample: Is genre involved at all? If it is, is the genre involved that of an 'article' from a 'constitution' or that of a 'motto'? If it is the 'motto' which is intended, what structure, forms of expressions, etc. would mottoes conventionally be associated with in English? The answers which have to be provided by the interpreter on the spot with least delay point us in the direction of the need to operate with generic structures such as the 'motto' and opt for a form of expression appropriate to this social occasion which has its own set forms of linguistic expression. Sample E2 provides a suggested rendering of the text sample in question:

Sample E2
    Riyad: And their motto is: Read not . . . Write not . . . Comprehend
    not . . .

It is the intertextual potential of genres and genrelets that may be utilized in situations such as this. Like the macro-signs text and discourse and the micro-signs subsumed within them, genres are psychologically real, are internalizable as part of textual competence and are effective controls which impose order on an otherwise unwieldy state of the language.

Micro-signs—A Final Word

Textual, discoursal and generic constraints are important macro-signals which regulate message construction and ensure that texts are efficient, effective and appropriate. But to operate bottom-up (as opposed to the top-down orientation we have been adopting), the language user needs to be aware of the various micro-signals which help in testing initial hypotheses and making sense of the text as it unfolds. Micro-signals have been alluded to in passing throughout the above discussion. It may, however, be worth reiterating our view of what constitutes these signals, and perhaps concluding with a word on the function of the micro-signal as the carrier of pragmatic and other register specifications while implementing or issuing semiotic/attitudinal instructions.

Within texts, micro-signals are those elements which realize overall structural and textural organization and thus implement the basic rhetorical purpose of a given text. Citing an opponent's thesis and then rebutting it are micro-signals in a counter-argumentative text. But for these elements to relay the values involved, they must be seen to carry within them clues pointing to a particular cultural code. These discoursal micro-signals enter text organization through the area of texture which enables us to 'read off' a given ideological stance, a commitment to a cause or simply an attitude to some aspect of the text-world as in literary or scientific communication.

Discourse is thus not seamless. We have textual demarcation lines, and we have generic constraints that ensure the appropriateness of the way a message is put together to serve both a given rhetorical purpose and a given social occasion. These textual and generic micro-signals infiltrate texts through texture as well, and some may even be active at the level of text structure. Riddles, mottoes, graffiti slogans, etc. have both an idiom and a structure of their own.

Now, where is pragmatics and register specification in all of this, and how do these relate to semiotic meaning posited here to be particularly distinct and indeed privileged? Regarding this matter, I suggest that, while the semiotic domain of attitudinal meaning is home to the 'universal', pragmatics is the domain of negotiating how best to make sense of semiotic values, given the importance here of who is talking to whom, in what circumstances and for what purpose. Register lends us the framework for the entire transaction, providing the vehicle of expression, the mode, the tenor, etc.

Let me illustrate this point briefly. Both the English interviewee and the Arab Minister in samples A1 and C1 respectively wished to counter-argue, engage in evaluative/committed discourse and operate within the rules of the genre in question. These are semiotic considerations behind attitudinal meanings which must be taken as universal. However, it is the area of pragmatics which tends to be more language- and culture-specific and in which divergence normally sets in between different languages and between different varieties within the same language. Speakers find themselves in actual situations where an element of who is speaking to whom must be catered for. This underlines the need to operate within, say, rules of 'politeness' that may not necessarily be equally operative for the two languages or varieties in question. For example, it is too abrasive to oppose explicitly in Arabic, not to mention the unvirtuous nature of telling lies which is in effect what people do when paying lip-service to the thesis of an adversary.

Wider Implications of Semiotic Analysis

The obvious conclusion to be drawn from the above kind of investigation is that negotiating text in context, with the latter taken *inter alia* to be a function of all the other relevant prior texts surrounding a given utterance, has an important role to play in the training and professional activity of the translator and the interpreter. More specifically, it is argued that training in skills such as liaison interpreting contributes most positively to the preparation of those who wish to concentrate on translation. Such a skill not only equips these practitioners with the added facility of handling oral/aural interaction if and when they are called upon to do so, but also makes them more aware of what is involved in translation—a skill on which they have chosen to focus.

But a less obvious, though perhaps more far-reaching, conclusion of this study is that the difference between translation and interpreting is often exaggerated. Of course, the two skills are somehow distinct in terms of self-evident factors to do with the mode of delivery and reception: interpreters work under pressure; there are constraints on perception and storage of information; recall can be problematic for all kinds of reasons. But in terms of the underlying strategies of approaching context, handling text type and negotiating both the structure and texture of communicative occurrences, the differences are simply too marginal to be worth the kind of exclusive treatment they sometimes receive (see Hatim and Mason 1997). Both the translator and the interpreter go about their textual business more or less in the same way. Texts are texts which change only slightly and, to all intents and purposes, almost negligibly when intended for translation or for interpreting.

The theoretical and practical implications of the position argued for in this chapter are simply too daunting to be ignored. Let us look at the issue of training possibilities and the difference between translation and interpreting raised in the previous paragraph. Leaving aside the extremely uninteresting question of territoriality (which institution is qualified to teach what), the problem facing translator and interpreter training simply becomes one of using time and effort most judiciously. In the world we live in at present, with numerous cut-backs and with higher education facing unprecedented pressures, can we really afford the kind of artificial over-compartmentalization which has led to separate so-called disciplines on either side of spurious professional divides?

Addressing this and similar matters takes on added urgency when what

211

we should be devoting a little more time to is the proper analysis of the texts and discourses of our diplomats, our scientists, our engineers, and our statesmen, and comparing these with other relevant texts and discourses representative of a given target culture. This should all be undertaken with the aim of developing a unified text strategy that can inform our theoretical models and enrich our techniques and procedures in the training of translators and interpreters alike. The need for such a more comprehensive approach to the study of translating and interpreting (and indeed other domains within translation studies such as literary or technical translating) must surely make us re-think our priorities and the bulk of received wisdom which we have uncritically accepted for far too long.

Summary

The aim of this chapter was to view liaison interpreting within a discourse processing framework and to argue for its inclusion as an important skill in all translator-training programmes. On a slightly more theoretical level, the chapter also sought to demonstrate that, within the various domains of context, semiotics has pride of place, with discourse being particularly privileged as a carrier of attitudinal meaning and a facilitator of interaction. In themselves, texts and genres are mere vehicles of linguistic expression, and it is only when language use becomes imbued with ideological and other kinds of discursive meaning that texts and genres begin to take on discoursal values and communication truly materializes. Once such a framework is in place, differences between technical or Bible translating, literary translating or conference interpreting and so on can be seen in perspective and become less important than that which unites these diverse activities: a common concern with the need to communicate another act of communication across both linguistic and cultural boundaries.

Glossary of Contrastive Text Linguistics and Translation Terms

ACTUAL: see **Virtual**

ANAPHORA: This is when a linguistic item (say, a pronoun) is used to refer to antecedent elements in the text (e.g. *The king spoke. In his speech, he said . . .*). **Cataphora**, on the other hand, is when a linguistic item is used to refer to subsequent elements in the text (e.g. *In his speech, the king said . . .*).

ARGUMENTATION: A text type in which concepts and/or beliefs are evaluated. Two basic forms of argumentation may be distinguished: **Counter-argumentation** in which a thesis is cited, then opposed; and **Through-argumentation** in which a thesis is cited, then extensively defended. Counter-arguments could be:

(1) **Explicit** (the concession is explicitly signalled by the use of concessives such as *although, while*, etc.). (Also referred to as the **Concessive argument**);

(2) **Implicit** (the opposition is introduced by the use of adversatives such as *but, however*, etc. following the citation of an opponent's thesis). (Also known as the **Strawman Gambit**);

(3) **Suppressed** (the implicit opposition is introduced without the use of an explicit adversative).

Through-arguments are basic argumentative formats which could either be **Detached** (objective) or **Involved** (subjective).

ASPECT OF THE SCENE: See **Text Structure**

ATTRIBUTES: see **Element**

AURAL TEXT: see **Visual Text, Literacy**

BACKWARD DIRECTIONALITY: see **Thematic Progression**

BLOOMFIELDIAN STRUCTURALISM: An approach to linguistics which stresses the importance of language as a system and which investigates the place that linguistic units such as sounds, words and sentences have within the system. In this framework, the work of the American linguist Leonard Bloomfield is by far the most prominent. The theory of psychology to which Bloomfieldian Structuralism subscribes is known as Behaviourism. This states

COMMUNICATION ACROSS CULTURES

that human and animal behaviour can and should be studied in terms of physical processes only.

BOTTOM-UP: see **Top-down**

BREAKING A MAXIM: see **Cooperative Principle**

CATAPHORA: see **Anaphora**

CHUNK: see **Element**

COHERENCE: see **Cohesion**

COHESION: The requirement that a sequence of sentences realizing a > * **Text** display grammatical and/or lexical relationships which ensure surface structure continuity. For example, in the exchange:

A. Where have you been?

B. To the Empire

there is an implicit link between *have been* and *to the Empire* which accounts for the cohesiveness of the sequence.

Coherence, on the other hand, stipulates that grammatical and/or lexical relationships involve the meanings of the various elements of text and not only continuity of forms. Thus, the > **Ellipsis** in the above exchange could conceivably be used to relay 'marital tension'. It is only **Contextual** glosses such as this which capture coherence relations adequately.

COMMUNICATIVE: see **Context**

COMMUNICATIVE DYNAMISM (CD): The phenomenon whereby sentences are made up of **Themes** followed by **Rhemes** and whereby, in the **Unmarked** case, Rhemes are more communicatively important (i.e. display a higher CD).

CONCESSIVE ARGUMENT: see Argumentation

CONNOTATION: Additional meanings which a lexical item acquires beyond its primary, referential meaning, e.g. *notorious* means 'famous' but with negative connotations. **Denotations**, on the other hand, cover the dictionary, contextless meaning of a given lexical item.

CONTEXT: The extra-textual environment which shapes and is in turn shaped by linguistic expression. The subject matter of a given text is part of > **Register** and can thus determine, say, the way the text presents who is doing what to whom (> **Transitivity**). Three domains of context may be distinguished:

(1) **Communicative**, including aspects of the message such as **Register Membership**;

(2) **Pragmatic**, covering **Intentionality**;

(3) **Semiotic**, accounting for **Intertextuality**.

CONTEXT OF CULTURE: A form of behaviour potential available to the individual text user and yielding a set of options. Once chosen, the various options provide the environment for actual lexico-grammatical selections. To shift the blame from a male perpetrator of a crime onto a woman and dehumanize the latter is a reading which the **Context of Culture** makes

---

*The symbol > stands for 'see the term indicated'. This term is fully defined elsewhere in the Glossary

available. To select a particular form of the passive (e.g. *Girl 7 killed while mum was drinking at the pub*), on the other hand, is an aspect of **Field of Discourse** related to **Context of Situation**.

CONTEXT OF SITUATION: see **Context of Culture**

CONTRASTIVE TEXT LINGUISTICS: An extension on the basic methods of linguistic analysis which show the similarities and differences between two or more languages. Approaching the idea of comparison and contrast from a text perspective entails that the primary object of the analysis become stretches of language longer than the sentence. Sequences of utterances are thus seen in terms of certain **Contextual** requirements and of the way these are implemented in text **Structure** and **Texture**, across both linguistic and cultural boundaries.

CONTRATEXTUALITY: see **Intertextuality**

THE COOPERATIVE PRINCIPLE: The assumption that interlocutors cooperate with each other by observing certain so-called **Conversational Maxims**. These are:

  Quantity: Give as much information as is needed;
  Quality: Speak truthfully;
  Relevance: Say what is relevant;
  Manner: Avoid ambiguity.

However, these Maxims may be **Broken** (inadvertently) or **Violated** (when the **Deviation from the Norm** of adhering to them is not communicated properly). Whether broken or violated, there would no indirect meaning or **Implicature** to be detected. Implicatures only arise when the Maxims are **Flouted** (i.e. not adhered to for a good reason). Thus, to say 'I am voting for Regan because Carter is the evil of the two lessers' could be:

  (a) a case of breaking the Maxim of Manner if uttered by someone who gets the idiomatic saying mixed up;

  (b) a case of violation if said to someone who is not familiar with the original idiomatic saying; or

  (c) a case of flouting, giving rise to an implicature which might be something like 'it is all a sad charade and not even worth discussing'.

CO-TEXT: The sounds, words or phrases preceding and/or following a particular linguistic item in an utterance. This may be compared with the > **Context** enveloping that particular utterance.

COUNTER-ARGUMENT: see **Argumentation**

CULTURAL CODE: A system of ideas which conceptually enables **Denotative** meanings to take on extra **Connotative** meanings and thus become key terms in the thinking of a certain group of text users, ultimately contributing to the development of **Discourse**.

DENOTATION: see **Connotation**

DEVIATION FROM THE NORM: Norms subsume what is conventionally considered appropriate in speech or writing for a particular situation or purpose. These are sometimes deviated from for a 'good reason' mostly to do with pursuing a particular rhetorical aim. For example, instead of an expected > **Argument**, the text producer may opt for an **Expository** narrative. Such expectation-defying choices are normally more interesting and highly dynamic. See > **Cooperative Principle**, and > **Informativity**.

DISCOURSE: Modes of speaking and writing which involve participants in adopting a particular attitude towards areas of socio-cultural activity (e.g. racist discourse, bureaucratese, etc.). The minimal unit of discourse analysis is the **Discourse Statement** (e.g. the racism of a remark). Also see **Text**.

DISCOURSE STATEMENT: see **Discourse**

DISCURSIVE COMPETENCE: see **Textual Competence**

DISTANCE: see **Politeness**

DISTRIBUTIONAL METHOD: A method of linguistic analysis which shows the distribution of phonological, lexical or grammatical elements within larger sequences of sentences, e.g. phonemes in words, or words in sentences.

ELEMENT: In dealing with > **Text Structure**, an element is the minimal unit of analysis and could in compositional terms be a phoneme, a word or a sentence. Within the hierarchic organization of texts, elements make up a **Chunk** and a number of chunks make up a **Text**. One-element, one-chunk texts are not uncommon: *No Smoking*, for example. Elements of an > **Argumentative** text are called **Steps**, those of an > **Expository Narrative** text are **Events**, and those of an > **Expository Descriptive** text are **Attributes**.

ELLIPSIS: The omission (for reasons of rhetorically- and/or linguistically-motivated economy) of linguistic items whose sense is recoverable from > **Context** or > **Cotext**.

EVALUATIVENESS: The comparison or assessment of concepts, belief systems, etc. It is the determining factor in distinguishing > **Argumentation** from > **Exposition**.

EVENT: see **Element**

EVIDENTIALITY: Building on the premise that truth is relative, evidentiality studies the ways in which this relativity is expressed in languages. Put simply, there are some things people are sure of, others they are less sure of and so on. See **Modality**

EXPLICATIVE: A term used here to refer to languages that tend to express what is intended in a fairly explicit and direct way. In such languages, the relationship between meaning and linguistic expression is fairly transparent. **Implicative** languages, on the other hand, tend to be less direct, and the lexicogrammar tends to be used less transparently in the expression of communicative intentions. For example, while a clause type such as SVO could be used in English both evaluatively or non-evaluatively (i.e. expressing involved or detached attitudes), in Arabic, the > **Nominal** clause type SVO tends to cater for evaluative functions and another structure, namely the > **Verbal** VSO, seems to be earmarked for the less evaluative, more detached forms of expression.

EXPOSITION: A text type in which concepts, objects or events are presented in a non-evaluative manner. Three basic forms of exposition may be distinguished:

   (1) **Description**, focusing on objects spatially viewed;

   (2) **Narration**, focusing on events temporally viewed;

   (3) **Conceptual Exposition**, focusing on the detached analysis of concepts and yielding a number of text forms. Starting with the most detached and moving onto the least detached, these conceptual expository text forms include: the Synopsis, the Abstract, the Summary, the Entity-Oriented Report, the Person-Oriented Report, the Event-Oriented Report. The Report can also be Formulaic (e.g. the Auditors' report), Executive (e.g. the company Chairman's annual statement) and Reminiscent (e.g. the memoires).

FACE: In the > **Pragmatic** theory of > **Politeness**, face involves the positive image which one shows or intends to show of oneself. If this image is not accepted by the other participants, feelings may be hurt and 'loss of face' is incurred.

FACE THREATENING ACT (FTA): see **Politeness**

FIELD OF DISCOURSE: see **Meta-functions**, **Register**

FLOUTING A MAXIM: see **Cooperative Principle**

FORMAT: see **Text Structure**

FORWARD DIRECTIONALITY: see **Thematic Progression**

FRAME: see **Script**

FREE TRANSLATION: see **Literal Translation**

FUNCTIONAL: Having a role to perform in the realization of > **Context** by a **Text**. Functional signals are in contrast with other purely organizational devices whose role is, as the term suggests, merely formal and cosmetic rather than rhetorically motivated.

FUNCTIONAL SENTENCE PERSPECTIVE (FSP): The assumption that a sentence is to be viewed within a particular communicative perspective, in which, in the unmarked form, whatever is mentioned first (> **Theme**) is normally of less communicative importance than what follows (> **Rheme**).

FUNCTIONAL TENOR: An aspect of > **Tenor** or level of formality used to describe what language is used for (e.g. persuading) and is thus very much akin to the notion of > **Text Type.**

GENRE: Conventional forms of text associated with particular types of social occasion (e.g. the news report, the editorial, the cooking recipe). Within a given genre (the **Master Genre**), subsidiary minor genres (Genrelets) may be identified. For example, a Letter to the Editor may employ a number of genrelets such as the 'auctioneer's falling gavel' genrelet: *going, going, gone.* Whether the genre is major or minor, the minimal unit of genre analysis is the **Genre Feature (e.g. the social occasion involved).**

GENRE FEATURE: see **Genre**

GENRELET: see **Genre**

HEURISTIC: A set of analytic principles that rely on variable and not categorical rules in dealing with texts, that help us to learn about and discover things in texts as we go along and that rely on hypotheses and options to be confirmed or disconfirmed in the light of unfolding textual evidence.

IDEATIONAL MEANING: see **Meta-functions**

IDEOLOGY: A body of ideas which reflects the beliefs and interests of an individual, a group of individuals, a societal institution, etc., and which ultimately finds expression in language. For example, the headline *Girl 7 killed while mum was drinking at the pub* relays a particular ideological stance (i.e. sexism) towards men and women which the newspaper in question arguably adopts and propagates (see > **Discourse**).

ILLOCUTIONARY ACT: see **Locutionary Act**

IMMEDIATE CONSTITUENT ANALYSIS: A method of analyzing sentences or words by dividing them into their component parts (a sentence's Noun Phrase and Verb Phrase, for example).

IMPLICATURE: see **Cooperative Principle**

IMPOSITION: see **Politeness**

INFORMATIVITY: The degree of unexpectedness which an item or an utterance displays in some context. See **Deviation from the Norm**

INSTRUCTION: A text type in which the focus is on the formation of future behaviour, either 'with option' as in advertising or 'without option' as in legal instructions (e.g. Treaties, Resolutions, Contracts, etc.).

INTENTIONALITY: A feature of human language which determines the appropriateness of a linguistic form to the achievement of a > **Pragmatic** purpose.

INTERPERSONAL MEANING: See **Meta-functions**

INTERTEXTUALITY: A precondition for the intelligibility of all texts, involving the dependence of one text as a semiotic entity upon another. The other text could be a prior independent text, in which case intertextuality is the appropriate term. But, the intertext could be within one and the same text, and here Intratextuality might be a more appropriate term. Finally, the intertextual reference, instead of evoking an image, can preclude it, parody it, or signify its exact opposite, cases which are all subsumed under what is known as **Contratextuality**. This may be illustrated from the tactics of some political speakers using the opponent's terms of reference for their own ends.

INTRATEXTUALITY: see **Intertextuality**

ISOMORPHISM: Similarities between two or more languages in their phonological, semantic or grammatical structure.

LIAISON INTERPRETING: A form of oral interpreting in which two speakers who do not know each other's language or know it only imperfectly communicate through an interpreter, normally in fairly informal conversational settings.

LITERACY: A condition which prevails in the use of certain languages. The study of literacy does not focus so much on the ability to read and write as on the facility which certain languages make available to their users for the appropriate handling of written **Texts**, **Genres** and **Discourses** and for acquiring and operating within the writing or speaking conventions regulating these wider structures. These skills are also referred to as **Socio-textual Practices**. **Orality**, on the other hand, covers those aspects of language use that rely more on the spoken mode and thus tend to promote a style which is less abstract, more additive, distinctly repetitive and with a greater dependence on the immediate situation. See **Visual Texts**.

LITERAL TRANSLATION: A rendering which preserves surface aspects of the message both semantically and syntactically, adhering closely to source text mode of expression. **Free Translation**, on the other hand, modifies surface expression and keeps intact only deeper levels of meaning. The choice of either method of translation is determined by text properties to do with text type, purpose of translation, etc.

LOCUTIONARY ACT: A distinction is made in **Speech Act Theory** between a **Locutionary Act** (the act of saying something—e.g. *It is hot in here*), an **Illocutionary Act** (what is intended by the locutionary act—'please open the window'), and a **Perlocutionary Act** (what the ultimate effect could be said to be—demonstrating who is 'boss' around here).

MACRO-SIGN: see **Sign**
MANAGING: see **Monitoring**
MANNER: see **The Cooperative Principle**
MARKED: see **Unmarked**
MASTER GENRE: see **Genre**
MAXIM: see **The Cooperative Principle**
META-FUNCTIONS: These are not to be seen as functions in the sense of 'uses of language', but as functional components of a semiotic system. They are modes of meaning which are present in every use of language. Thus, the **Ideational** function, which emanates from **Field of Discourse**, represents the speaker's meaning potential as an 'observer': language is about something (e.g. *Ten Blacks Shot By Police* and *Police Shoot Ten Blacks* are two different ideational structures, one generally catering for a white perspective, the other for a black perspective). The **Interpersonal** component, which emanates from **Tenor of Discourse**, represents the speaker's meaning potential as an 'intruder': language as doing something (e.g. different uses of **Modality** relay different interpersonal meanings). Finally, the **Textual** component, which emanates from **Mode of Discourse**, represents the text-forming potential which speakers possess as part of their communicative competence: how language is made both relevant and operational (e.g. choices of what occupies the slot > **Theme** in the text is a textual orientation).
MICRO-SIGN: see **Sign**
MODALITY: Expressing distinctions such as that between 'possibility' and

'actuality', and, in the process, indicating an attitude towards the state or event involved. Modality constitutes one set of means for relaying > **Evidentiality**.

MODE OF DISCOURSE: see **Meta-functions, Register**

MONITORING: Expounding in a non-evaluative manner. This is in contrast with **Managing** which involves steering the discourse towards speaker's goals.

MOOD: The basic choice we make between using a statement, a question or a command. This choice is not without significance in the analysis of > **Ideology** and the **Interpersonal Meaning**.

MOTIVATEDNESS: The set of factors which rhetorically regulate text user's lexico-grammatical as well as textual/rhetorical choices.

MYTH: The way in which a given **Sign** undergoes a series of transformations until it achieves cultural status in the collective mentality of a community (e.g. the myth 'honour' in the **Cultural Code** of a number of language communities around the world).

NEGATIVE POLITENESS STRATEGIES: see **Politeness**

NOMINAL SENTENCE: In Arabic this consists of a Subject + Verb + Complement in this order, and is normally associated with **Evaluative contexts** (e.g. **Argumentation**). The Verbal Sentence, on the other hand, has a Verb + Subject + Complement structure and is normally associated with > **Non-evaluative** contexts (e.g. **Exposition**).

NOMINALIZATION: The condensed reformulation as a Noun Phrase of a verbal process and the various participants involved. This is an important grammatical resource for the expression of **Ideology** as when in saying *There has been criticism of...*, the speaker not only passivizes but also nominalizes, thus gets round having to state explicitly who the critics are.

NON-EVALUATIVENESS: see **Evaluativeness**

OPPOSITION: see **Text Structure**
Orality: see **Literacy, Visual Texts**

PERLOCUTIONARY ACT: see **Locutionary Act**
PLAN: A global pattern representing how events and states lead up to the attainment of a goal. To criticize, say, the inefficiency of the educational system, a text producer has to define what the goal is and has then to decide on the most effective way of attaining this. Plans are thus predominantly utilized in putting together **Argumentative** texts.

POLITENESS: A **Pragmatic** theory which is centered on the notion of > **Face**, that is, the attempt to establish, maintain and save face during interaction with others. Two main factors regulate the degree of **Imposition** which is ideally kept at a minimum: **Power** and **Distance**. In handling these, two basic sets of strategies are in use: **Positive Politeness Strategies** (those which show intimacy between speaker and hearer) and **Negative Politeness Strategies** (those which underline social distance between participants). Any irregularity in dealing with Power and/or Distance would result in compromising the degree of Imposition in a wide range of what is known as **Face Threatening Acts (FTAs)**.

POSITIVE POLITENESS STRATEGIES: see **Politeness**

POWER: In the analysis of **Politeness, Tenor** or, more specifically **Interpersonal Meaning**, two basic types of relationship may be distinguished: **Power** and **Solidarity**. Power emanates from the text producer's ability to impose his or her plans at the expense of the text receiver's plans. Solidarity, on the other hand, is the willingness of the text producer genuinely to relinquish power and work with his or her interlocutors as members of a team. Particular choices within > **Mood** and > **Modality** are relevant to the expression of either power or solidarity.

PRAGMATICS: The domain of **Intentionality** or the purposes for which utterances are used in real contexts.

PROPOSITIONAL CONTENT: What is involved in saying something that is meaningful and can be understood. Not necessarily included here is the function which the particular sentence performs in some specified context. For example, within propositional content analysis, *It is hot in here* would be analyzed as a comment on the temperature of the room and not, say, an attempt to get someone to open the window.

QUALITY: see **Cooperative Principle**
QUANTITY: see **Cooperative Principle**

REGISTER: The set of features which distinguish one stretch of language from another in terms of variation in > **Context** to do with the language user (geographical dialect, idiolect, etc.) and/or with language use (> **Field** or subject matter, > **Tenor** or level of formality and > **Mode** or speaking v. writing).

RELEVANCE: Sperber and Wilson (1986) define this as an expectation on the part of the hearer that his or her attempt at interpretation will yield adequate contextual effects at minimal processing cost. We adopt this sense, but we also take a rather less stringent view and define relevance both within the Gricean > **Maxims** and as part of text-type > **Politeness**, thus: it is the compliance by text users with rhetorical conventions regulating what one can or cannot say within the parameters set by a given > **Genre**, a given > **Discourse** and a given > **Text**, a matter which is ultimately regulated by a wide range of > **Socio-cultural** factors. For example, relevance is compromised when unmotivated emphasis is used in what is otherwise a fairly detached news report.

RELEVANCE AS A MAXIM: see **Cooperative Principle**

RHEME: That part of a sentence which, in the > **Unmarked** case, occurs last in an utterance and carries maximal communicative importance.

RHETORICAL CONVENTIONS: A set of variable rules and strategies which conventionally regulate the way a given stretch of textual material is put together (> **Text Structure**) and is made to hang together (> **Texture**), ultimately contributing to the efficiency of communicative behaviour and to its appropriateness to a given context of situation. In Arabic, for example, almost every sentence of a news report is introduced by a verb of saying (*He said . . .; he continued . . .; he added . . .*, etc.). English news reporting, on the other hand, tends to introduce a whole sequence of sentences with one verb of saying. What is involved here are two different sets of rhetorical conventions.

RHETORICAL PURPOSE: see **Text**

SCENARIO: see **Schema**

SCENE-SETTER: see **Text Structure**

SCHEMA: A global pattern representing the underlying structure which accounts for the organization of a text. A story schema, for example, may consist of a setting and a number of episodes, each of which would include events and reactions. Schema are predominantly utilized in putting together texts of the **Expository Narrative** type.

SCRIPT: Another term for 'frame'. These are global patterns realized by units of meaning that consist of events and actions related to particular situations. For example, a text may be structured around the 'restaurant script' which represents our knowledge of how restaurants work: waitresses, cooks, tables where customers sit, peruse menus, order their meals and pay the bill at the end. Scripts and frames are predominantly utilized in putting together texts of the > **Expository Descriptive** type.

SEMIOTICS: A dimension of context which regulates the relationship of texts and elements within texts to each other as signs. Semiotics thus relies on the interaction not only between speaker and hearer but also between speaker/hearer and their texts, and between text and text. This **Intertextuality** is governed by a variety of **Socio-cultural** factors (e.g. > **Politeness**), and **Rhetorical Conventions** (the way news reporting is handled in a given language). These factors and conventions are ultimately responsible for the way **Socio-textual** practices develop within a given community of text users (see > **Genre**, > **Text**, > **Discourse**).

SIGN: A unit of signifier and signified, in which the linguistic form (Signifier) stands for a concrete object or concept (Signified). When the notion of sign is extended to include anything which 'means something to somebody in some respect or capacity', we are able to refer through signs to cultural objects such as *honour* (Micro-signs), as well as to more global structures such as text, genre and discourse (Macro-signs), and to even more global structures such as that of > **Myth**.

SOCIO-CULTURAL FACTORS: see **Semiotics**

SOCIO-TEXTUAL PRACTICES: see **Literacy, Semiotics**

SOLIDARITY: See **Power**

SPEECH ACT THEORY: see **Locutionary Act**

STEP: see **Element**

STRAWMAN GAMBIT: see **Argumentation**
STRUCTURE: see **Text Structure**
SUB-GENRE: see **Genre**
SUBSTANTIATION: see **Text Structure**
SUPPRESSED COUNTER-ARGUMENT: see **Argumentation**
SUPPRESSION OF AGENCY: See **Nominalisation**

TENOR OF DISCOURSE: see **Meta-functions, Register**
TEXT: A set of mutually relevant communicative functions that hang together
(> **Texture**) and are put together (> **Structure**) in such a way as to respond
to a particular **Context** and thus achieve an overall **Rhetorical Purpose**. For
example, in response to a thesis which the text producer takes to be flawed,
he or she may attend to > **Counter-arguing** as a rhetorical purpose, which
entails the use of particular > **Evaluative** forms of linguistic expression with
a particular structure format that starts with the citation of an opponent's
thesis and moves on to a rebuttal. The minimal unit of text analysis is the
text Element **(e.g. thesis cited to be opposed)**. See **Discourse**.
TEXT ELEMENT: see **Text**
TEXT HYBRIDIZATION: Text Types are rarely if ever pure. More than one
text-type focus is normally discernible, a situation that is not as open-ended
as it may seem. In the event that more than one text-type focus is in evidence,
one and only one is bound to be predominant, with the others being subsidiary
if not totally marginal.
TEXT STRUCTURE: The compositional plan of a text. Different > **Text types**
exhibit different structure formats. Some of these are formulaic as in the
structure of the **Preamble** in legal documents: *X and Y, having met . . .,
considering . . ., re-emphasizing . . ., have agreed . . .* Other formats are less
formulaic, though fairly predictable. For example, a **Counter-argument** has
the following **Structure**: Thesis Cited, Opposition, Substantiation,
Conclusion. A **Through-argument** simply has Thesis Cited, Thesis Extensively
Defended. Whether to be rebutted or defended, the thesis cited always Sets
a Tone. **Monitoring Exposition**, on the other hand, displays the most
open-ended of formats: Scene Set, Aspects of the Scene Tackled.
TEXT TYPE: The way > **Text** > **Structure** and > **Texture** are made to respond
to their **Context** and to display a particular > **Text-type Focus**. Three basic
text-type foci may be distinguished: > **Exposition**, > **Argumentation** and
> **Instruction**.
TEXT-TYPE FOCUS: see **Text Type**
TEXTUAL COMPETENCE: The ability not only to apply the lexico-
grammatical rules of a language in order to produce well-formed sentences,
and not only to know when, where and with whom to use these sentences,
but also to know how to make the sentence play a role within a sequence
that is eventually part of a well-formed text, discourse and genre.
TEXTUAL MEANING: see **Meta-functions**
TEXTURE: Aspects of **Text** organization which contribute to the overall effect

223

of texts hanging together and reflect the **Coherence** of text > **Structure** and the way texts are responding to their > **Context**. Texture includes aspects of message construction such as > **Cohesion**, > **Theme- Rheme** organization, as well as Text idiom and diction.

THEME: That part of a sentence which, in the > **Unmarked** case, occurs first and which normally has less communicative importance than the > **Rheme**.

THEMATIC PROGRESSION (TP). The tendency for > **Themes** or > **Rhemes** to concatenate in particular patterns, relating to > **Text-type Focus**. In **Exposition**, for example, the tendency is for the discourse to display **Backward Directionality**, that is, Themes are redeployed as themes in the subsequent discourse (Uniform Pattern). In > **Argumentation**, on the other hand, the tendency is for the discourse to have **Forward Directionality**, that is, Rhemes are deployed as Themes in the subsequent discourse (**Zig-Zag Pattern**).

THESIS CITED TO BE OPPOSED: see **Text Structure**

THROUGH-ARGUMENT: see **Argumentation**

TONE-SETTER see **Text Structure**

TOP-DOWN: In cognitive psychology and adjacent disciplines, two different ways in which humans analyze and process language are distinguished. Top-down processing involves the reliance by the text user on > **Contextual information** (higher-level knowledge) in actually dealing with the information received (words, sentences, etc.) In **Bottom-up** processing, on the other hand, text users mostly utilize presented information as a point of departure towards the discovery of some contextual knowledge. Needless to say, both types of process are involved in any meaningful act of, say, reading or translating.

TRANSFORMATIONAL GRAMMAR: A theory of grammar proposed by the American linguist Noam Chomsky in 1957. Chomsky attempted to show how, with a system of internalized rules, native speakers of a language put their knowledge to use in forming grammatical sentences.

UNIFORM PATTERN: see **Thematic Progression**

UNMARKED: The state of certain lexical or grammatical items or structures considered to be more basic or common than other structures, **Marked** for particular effects. The cleft sentence *It was John who did it* is a marked form of *John did it*.

VERBAL SENTENCE: see **Nominal Sentence**

VIOLATING A MAXIM: see **Cooperative Principle**

VIRTUAL: A term used to refer to systemic aspects of language structure or *langue* before context is brought in to add another, deeper dimension to meaning. When this happens, and linguistic structures are seen as part of *parole*, we would be in the domain of the actual.

VISUAL TEXT: A text that is put together in such a way as to satisfy the requirements of literate (as opposed to orate) rhetorical conventions at work in societies characterized by literacy (as opposed to orality). In such societies, texts are normally heavily subordinated, possessing minimal unnecessary repetition and being generally tighter (or more complex) in terms of both > **Structure** and > **Texture**. Orate communities of language users, on the other hand, would be content with so-called **Aural texts** that tend to be heavily coordinated, that exhibit a great deal of repetition and that are generally looser (or simpler) in terms of both > **Structure** and > **Texture**. See **Literacy, Orality**.

ZIG-ZAG PATTERN: see **Thematic Progression**

References

al-'Askarii, A. (d. AH 395) *al-Sinaa'atayn* ('The Two Crafts: Prose and Poetry'), edited by A. M. al-Bajjawi and A. Ibrahim. Cairo: al-Babi al-Halabi Press, 1952.

Barthes, R. (1957) *Mythologies*. Paris: Seuil (London: Paladin, 1973).

Bateson, M. C. (1967) *Arabic Language Handbook*. Washington D.C.: Centre for Applied Linguistics.

Bauman, R. (1977) *Verbal Art as Performance*. Rowley, Mass.: Newbury House.

Beaugrande, R. de (1978) *Factors in a Theory of Poetic Translating*. Assen.: van Gorcum.

Beaugrande, R. de and Dressler, W. (1981) *Introduction to Textlinguistics*. London: Longman.

Beeston, A. F. L. (1970) *The Arabic Language Today*. London: Hutchinson.

Bloomfield, L. (1933) *Language*. London: Allen & Unwin.

Britton, J. (1963) 'Literature', in J. Britton (ed.) *The Arts and Current Tendencies in Education*. London: Evans, pp. 34–61.

—(1982) 'Spectator role and the beginnings of writing', in M. Nystrand (ed.), *What Writers Know: The Language, Process and Structure of Written Discourse*. New York: Academic Press.

Brown, G. and Yule, G. (1982) *Discourse Analysis*. Cambridge: Cambridge University Press.

Brown, K. (1984) *Linguistics Today*. London: Fontana.

Brown, P. and Levinson, S. (1978) 'Universals in language usage: politeness phenomena', in E. N. Goody (ed.), *Questions and Politeness: Strategies in Social Interaction*. Cambridge: Cambridge University Press, pp. 56–288.

Candlin, C. N. (1976) 'Communicative language teaching and the debt to pragmatics', in C. Rameh (ed.), *Semantics: Theory and Applications*. Georgetown University Round Table on Language and Linguistics, pp. 237–57.

Carter, R. (1988) 'Front pages: lexis, style and newspaper reports', in M. Ghadessy (ed.) *Registers of Written English: Situational Factors and Linguistic Features*. London: Pinter Publishers, pp. 8–17.

Catford, J. C. (1965) *A Linguistic Theory of Translation*. Oxford: Oxford University Press.

REFERENCES

Corder, S. P. (1973) *Introducing Applied Linguistics*. Harmondsworth: Penguin.

Crystal, D. and Davy, D. (1969) *Investigating English Style*. London: Longman.

Crombie, W. (1985) *Process and Relation in Discourse and Language Learning*. Oxford: Oxford University Press.

Daneš, F. (1974) 'Functional Sentence Perspective and the organization of the text', in F. Daneš (ed.) *Papers on Functional Sentence Perspective*. The Hague: Mouton, pp. 106–128.

Deyes, A. (1978) 'Towards a linguistic definition of functional varieties of written English', *IRAL*, Vol. XVI/4, pp. 313–329.

Emery, P. (1991) 'Text classification and text analysis in advanced translation teaching', *META*, XXXVI, 4, pp. 567–577.

Enkvist, N. E. (1973) *Linguistic Stylistics*. The Hague: Mouton.

—(1991) Discourse type, text type, and cross-cultural rhetoric', in Sonja Tirkkonen-Condit (ed.) *Empirical Research in Translation and Intercultural Studies*. Tubingen: Gunter Narr Verlag, pp. 5–16.

—(1992) Review of *Discourse and the Translator* by B. Hatim and I. Mason, *Target* 4: 1, pp. 124–126.

Fairclough, N. (1989) *Language and Power*. London: Longman.

Farghal, M. (1991) 'Evaluativeness parameter and the translator from English to Arabic and vice-versa', *Babel* 37, pp. 138–151.

Firbas, J. (1975) 'On the thematic and non-thematic sections of the sentence', in H. Ringbom (ed.) *Style and Text* . Stockholm: Skriptor, pp. 317–334.

Firth, J. R. (1957) *Papers in Linguistics 1934–1951*. Oxford: Oxford University Press.

Fowler, R. (1985) 'Power', in T. van Dijk (ed.), *Handbook of Discourse Analysis*, vol. 4: *Discourse Analysis in Society*. New York: Academic Press, pp. 61–82.

—(1986) *Linguistic Criticism*. Oxford: Oxford University Press.

Gregory, M. and Carroll, S. (1978) *Language and Situation: Language Varieties and their Social Contexts*. London: Routledge & Kegan Paul.

Grice, P. (1975) 'Logic and conversation', in P. Cole and J. Morgan (eds), *Syntax and Semantics 3: Speech Acts*. New York: Academic Press, pp. 41–58.

Grimes, J. (1975) *The Thread of Discourse*. The Hague: Mouton.

Halliday, M. A. K. (1971) 'Linguistic function and literary style: An inquiry into the language of William Golding's *The Inheritors*', in S. Chatman (ed.) *Literary Style: A Symposium*. Oxford: Oxford University Press, pp. 330–68.

—(1973) *Explorations in the Functions of Language*. London: Edward Arnold.

—(1978) *Language as Social Semiotic*. London: Edward Arnold.

Halliday, M. A. K. and Hasan, R. (1976) *Cohesion in English*. London: Longman.

Halliday, M.A.K., McIntosh,A. and Strevens, P. (1964) *The Linguistic Sciences and Language Teaching*. London: Longman.

Hartmann, R. R. K. (1980) *Contrastive Textology*. Heidelberg: Julius Groos Verlag.

Hasan, A. (1975) *Al-NaHuu al-Waafii*. Cairo: Daar al-Maʿaarif

Hasan, R. (1975) 'The place of stylistics in the study of verbal art', in H. Ringbom (ed.) *Style and Text*. Stockholm: Skriptor, pp. 49–63.

Hatim, B. (1991) 'The pragmatics of argumentation in Arabic: The rise and fall of a text type', *Text* 11 (2), pp. 189–199.

—(forthcoming) 'Politeness of texts', in L. Hickey (ed) *New Horizons in Pragmatics*. Multilingual Matters.

Hatim, B. and Mason, I. (1990) *Discourse and the Translator*. London: Longman.

—(1997) *The Translator as Communicator*. London: Routledge.

Hill, A. A. (1958) *Introduction to Linguistic Structure: From Sound to Sentence in English*. New York: Harcourt Brace & Co.

Hoey, M. (1983) *On the Surface of Discourse*. London: George Allen & Unwin.

Horman, H. (1975) *The Concept of Sense Constancy*. Memeo. University of Bochum.

Hymes, Dell H. (1967) 'Models of interaction of language and social setting' *Journal of Social Issues* 23.

James, C. (1989) 'Genre analysis and the translator', *Target* 1: 1.

Johanesson, Nils-Lennart (1985) 'Pragmatics', *Stockholm Papers in English Language and Literature*, Publication 5.

John, G. C. (1978) 'Towards a Linguistic Typology of Prose and Poetic Texts'. Unpublished MA dissertation. University of Exeter.

al-Jurjaanii, A. (d. AH 471) *Dalaa'il al-I'jaaz* ('Signs of Qur'anic Inimitability'), edited by M. R. al-Daya and F. al-Daya. Damascus: Maktabat Sa'd al-Din, 1987.

Kennedy, G. (1969) *Quintilian*. New York: Twayne Publishers, Inc.

Koch, B. (1983) 'Presentation as proof: The language of Arabic rhetoric', *Anthropological Linguistics*, Vol. 25, No. 1, pp. 47–60.

—(1986) 'Arguments with Khomeini: Rhetorical situation and persuasive style in cross-cultural perspective', *Text* 6, pp. 171–187.

Kress, G. R. (1985a) 'Ideological structures in discourse', in T. van Dijk, (ed.), *Handbook of Discourse Analysis*, vol. 4: *Discourse Analysis in Society*. New York: Academic Press, pp. 27–42.

—(1985b) *Linguistic Processes in Sociocultural Practice*. Victoria: Deakin University Press.

Kress, G. R. and Jones, G. (1981) 'Classification at work: The case of middle management', *Text* 1 (1).

Langendoen, D. T. (1970) *Essentials of English Grammar*. New York: Holt, Rinehart & Winston.

Lemke, J. L. (1985) 'Ideology, intertextuality and the notion of register', in J. D. Benson and W. S. Greaves (eds) *Systemic Perspectives on Discourse*, Vol. 1. Norwood, N.J.: Ablex Publishing Corporation, pp. 275–294.

Longacre, R. E. (1976) *An Anatomy of Speech Functions*. Lisse: Peter de Ridder Publishing Co.

Martin, J. R. (1985) *Factual Writing: Exploring and Challenging Social Reality*. Victoria: Deakin University Press.

REFERENCES

Myers, G. (1989) 'The pragmatics of politeness in scientific articles' *Applied Linguistics*, Vol. 10, No. 1, pp. 1–35.

Nash, W. (1980) *Designs in Prose*. London: Longman.

Nu'aimi A. and Kayyal, D. (1984) *al-'Imlaa' al-WaaDiH*. Baghdad: al-Russafi Press.

Ochs, Elinor (1979) 'Planned and unplanned discourse', in Talmy Givon (ed.) *Discourse and Syntax*. New York: Academic Press, pp. 50–80.

Ong, W. (1971) *Rhetoric, Romance and Technology*. Ithaca, N. Y.: Cornell University Press.

Palkova, Z. and Palek, K. (1977) 'Functional Sentence Perspective and text-linguistics', in W. Dressler (ed.) *Current Trends in Textlinguistics*. Berlin: de Gruyter, pp. 212–227.

Prince, E. F. (1981) 'Toward a taxonomy of given-new information', in P. Cole (ed.), *Radical Pragmatics*. New York: Academic Press, pp. 223–255.

Qudaama b. Ja'far (d. 237 AH) *Naqd al-Nathr* ("The Criticism of Prose"), edited by A. al-Khafaji, Cairo (undated).

Quintilian *De Institutione Oratoria* (On the Education of the Orator) [cited in G. Kennedy (1969)].

Robinson, P. C. (1980) *ESP (English for Specific Purposes): The Present Position*. Oxford: Pergamon Press.

Sa'adeddin, M. A. (1989) 'Text development and Arabic-English negative interference', *Applied Linguistics*, Vol. 10, No. 1, pp. 36–51.

al-Sakkakii, Y. (d. AH 626) *MiftaaH al-'Uluum* ('The Key to the Rhetorical Sciences'). Cairo: al-Babi al-Halabi Press, 1937.

Saussure, Fredinand de *Course in General Linguistics* (translated by Wade Baskin, McGraw Hill, New York, 1966).

Sell, Roger D. (1993) *Literary Pragmatics*. London: Routledge.

Shouby, E. (1951) 'The influence of the Arabic language on the psychology of the Arabs', *Middle East Education* 5, pp. 284–302.

Siddiq, M. (1986) '"Deconstructing" *The Saint's Lamp*', *Journal of Arabic Literature*, Vol. XVII, pp. 126–145.

Sinclair, J. and Coulthard, M. (1975) *Towards an Analysis of Discourse*. Oxford: Oxford University Press.

Stalnaker, R. C. (1972) 'Pragmatics', in D. Davidson and G. Harman (eds), *Semantics in Natural Language*. Dordrecht: Reidel.

Sperber, D. and Wilson, D. (1981) 'Irony and the use-mention distinction', in P. Cole (ed.), *Radical Pragmatics*. New York: Academic Press, pp. 295–318.

—(1986) *Relevance: Communication and Cognition*. Oxford: Basil Blackwell.

Stubbs, M. (1983) *Discourse Analysis: The Sociolinguistic Analysis of Natural Language*. Oxford: Basil Blackwell.

Sykes, M. (1985) 'Discrimination in discourse', in T. van Dijk (ed.), *Handbook of Discourse Analysis*, vol. 4: *Discourse Analysis in Society*. New York: Academic Press, 83–101.

Turner, G. J. (1973) 'Social class and children's language of control at age five and age seven', in B. Bernstein (ed.) *Class, Codes and Control 2: Applied*

Studies—Towards a Sociology of Language. London: Routledge & Kegan Paul.

van Dijk T. (ed.) (1985) *Handbook of Discourse Analysis,* Vols 1–4: *Discourse Analysis in Society.* New York: Academic Press.

Volosinov, V. N. (1921) *Marxism and the Philosophy of Language* (translated by L. Matejka and I. R. Titunik, Seminar Press, New York 1973).

Werlich. E. (1976) *A Text Grammar of English.* Heidelberg: Quelle & Meyer.

Widdowson, H. G. (1979) *Explorations in Applied Linguistics.* Oxford: Oxford University Press.

Winter, E. O. (1982) *Towards a Contextual Grammar of English.* London: Allen & Unwin.

Young, D. E., Becker, A. L. and Pike K. L. (1970) *Rhetoric: Discovery and Change.* New York: Harcourt, Brace and World.

Young, David, J. (1985) 'Some applications of systemic grammar to TEFL, or whatever became of register analysis?', in James D. Benson and William S. Greaves (eds) *Systemic Perspectives on Discourse,* Volume 2. Norwood, N.J.: Ablex Publishing Corporation, pp. 282–294.

Index

231

solidarity, 28, 29, 126, 166, 169, 234
speech acts, 22, 33, 110, 127–130, 176, 197, 216, 231
staging, 76, 100, 177
state predicate, 179
strawman gambit, 6, 50, 63
structuralism, 16, 17, 222
style, xiv, 13, 15, 16, 21, 47, 95, 116, 119, 136, 162, 180, 183, 187, 215–218, 230
subordination, 116, 162–164, 240

tenor, 22, 25–29, 56, 126, 128, 169, 176, 197, 202, 210, 228, 234
text receiver, 24, 25, 27, 32, 33, 48, 50, 55, 58, 82, 84, 92, 93, 106, 108, 117, 118, 121, 122, 127, 128, 142–149, 166, 169–172, 176, 188, 195, 234
text structure, xiv, 6, 11, 22, 54, 55, 58, 62, 65, 67, 69, 75, 76, 82, 88, 90, 101, 134, 136, 149, 166, 210
text type, xiv, 4, 7, 9, 11, 12, 16, 22, 35, 36, 38, 39, 41–44, 46, 48, 50, 52, 54, 63–66, 75, 76, 86, 88, 89, 91–93, 97, 99, 101–103, 105, 107, 108, 117, 139, 140–142, 145, 148, 151, 153, 155, 158, 163, 165–167, 171–173, 206, 211, 217, 221, 227, 229, 231, 237

textual competence, 7, 8, 18, 25, 93, 144, 209
textual transfer, xiii, 124, 127, 130, 132, 197, 198
texture, xiv, 4, 7, 9, 11, 12, 22, 29, 56, 62, 65, 66, 72–76, 80–85, 87–92, 99, 100–102, 105–108, 113, 115, 117, 120, 125, 132, 136, 145, 158, 172, 206, 210, 211, 224, 235, 237, 238, 240
The cooperative Principle, 222, 225, 228, 229, 231, 234, 235, 239
The Cooperative Principle (CP), 192, 222, 225, 228, 229, 231, 234, 235, 239
Theme–Rheme, 80–82, 222, 228, 239, 240
Thesis Cited, 4, 6, 9, 51, 56, 57, 59, 60, 91, 93, 100, 134, 205, 237
transitivity, 29, 114, 179, 180–184, 223
translation assessment, 1
translation theory, xi

universe of discourse, 30, 86, 87, 142

variation, 7, 13, 16, 20–23, 25, 65, 82, 89, 99, 139, 150, 151, 234
Verbal sentence, 77, 78, 87, 119, 121
visual text, 166, 167

word order, xv, 9, 79, 115, 117, 119